The White Mosque

The White Mosque

· *A Memoir* ·

Sofia Samatar

CATAPULT  NEW YORK

This is a work of creative nonfiction. Names of living persons who are not public figures have been changed. In some cases, two people have been compressed into a single character. The stories are true to the best of the author's knowledge. The places are real.

Copyright © 2022 by Sofia Samatar

Grateful acknowledgment for reprinting materials is made to the following:
To the Pennsylvania German Society and editor John J. Gerhart
Excerpt from *Mennonite Identity and Literary Art* by John L. Ruth. Used by permission of Herald Press. All rights reserved.

First Catapult edition: 2022

Hardcover ISBN: 978-1-64622-097-7
Paperback ISBN: 978-1-64622-203-2

Library of Congress Control Number: 2021952950

Cover design by Dana Li
Cover pattern of dots © iStock / artishokcs
Book design by Laura Berry

Catapult
New York, NY
books.catapult.co

Printed in the United States of America

1 3 5 7 9 10 8 6 4 2

For my mother,
Lydia Samatar

for my parents-in-law,
Annetta Miller and Harold F. Miller

and in memory of my father,
Said Sheikh Samatar

✳

Combining an angular 16th century Gothic letter type known as "Fraktur"—familiar to them through written and engraved copybooks, letters of apprenticeship, deeds, and official edicts—with the somewhat Oriental motifs of 18th century European hand-blocked and woven textile designs, the Pennsylvania Germans produced a new art form of such great richness, and in such great quantities, that it should be regarded more as a *revival*, than as a *survival* of Medieval illumination.

—DONALD A. SHELLEY, *The Pennsylvania German Style of Illumination*

The story has become luminous.

—JOHN L. RUTH, *Mennonite Identity and Literary Art*

Contents

The White Mosque

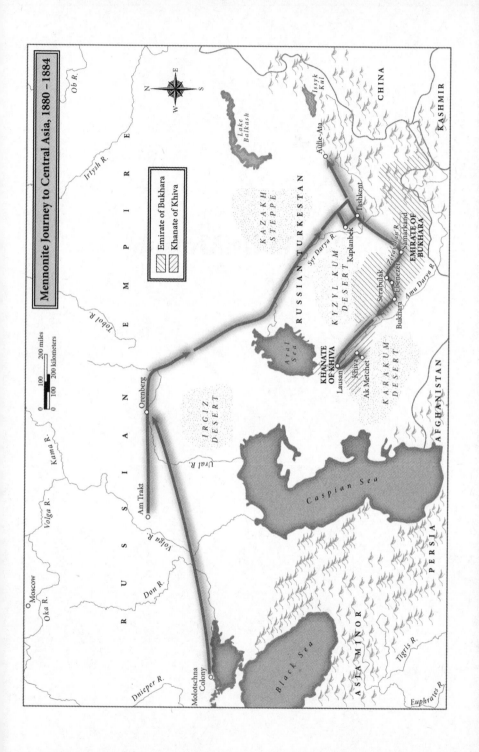

Mennonite Journey to Central Asia, 1880–1884

Emirate of Bukhara
Khanate of Khiva

PART ONE

*

Wanderers

ONE

Tashkent

a more dazzling vision

Begin with the glow

Begin with the glow: the faint beam of a half-forgotten history. In this darkened hotel room, a trace of ochre outlines the curtains. Push them aside and a fawn-colored radiance blooms against my arms, revealing the city below, the dust and juniper trees, the loops of traffic. The light seems to flow from the streets as much as the sky, a tint in the air, less a brightness than a universal softening of the atmosphere, it appears to have no single source, it arrives everywhere at once, from all the ends of the earth, from the future and the past.

Rumpled sheets. Silky, patterned walls. A decorative chair in the corner, rigid and remote, like a lady-in-waiting. I've traveled before—as a tourist, a student, a volunteer English teacher—but never for research, never as a pilgrim.

Outside, a bus called Golden Dragon. Tree trunks painted white. The heat of June. And the vastness of Tashkent, its miles of tended parks, the giant mosques that seem akin to the lonely Soviet structures, buildings marooned in the sky, much taller than the trees. The larger everything is, the smaller I feel, the more I sense the glow. My insignificance brings me close to stray, discarded things, to the story that brought me here, to this blade of grass I pluck by the statue of Amir Timur, the conqueror, guarded by angels, born with his fists full of blood.

Pilgrims

Lunch with Kholid. The restaurant, curtained off from the midday glare, seems like a cavern at first, then slowly the tablecloths emerge from the gloom, the glint of teapots, the red and purple and rose-pink of the cushions, dizzying patterns that ought to clash, but it all looks wonderful. Kholid is a PhD student in history. We discuss Edward Said's *Orientalism*, drinking cup after cup of tea. Kholid accompanies the tour as a local expert; he's courteous and assured in his role, his shirt pressed, his purpose clear. And me, I'm the traveler, earnest, sweaty, disheveled, sipping beef soup, eating the dollops of cream cheese sprinkled with paprika, the Uzbek samosas out of a basket (samosas, Kholid informs me, originated in Uzbekistan, not India), consuming everything with the haphazard, distracted air of a person flung through the atmosphere, sleep-deprived, cockeyed with jet lag, with that peculiar weightlessness and tension, that sensation of being both empty and distended, like a balloon, that translates itself as a headache. A languid, buzzing headache, streaked with currents of elation. In 1941, Kholid tells me, Stalin sent an expedition to open the tomb of Timur, the fourteenth-century military giant known in the West as Tamerlane. Ignoring the warning inscription—"Whoever disturbs my tomb will unleash an invader more terrible than I am!"—a team of scientists broke into the sarcophagus. Two days later, Hitler invaded the Soviet Union. Moreover, the grave robbers' crane mysteriously broke down, their lights went out, and the odor of musk issuing from the coffin knocked the whole team unconscious.

The sweetness welling from the past can knock you flat. It can hurl you across the planet. Now the *plov* arrives, the national dish, studded with raisins, each grain of rice gleaming darkly with oil and spices. Plov tastes best eaten with the fingers, Kholid remarks, but he eats it with a fork, so I do too. He tells me that, as a child, Amir Timur—the title *Amir* means prince—was visited by the ghost of Alexander the Great. This must have happened at the conqueror's birthplace, Shakhrisabz. I've read of this city, and of the residence Timur built there, Ak Saray, the White Palace, of which a Spanish ambassador wrote, "The workmanship of this palace was so rich that it would be impossible to describe it, without gazing and walking over everything, with slow steps."

I want to walk over everything with slow steps. But this is a tour; we have a schedule to keep. I can't stop for the man in the park to sketch my portrait, can't linger in the shade of the bridge where young couples stroll together near the Museum of the Victims of Repression. Our tour guide, Usmon, explains how a mass grave was discovered here when the ground was dug up for a tennis court—tennis being the favorite sport of Islam Karimov, who became the first president of independent Uzbekistan in 1991. He's still president now, in the summer of 2016. The domes of the museum throb against the sky, they're the same strong, fresh blue as the dome of Timur's museum, a turquoise I will come to associate indelibly with Uzbekistan, a blue with the vitality of a leaf. In the hot summer sky, this blue exudes a coolness almost green. A railway line runs nearby. In Stalin's time, says Usmon, people were brought to this place at night, transported secretly from concentration camps in Kazakhstan, and murdered under the noise of passing trains.

Legends of the conquerors, preserved in pride and fear. Timur's tomb, the one he built for himself, stands empty at Shakhrisabz; instead he was buried in Samarkand beneath a slab of jade. The site was discovered when a child fell into the crypt. I write these stories in my notebook, occasionally adding a star to mark the moments when the great tide of history merges with my own, when my research flashes up, the wayward tributary that's brought me to this place, for this is a double tour, a palimpsestic quest. On the one hand, it's a visit to the major sites of Uzbekistan; Usmon is our leader in this area. On the other hand, it's a Mennonite heritage tour, reconstructing the journey of a group of Mennonites who moved here from southern Russia, now Ukraine, in the 1880s. Kholid, whose father is writing a monograph on the Mennonites, joins us to comment on this minor history. And we have a third leader, as well: Frank, an American Mennonite historian, an expert on that strange, small story.

I write in my notebook: *Shakhrisabz*. Mark it with a star.

Most of the people on the tour are descendants of the Mennonites who settled here more than a century ago. They have come to see where their ancestors walked, to taste the air, the fruit, to photograph any traces that remain. They are Americans and Canadians. Like their ancestors who migrated here from Russia, they have pale skin, Germanic surnames, and roots in Central Europe. There are also two Uzbek bus drivers on this trip, and our guides, Usmon and Kholid. There's Nozli, a young Uzbek woman, a tour guide in training. And then there's me.

Beautiful error

What brought me here? In a way, I've arrived by accident. I'm haunted by a little piece of history, the story of a small, hardy, stubborn group of people who traveled here more than a hundred years ago. I am haunted by a photograph of their church, blanched with whitewash, standing among the poplars of an arid village square. When I first saw it, I imagined its thick walls were made of crystal, that its surface would taste of salt, and that it could contain more than was physically possible, like a word.

Because I saw this church in a photograph, I felt I could hold it in my hand. Because the photograph was a century old, I felt I was holding my century, the one in which I was born, the twentieth century. Because the church was located in Central Asia, in what is now Uzbekistan, a place I had never seen and of which I knew practically nothing, I felt it was very foreign. Because the church was a Mennonite church, belonging to my own denomination, the faith tradition of my mother's family, I felt it was very close.

To be very close to the very foreign is one definition of haunting. As the most prominent landmark of the village where it stood, the church in the photograph gave the place its name: *Ak Metchet*, the White Mosque. To the local population, largely Muslim, the church was a white mosque.

Beautiful error, radiant mistake! Whether one is Christian or Muslim or neither, churches and mosques form nodes of powerful feeling. Passions cluster about them. Some perceive them as violently opposed, charged in such a way that they must repel one another. Others would place them together, as representatives of the same monotheistic, extremist, world-conquering impulse. But whether you see the forces these places emit as wildly different in character, generating worldviews that can never touch, or whether you see them as unified at a deep level, amplifying one another in a sizzling sibling rivalry, or whether your opinion partakes of both notions, I'm in this electrical storm. My mother's family are Swiss-German Mennonites, my father's Somali Muslims. I stand amid this lightning which, here in the twenty-first century, only seems to be growing more intense.

And so I wished to go inside the church that was a mosque. Its simplicity. Its almost blinding pallor.

The church crumbled decades ago. It no longer exists.

A pilgrimage, then, to error, to ghosts, to the accidental, to the glow.

The implausible story

The first time I came across the story of the Mennonites of Ak Metchet, I hardly noticed it. I was sixteen then, a student at Lancaster Mennonite School in Pennsylvania, taking the required course in Mennonite history. This history began with an immense amount of flogging, tongue screws, and burning at the stake. The Mennonites, we learned, were persecuted to pieces by both Catholics and Protestants because they rejected infant baptism, which is why they are known as Anabaptists, or re-baptizers, since people like Menno Simons, for whom the denomination is named, went around baptizing adults in the ponds of the Dutch provinces. Mennonites also rejected violence—Menno was appalled by the behavior of some of the other Anabaptists of his day, like the notorious Jan van Leyden, who took over the city of Münster, practiced polygamy, abolished property, and ran around stark naked. Menno was a far less exciting figure, but he had a certain sly charm, like the hero of a folktale. According to legend, he was once stopped on the road by some Anabaptist-hunters who demanded to know "if Menno Simons was in the coach." Menno happened to be driving the coach. He leaned down and asked the people inside, "Is Menno in there?" "No!" was the answer. Thus he got out of his predicament without lying. He wrote a book with the marvelous title *Why I Do Not Cease Teaching and Writing*, died peacefully, and was buried in his garden.

When the class began, it was easy to pay attention: there were so many grisly stories of martyrdom, of Mennonites living in hiding like underground revolutionaries. But then it was spring, the classroom got hotter, the atmosphere soporific, Mennonite history so boring, just people leaving their homes time after time. Usually, they got into trouble for refusing to join the army of whatever country they happened to be in. Then they'd be forced to move again: to Prussia, Russia, the Americas. We had to memorize all the treks for the final exam. Outside, the parking lot simmered. Flies bumped the windows. Our textbook was a terrible chalky pink, the color of bathroom tile. In the catalogue of miseries and migrations, the Mennonite journey to Central Asia was almost buried, mentioned only briefly, and with disapproval. The group that made that journey had been led, I read, by a false prophet, a man named Claas Epp Jr., who had dared to predict the date of Christ's return. His prophecies failed, of course. The book described the trek as a sad misstep, "a monument of warning."

A repetitive history, flat like a plain, like wheat. I yawned my way through it, fanning myself with a piece of notebook paper. And yet, years later, the story of this trek would leap out to me. I was in Nairobi, on my way to take up a teaching position in South Sudan, when my father-in-law gave me a book: *The Great Trek of the Russian Mennonites to Central Asia, 1880–1884*. I remember reading it there, in the small room with the plywood wardrobe, under fluorescent light. Before you got into bed there was the ritual mosquito hunt. They were so fast your hand couldn't possibly hit them. We smacked them with our pillows. Walls and pillowcases dotted with blood, and the book in my hands, a tale of wonder and terror, pilgrimage and exile, apocalyptic fervor and failure, a story removed from me in time and space yet calling out with its domed cityscapes, camels, German hymns, and snow. By that time, I was accustomed to living a fragmentary life. I was a Mennonite, a Somali American, a recent student of African literature, and a writer of as-yet-unpublished fantasy novels, and I had learned that these things, while they might stand beside one another, could never be combined. There was really no way to put them together, except as mosaic: that is, as a shattering. I learned this whenever I was questioned about my origins, or, as people said with careful emphasis, my "ethnic background"—an experience I had, and still have, almost daily. Meeting a new person requires an explanation of who I am, and how I came to exist, so prolonged and elaborate it feels like a fantasy novel. How my mother, a Mennonite of Swiss ancestry from North Dakota, traveled to Somalia as a missionary English teacher. How she met my father, who taught the Somali language to the missionaries, who had grown up herding livestock in the desert. He was raised on meat and milk. His primary school met under a tree. He had memorized the Qur'an. She wore, on her hair, which was coiled into a bun, the traditional Mennonite covering, a soft curve of white netting. The more I tell it, the more implausible it sounds. I wonder about the effects of telling repeatedly, over a lifetime, a story this odd, of having to make an identity out of such a story, and of seeing, again and again, on the faces of listeners, expressions of wonderment: slack mouths, wide eyes, the brief shocked laughter. I think it might make someone feel like a mistake, a cosmic gaffe. It might make a person feel like a sort of traveling theater, exotic and ephemeral, pitching camp in the scrub where the forest meets the road, belonging to no town. It might make you feel like a carnival mask, too gaudy for everyday use. It might make you love such things. You might become a devotee of the bizarre. The tale that provokes a gasp of disbelief might feel like *yours*. You might become happiest, most at home, with the implausible.

I began to read the story of the Mennonite trek from Russia to Central Asia, and then I began to tell it. I told it everywhere, in airplanes, in cafés, at job interviews, at academic conferences, in churches. Everywhere, it received the same expression of astonishment, the same amazed shake of the head, laced with curiosity or skepticism, that had always greeted my own story. This gave me an obscure and childlike pleasure. I would describe how the Mennonites settled in what was then the Khanate of Khiva, how they were cast up at the edge of the desert on the winds of prophecy, how their village persisted there for fifty years.

Every three days they would go into town to sell their butter, the fruit from the trees they had planted. In the bustling market of Khiva, wearing their dark suits and hats. I see them with their wagons, the local *arbas* with large spokes. Around them the maze of languages: Uzbek, Turkmen, Kazakh, Russian.

It's the contrast, the incongruity, that delights. Beyond the initial shock of the story of reckless prophecy, this story that makes my listeners shake their heads, recoil, or laugh, there's the reverberation of *Mennonites in Uzbekistan*. Many of my listeners are Mennonites who have never heard this story, or who think they have never heard it, just as I thought, having forgotten my high school textbook, that I'd never heard it when I picked up *The Great Trek of the Russian Mennonites to Central Asia*. Other listeners are people who have never, or very infrequently, heard of Mennonites. They want to know, first, what a Mennonite is, and I give them my quick summary: Europe, Radical Reformation, adult baptism, pacifism, farmers, missionaries, kinship with the Amish. These bits of information, mixed with a few images gleaned from popular culture, such as Kelly McGillis in her bonnet in the movie *Witness*, and overlaid with the sound of the word *Mennonite* itself, which, like *Israelite* or *Luddite*, carries a dogmatic, tribal, and cultish aura, is enough to impress on my audience how extremely weird it is that a group of such people should wind up in Uzbekistan. For Uzbekistan, usually even foggier to my listeners than Mennonites, signifies the East, the Silk Road, and Genghis Khan. Uzbekistan is "the golden road to Samarkand." It's there, somewhere, among the other "-stans," in the cartographic rubble left behind by the Soviet Union.

We are, of course, in the realm of stereotypes. But what's significant here is the conjunction of clichés. When two sets of images, assumed to be fixed and separate, nonetheless come together, it suggests that a third term is possible. This is the source of light.

A magpie existence

Around the time I first read about the Mennonite trek to Central Asia, only to forget it completely, I also read Gertrude Stein's "Melanctha." I read this story on high alert. It was my first time reading about a mixed person like myself, and I was ready to seize all the wisdom it divulged. My English teacher said "Melanctha" was considered the best story in *Three Lives*, at which I felt gratified, as if I were somehow responsible for its success, as if I'd personally assisted Melanctha in beating both the Good Anna and the Gentle Lena, two dull ladies of German extraction. Melanctha, I noticed, had no defining adjective, only her name—a brownish, pensive, unpronounceable appellation, which seemed to presage great trials in her future. And in fact, though her subtitle, "Each One as She May," sounded promising, Melanctha turned out to be a figure of sorrow. According to my teacher, she represented the "tragic mulatto," or, in this case, the "tragic mulatta," who can never fit into any American society, Black or white, but is doomed to founder between them. *Mulatto* comes from *mule*, because mules are sterile. This is a way of saying that mixed people have no future. I worried about this, especially because I felt someone could easily describe me just as Gertrude Stein described Melanctha. I, too, was a graceful, pale yellow, good looking, attractive negress, a little mysterious sometimes in my ways, and always good and pleasant, and always ready to do things for people. Also, I was complex with desire. The end of this paragraph should describe how I've changed, but I am still the same.

To say "it's just fiction" is useless; there's nothing more powerful than a story, especially if one encounters it in an open, impressionable state. Today, I'm aware of the dangers of taking Melanctha as a model, but the thought of her still occasionally gives me a superstitious chill, because she was always seeking rest and quiet, but all she could do was make trouble for herself, flitting from place to place until she died of TB. In Tashkent, I photograph the immense portal of a sixteenth-century *madrasa*, its terracotta surface inlaid with blue glazed tiles, a cross-stitch pattern rising from a vast expanse of grayish brick that seems designed to represent a desert. Heat boils up from this modern, well-swept wasteland. On the opposite side, in the Muyi Mubarak Museum, named for the "Blessed Hair" of the Prophet, my tour group views the world's oldest Qur'an, written in heavy Kufic script on gazelle skin swollen with age. The Qur'an belonged to the Caliph Uthman, who was stabbed to death while reading it; his blood flecks a page like the shadow of a moth. It was this caliph, Usmon explains, who ordered the verses revealed by the Prophet to be compiled into the Qur'an, instead of just memorized or passed around on pieces of camel bone. Now the huge book, each page as long as my arm, reclines under glass in a climate-controlled sarcophagus imported from Germany. I remember, when I took my first Arabic class, I was enraptured by the thought of a script both ancient and alive. I'd found a form of writing preserved so immaculately and so long that a literate person today can read poetry written down in the eighth century. Try reading English poetry from the eighth century sometime. I had tried this in an Anglo-Saxon class, and it was brutal. It's worth noting that I did not need to take an Anglo-Saxon class, as I was majoring in Swahili. I didn't need to take an Arabic class, either, but in the end it didn't much matter, because during a study abroad program, I ran across an old college boyfriend in Zanzibar, married him a few months later, quit my PhD program, and moved to South Sudan.

A magpie existence. Never in the same place for more than five years—I managed that stretch in New Jersey, as a child. The decision to teach Swahili, no, Arabic, no, English, no, Arabic after all, but then no, English. The career as a scholar, or else a novelist. Can't I do both at once? Of course, do as many things as you like—but you'll do them badly. So I tell myself in my more dejected moments, for example while sewing up the arm of a couch from which my husband has extracted a dead mouse. The mouse got into the couch and died, it rotted there for days, and instead of throwing the couch away once our son had located the tiny corpse, we cut open the arm, replaced the foam, and scrubbed the fabric, hiding the whole process from our sensitive, animal-loving daughter. Repairing the arm of this shabby, mouse-colored, bargain-basement couch, purchased from one of those ill-lit dens where each stick of remaindered furniture mourns the fall of its tribe, I can't help reflecting that people who've been raised in a single tradition may be predisposed toward a stable and organized life. I know some of these people, cousins on both sides of my family, and it seems to me that they are not plagued by mice, fruit flies, or poison ivy, that their days have a regular rhythm, structured around the church or mosque, and that their basement pumps don't mysteriously shoot out more water than any other house on the street. These people have solid careers, because each of them has selected just one. They keep track of crucial meetings at their children's schools, they know when it's picture day, they remember when to turn in the box tops, they have actually taken the trouble to collect the box tops, while we lumber after the school bus, waving forgotten backpacks and yelling. My husband is Swiss-American, the grandson of Mennonite missionaries, raised in Nairobi, multilingual, a total rootless cosmopolitan. We're both secular Mennonites, but he's a staunch atheist, while I, in accordance with my magpie disposition, pick and choose: I go to church every Sunday, I love the music, I sing, I drift, I take notes on the church bulletin, I lose myself, I write. Our children are being raised with no religious tradition to speak of, but sometimes we test them at dinner; suddenly we're scared they'll be cultural nitwits. Hey, we demand, what's the story of Samson? Can anybody tell me the story of Joseph and his brothers? This, not for religious reasons, but so they'll be able to understand Western literature. We've taken such care not to oppress them with a sense of identity, we don't know who they'll be. When a friend asked my ten-year-old daughter what race she was, my daughter said, "I'm a fruit pie."

Once, the Arabic language seemed to promise me a certain stability: I thought I'd spend my life immersed in the splendor of its grammar, in a labyrinth of literature extensive enough to satisfy even me. If I'd really concentrated on Arabic for all these years, what skills I'd possess! But I can't read the block-like script of the Caliph Uthman's Qur'an, I can only pick out a few letters, I'm not even sure about all of those, I shouldn't be here, I should be home, something always goes wrong when I'm away, I communicate poorly, I mix up dates, when I went to that academic conference the kids missed a birthday party, we'd bought a present, I cried on the train, if I'm going to travel it should at least be for reasons related to my career, but a photograph caught my eye and here I am. Here I am, peering at words so precious they were passed from hand to hand, repeated until their shapes were set in the mind like jewels, held close in the body before the book. Words my father knew by heart. And that feathery stain, the print of blood.

It's the mental disorderliness that worries me most of all. My suitcase crammed with notes. When I first began to read about Claas Epp Jr., the preacher who led the Mennonites into Central Asia, I was fascinated by his prophecies, but even more by his singleness of purpose. This was a man who knew what he had to do. His firmness exerted a power over others. He'd ride up and down the Mennonite farms of southern Russia, handing out copies of his treatise *The Unsealed Prophecy of the Prophet Daniel and the Meaning of the Revelation of Jesus Christ*. He carried a sumptuous atlas, which he'd unfold on kitchen tables, his hand brushing over the deserts of Central Asia. That was their destiny.

There, in the East, in the land of the rising sun. There, in the spring of 1889, Christ would come again. It strikes me that when the journey began, this migration that would become known among Mennonite historians as the Great Trek to Central Asia, Claas Epp Jr. was forty-two years old, and that when I began my research, I was the same age. I was forty-two, and I'd just finished school. At my age, Epp had a thriving farm and a brick factory. I have two nascent careers and mice. In the low light of the museum, gripped by the sight of blood on skin, I pursue my magpie, my—dare I say it—mulatta existence.

Corrective

Of course, Melanctha is a stereotype, the myth of the "tragic mulatto" an insult to people like myself. Indeed, to say "a magpie existence" is an insult to magpies. Magpies are curious, but not particularly entranced by shiny objects. They got that reputation from a French play, in which a magpie takes off with the silverware and a servant gets the blame. This play was performed at the Théâtre de la Porte Saint-Martin in Paris in 1815, on the same stage where, ten years later, theatergoers could watch *Ourika, or the African Orphan*, the tale of a Senegalese girl raised as white by her aristocratic parents. Ourika's happiness receives a fatal blow when she overhears her parents' friends talking about her: she discovers that, having treated her as white, her parents have doomed her to lifelong suffering, for now she'll never fit into any world, never marry, never have a home. She begins to avoid mirrors, as if she's a vampire. Sometimes it's exhausting to pretend that stereotypes mean nothing, as if the mere words "that's a stereotype!" create a magic spell sufficient to exorcise the power of the image. Ourika tucks her hair inside her hat. She hides her hands with gloves; to her, they have begun to look like paws. She will die of melancholy in a convent. I'm aware of the caustic tone that creeps in when I describe myself, a bitterness that, if it's not too late, I would transform.

(Un)homelike

But what was it that drew me to this story, if not a sense of wholeness? At the hotel, I spread my papers on the bed. Printouts of articles, two worn notebooks scored with lines and circles, thick with photocopied pictures taped inside. The tiny lamp with the burn mark on the shade casts an orange lozenge that only covers half the bed. Shift the papers toward the light. On the back of my photocopy of Claas Epp Jr.'s prophetic treatise, I find a pair of scribbled lists:

MENNONITE	UZBEKISTAN
simple	ornate
frugal	lavish
pacifist	warlike
quiet	turbulent
farm	market
bland food	spices
hat	turban
cow	camel
white	colored
West	East
Christian	Muslim
church	mosque

What obnoxious lists, reductive, misleading, false! But what else makes the story of Mennonites in Central Asia so implausible? What but the hovering presence of such lists of opposing images, which can never meet except as mosaic? I'm ashamed of my lists, they make me happy, I carry them to the window, the paper still has the smell of my house, my clothes, I look out on the glitter of Tashkent, the circling lights of traffic, the apartment blocks with glints in the high windows. Why, from where, this extraordinary sense of wellbeing?

For Freud, a blend of opposing images creates a ghostly feeling. One night, he was making a long journey by train. He was alone in his sleeping compartment when the train gave a violent lurch, so that the door of the toilet between the compartments swung open. An elderly gentleman wearing a dressing gown and traveling cap burst in upon Freud. Thinking the old man must have lost his way in the dark, Freud jumped up to set him right, only to discover that the man was his own reflection in a mirror.

"I can still recall," wrote Freud in his famous essay on the uncanny, "that I found his appearance thoroughly unpleasant." The uncanny is a species of fear. It's the wary shiver you feel upon encountering something both like and unlike yourself, both foreign and very close. The uncanny flows from an unclear threat. It's not the fear of a wolf, which you know will eat you; it's something altogether more intimate and voiceless, the fear of something without a name, of a threat against your identity, an attack on your idea of yourself. That's not me, thought Freud—yet it was, and on some level, he *knew* it was. The uncanny is a symptom of repression. It's eerie, unhomelike—*unheimlich*—precisely because it leads you home, to what you wish to forget: the revenant, the ghost.

But what if you didn't want to forget? What if you were desperate to remember, in order to go on living, to be less afraid? I long to reimagine the conjunction of *close* and *foreign* as survival strategy, illumination, and hope. To embrace the elderly traveler who springs into the compartment, with his disordered clothes and strange, repellent face. To think with a shout of laughter, Why, it's me! As the train goes hurtling through a darkness spotted here and there with stars.

Shakhrisabz

Drag my suitcase along the corridor, bounce it down the single step to the courtyard, into a pallid morning that smells of leaves and exhaust. Outside the gate, the Golden Dragon waits, chugging by the curb. There's the gentle humidity of gardens being watered, the excitement of a journey. One of the drivers takes my suitcase and shoves it snugly into the compartment under the bus. We're leaving today, south toward Samarkand, the first leg of a journey that will take us to the village of Ak Metchet, where the Mennonite travelers settled. I choose a seat, arrange my backpack, take out a sheaf of notes. We will spend so much time on the Golden Dragon, which now pulls into the traffic with an easy, shouldering movement and sets off along the tree-lined boulevard. The Mennonite travelers needed two years for their journey; we've got two weeks. The shadows of passing branches flicker over my notes. I'm reading about the city of Shakhrisabz, the birthplace of Timur, the original goal of Claas Epp Jr. and his followers.

The tour is designed to make the most of time, even time on the bus: there's a microphone up front, our guides will talk to us as we ride, either Usmon or the American historian, Frank, who now clears his throat to lead us in the daily devotion. Each morning of our trek will begin with scripture. Frank can't stand up straight on the bus, he's too tall, he bends, he braces himself on the back of a seat. The day begins with the crackling mic, his energetic figure swaying along with the bus, his kind eyes behind his glasses. He has the tweedy charm of professors I remember from college, the close-cropped beard, not at all the broad whiskers of a Mennonite patriarch in a stock photo, but a beard that gestures modestly toward the past, as if to say, far be it from me to adopt the grand proportions of the beards of my fathers, and yet, forgive me,

I can't leave this face quite naked. It's the kind of beard my husband has, the kind preferred by most of the Mennonite men I know. Frank speaks to us of migration, of loss, of Babylon, of exile. He links our trip to the Great Trek that preceded ours, and then to even earlier, biblical journeys, Paul and Silas, the Christ Child in Egypt. Abraham, he says, was a wandering Aramean.

I hear the words wrong: *a wandering error man.*

The trees grow thinner as we leave Tashkent. Trucks roar past us, piled with bales of hay. I read of Shakhrisabz, which the Mennonite travelers called Shar-i-Sabs, where they intended to go when they started out from Russia. This was the site selected by Claas Epp Jr. in his prophecies, the place of refuge, where Christ would soon return. Valley of the Carrots, they thought it meant, but this is a mistranslation: Shakhrisabz means Green Town. They meant to go there, to this mistranslated valley, but circumstances forced them to change their route, they wandered, they were thrown off course, toward Khiva, error upon error, mistakes of language, direction, purpose, plan, a formidable misreading of the world.

Shakhrisabz, that missed destination, will not be part of my journey. It remains imagined, casting its green aura through my notes, a city that lies approximately eighty kilometers south of Samarkand. Some translators call it the Emerald City. Nearly three thousand years old, it was once known as Kesh, which means heart-pleasing. It has sometimes been identified with the lost city of Nautaca, the site of a famous Persian horse race, where Alexander the Great replaced his exhausted horses. The local breed was known in China as heavenly horses; they sweated blood.

"A fertile land," wrote the Arab geographer al-Maqdisi, "which exports early fruits."

I read of the ruddy clay of Shakhrisabz, the bleached muslin, the seventh-century coin with a hole in the center. Three kinds of salt were traded to China: red, green, and black.

The city had four gates: the Iron Gate, Abdullah's Gate, the Butcher's Gate, and the Town Gate.

Outside, purple pansies dance before a farmhouse door, and I think of the embroidery patterns of Shakhrisabz: flowers, vases, palms, and the *chahar-chirag*, the four lights motif, based on the shape of a lantern.

I dream of the language of ancient Shakhrisabz, that clement place. I read that slavery was never legal there, even at the height of the Silk Road trade. The mountains around the city glimmered with porcelain snow, reported the traveling monk Xuanzang, and the gates were reinforced with iron and hung with bells. The climate was warm and damp; epidemics prevailed. During the spring rains, priests retired for their "rain rest" to avoid disease. The appearance of the people was simple and rustic. Their language had twenty-five letters; by combining these, they could describe everything around them.

Imagine it's possible to speak of wholeness. Dream of a language that does not shatter.

Kholid, seated across the aisle from me, points out an orchard like a row of verdant flames. We are traveling through the region that produced the first apple. "According to our poets," says Kholid, "this is the Garden of Eden."

TWO

The Hunger Steppe

to transform the world into signs

The raven's claw

In the evening, dinner in a Kyrgyz yurt, a broad tent covered with felt. We are on the border of the Hunger Steppe, an area devoted to farming, though it was a desert when the Mennonite travelers came this way, inhabited only by nomads. Slender struts radiate from the domed center of the yurt, where the electric light spreads its branches, its rays reflected in our flat bowls of *beshbarmak*, described to us as "typical Kyrgyz food." *Beshbarmak* means five fingers, because that's what you're supposed to eat it with. We use spoons. Squares of pasta and strips of meat glisten in the broth, a liquid so clear and shallow it doesn't read to us as soup; it's as if someone's overturned half a glass of water into every plate. I try to stand up for the typical Kyrgyz fare, arguing that, with its bland flavor, easily digestible noodles, and nourishing scraps of meat, beshbarmak is probably a great comfort food, exactly what you'd want if you were in bed with a cold.

Arnie gives me a wry look from under his white eyebrows. "If you're miserable anyway," he agrees, "you might as well have some." But we eat heartily of the "five fingers," introducing ourselves, swapping histories with the interest of people brought together by an offbeat enthusiasm. Our decision to join this peculiar tour creates an instant trust. And there is, as well, in this brightly colored cocoon on the edge of the steppe, the inevitable unfolding of a deeply familiar practice: a form of inquiry known as the Mennonite game. In this game, two strangers trade the names of their hometowns, parents, in-laws, churches, and schools, until they find a connection between them. They'll settle for having met or taught or worked with each other's relatives, but the highest goal is to find out they're related. Of course, many cultures play some form of this game; the intricacies of the Somali game, played by people who have memorized their paternal lineage going back ten generations or more, make the Mennonite game look simple, though the Mennonite version is full of unexpected twists, as it's played by a smaller group with a higher degree of inbreeding.

Diane, who will be my roommate on the trip, smiles as the table goes through several rounds of the native sport. Her mother was Greek Catholic, but her father's family has been Mennonite since the seventeenth century. She is the fourth cousin, three times removed, of Claas Epp Jr.

Exchanges of names like playing cards. The significance of the name *Epp* turned over suddenly, heavy as a spade. And then there's my *Samatar*, glitteringly revealed at one end of the table, an ornate and fanciful queen from a different deck. I'm used to the effect of this name in churches and Mennonite gatherings where, in combination with my

Somali features, it suggests I'm a new or potential convert to the faith, or perhaps a visitor from one of our church offices abroad. I'm greeted with hesitant smiles until I play my hidden cards, my husband's *Miller* or, better, that magic phrase: "My mother was a Glick." The Germanic click of the name, so neat and *heimlich* on the tongue, opens the latch. All hesitation dissolves in warmth, surprise, and love. They look at me in a completely different way. I'm in, I win. It takes Arnie ten seconds to figure out he knows my uncle.

Mennonite names, the ones I know so well, they speak to me instantly, but they don't know me, I have to work my way into their fabric every time: that sonorous material, densely wadded like a quilt, in which I wrap myself, achy yet comfortable, like a sick child.

These names form a symbolic code, impenetrable to outsiders. And under our seats, as we sip our cooling soup and dab our lips with napkins, another code extends, embroidered on carpets that deepen the air with color, an emblematic language I can't read. Beneath the feet of the jolly tourists who patronize the yurt-restaurant, wondering if their traditional Kyrgyz dinner has been prepared with horsemeat, beneath the passing waiter who, overhearing, cries out, "Beef! Only beef!" with a haste that raises a laugh all down the table, the carpets go on silently uttering the ram's horn, which means prosperity, the comb for cleanliness, the spinal column for strength.

I have read of Kyrgyz symbols so complex they tell a story. They can say "a tiger has torn two cows in the pasture." There is a sign for "an eagle dispersing pheasants." A rising moon, to protect children. And the raven's claw, which means "to leave a trace."

Back at the hotel, I page through the history of the Great Trek: memoirs by Franz Bartsch, Herman Jantzen, Jacob Jantzen, Jacob Klaassen, and Elizabeth Unruh. Treasured photocopies of books borrowed from libraries, scanned in special collections, emailed to me by archivists in Kansas. These, with their repetitive names—they are my guides, my waymarks. They are the ones who wrote the story of the trek. I curl up with them in bed, in the murmur of water from Diane's shower and the beat of plaintive pop music through the wall.

Shadows of earthly things

Wanderers. They left their farms in Russia, the Am Trakt settlement, the villages nestling in the valleys, the bubbling Creek Tarlich. In his memoir of the trek, Franz Bartsch records the death of his infant daughter, who succumbed to a sudden fever on the eve of the migration. "Then we went to the cemetery where we took leave of our little one." They buried her at dawn, on a summer day in 1880. By ten o'clock, Bartsch and his wife were on their way to Central Asia with a group that would become known as the Bride Community.

They were sojourners and pilgrims. They were Germans from the Volga, they would explain to people they met along the way, who were seeking a place where they could practice their faith. They were leaving Russia, for the czar had revoked the law that exempted them from military service. All over the Mennonite settlements there, people were selling their farms and moving away, most going west, to the Americas, but these, raising the dust with their line of eighteen covered wagons, had chosen a different path, a more dazzling vision.

It was a vision of the end of the world. For decades, millenarian fever had been rippling across Europe, intensified by a series of populist revolutions that were seen by some as the footprints of Antichrist. One of these prophets was the Mennonite preacher Claas Epp Jr. He urged the faithful to abandon the West, with its sick, collapsing empires, and take refuge in the free wilderness of the East, in the desert, like the woman clothed with the sun in the Book of Revelation. *The moon under her feet, and upon her head a crown of twelve stars.* There they would await the Second Coming. Through his study of Revelation and the Book of Daniel, Epp predicted Christ's return with increasing precision, until he reached a date: March 8, 1889.

Franz Bartsch, a teacher, had at first been skeptical of Epp's prophecies, but had gradually become one of his most loyal followers. He was in the first wagon train, the core, made up of families who had attended a special communion service led by Epp. There they had bound themselves together with ties of love and destiny. They had shared in the new ceremony of foot-washing. They had given up the formal German pronoun, *Sie*, and addressed one another as *du*. They were turned toward the future, when they would meet Christ, their Bridegroom, in Central Asia.

I see them setting off in their covered wagons. A line of futurists, of idealists. There were more children than adults. Several sympathetic friends accompanied them part of the way, and a woman left them some fresh cream waffles on a stump. Claas Epp, too, was there, though he would soon return to the settlement to encourage others to undertake the journey. At the place of the three wells—a place which, Bartsch writes, "remained deeply engraved in our memories"—Epp gave a sermon called "Shadows and Essence." He used Hebrews 8:5, a text on *the shadow of heavenly things*. A document, I think, is a shadow of earthly things. I read Franz Bartsch in the morning, in a pale light barred by the lines between the windows, as the bus rolls down a highway lined with farms. An open landscape, dun and green, basking in the heat. Mounds of yellow clay piled up where they have been cleaning the canal. The houses are gray brick, with roofs of corrugated iron, sometimes painted, so they make quilt-like squares of lavender, orange, maroon. In the shade of a copse, black sheep clump together, richly colored like handfuls of dates. All movement seems slow compared to the rush of the Golden Dragon: the old men in white caps, chatting together on wobbling bicycles piled with clover; the boy pushing a cart of bottled water; the trotting donkeys.

This is Franz Bartsch's atmosphere, this his light. I read his memoir here, and I listen to it, too, for Frank, our historian, has the same books I do, the ones layered in my suitcase, he reads aloud from them into the microphone. He reads Bartsch's description of everyday things: the covered wagon, the samovar packed inside, the spring-filled cushion on the box. This is what we want to know. I can sense Frank's excitement, the historian's alertness to those small details that clarify the past. There is no sermon, no theological argument, that can make a moment suddenly come together in this way, the way Bartsch draws us close, writing of the tin ladle, the pails hanging on hooks, and the lopsided wagon cover, so poorly made, its thin struts buckling like leather.

Before the departure, Epp referred to Bartsch's dead infant in a sermon, as a metaphor for the old life, which must be left behind like a field of bones. But Bartsch is a documentarist. His heart loves the earthly things. He craves memorial. Later, on the trek, when the children begin to die, he will give thanks that his own little girl is buried at Am Trakt, in a grave, with a name, instead of on the desolate steppe without a cemetery.

The road, their road, fine and dry. Long ox caravans bearing pink salt to Orenburg. Kyrgyz nomads riding their shaggy camels to market. At Irgiz, the last town before the desert, the Mennonite travelers hired a camel caravan and several Kyrgyz drivers. They had to cross the waste to reach Tashkent. The camels would carry their provisions and feed for the horses across the sands. For cooking, the travelers would build fires of dried dung and the brittle desert shrub, *saxaul*, which burned a nitrous green.

Kara Kum: Black Sand. Kyzyl Kum: Red Sand. The names of deserts. Earth blistered and parched with sun, encrusted with salt crystals. A punishing glare, the plodding camels' feet leaving barely a trace. In the evenings, the wagons drawn into a circle, a *Wagenburg*.

Hymns on the air as the day cools.

Without the Kyrgyz drivers who led them to the wells, the travelers would have perished. Franz Bartsch recalls the names of these wells: Utsch Kuduk, Bish Kuduk, Kup Kuduk, Kara Kuduk, Kap Kara Kuduk. Three Wells, Five Wells, Many Wells, Black Wells, All Black Wells. The water of Kap Kara Kuduk was truly black. When his wife held the lantern close to the samovar, Bartsch recalls, they saw that the water was dark before they added the tea.

As the sands grew deeper and the journey more demanding for the horses, the Mennonites devised a relay system. Five horses would pull a wagon over a stretch; then men would ride the horses back, hitch them to another wagon, and pull it forward. Three weeks like this, back and forth over the sand. Such agonizing slowness, the steps constantly retraced, the same ground traveled over again and again, the stupidity of using horses and wagons instead of camels, the scarcity of water, the unremitting heat. In his history of the trek, Fred Belk records that eleven children died between Russia and the end of the desert. Bartsch includes his own lost infant to make twelve. He quotes a letter from Epp, received by the community once they had crossed the sands, which compares these twelve lost children to twelve stones. "When Israel entered Canaan through the Jordan, God commanded them to lay down twelve commemorative stones in the Jordan. We, the spiritual Israel, also had to leave twelve stones—the twelve bodies of little children—of which the biblical stones were but prototypes."

Words of—what? Comfort? "But what could possibly be the purpose of this interpretation?" asks Bartsch. "What good could it possibly effect?" Signs point to things—shadows indicate essence—very well, but why these signs? Every child under the age of four died before the end of the trip.

Who was this man Claas Epp Jr., who was so quick to transform the world into signs? In the photograph I hold, he sits with his wife and daughter. His hair, parted on the left, sweeps above his wide, white brow. His ears are prominent, his face rather flat, his beard so slight it might be a shadow. I am drawn to his left hand, resting on his knee, the first and second fingers slightly parted to cover his daughter's hand, perhaps to remind the little girl to stand still for the camera, or to add a warmer note to the stiff, conventional family portrait. His eyes are large. His shoulders slope. He wears a black cravat. His wife is the only one looking at the camera. You can tell almost nothing from a face. Somewhere behind or beyond this photograph he rides his handsome horse. He rides up and down the roads of the Mennonite settlements in Russia, distributing copies of his book *The Unsealed Prophecy of the Prophet Daniel and the Meaning of the Revelation of Jesus Christ.* He enters homes with his atlas. He speaks of the woman clothed with the sun, the beast Napoleon, the trials of the Last Days. The photograph tempts me to reverse engineer the past, to perceive the blanched light of prophecy in his motionless, formal gaze, to read in the line of his shaven lip the ambition of a wealthy, successful man who has discovered a spiritual calling. How he hurried his followers out of Russia! He wasn't the only preacher calling for an eastern journey, but he was the first to get people moving. I'm tempted to read a hunger in the crook of his arm. Something fierce or disturbed in his eye. The problem is, I know the future.

When you know the future, everything looks like a sign. The event becomes the inevitable. Prophecy differs from the documentary impulse. Even when looking backward, the documentarist is less interested in the result than in preserving the details of each passing moment. Jacob Jantzen, who was a teenager at the time of the trek, recalls the thickening atmosphere of death. "The children became poorer and poorer and finally died," he records in his memoir, written years later in

Oklahoma when he was seventy-five years old. "Many a mother had to lay her dear little ones beneath the ground." Sometimes they traveled with the corpses, hoping to find a town, to buy wood for a coffin. Sometimes they gave up and buried the bodies in sand. This was the case with the Kopper children, three little siblings who died within three days.

Lay your stones in the river. Three little children in three days, slipping away, chasing each other as in a game. They were buried together in the desert. Bartsch, still mourning his own child, writes of them tenderly. "Surely the resurrection morning will find them there."

On one of the wagons, a child, perhaps one who survived, or perhaps one of those who would sicken and die before reaching the end of that wasteland, pointed at the dunes, impressed by their smooth, regular waves, and cried out to the woman beside her, "Look at all the little doll-graves, Tante!"

The day feels stretched, boundless. How different, I think, from the days of those travelers who didn't have our comforts, our speed, the blur of the afternoon in the window, as we fly past the peaked metal bus stops that look like municipal sculptures, stopping only at a police checkpoint adorned with a potted fern. Tracing the path of the travelers, we immerse ourselves in their story. How they reached the Aral Sea at last, where the famished horses, driven to gnaw the wagon shafts, tore up greenery, careless of how the harsh reeds cut their mouths. Farther on, the travelers found pheasants, deer, and berries in the woods. At Kaplanbek, near Tashkent, they settled for the winter and were joined by two more wagon trains from Russia. Among the newcomers were three young people, all around fourteen years old, who would one day write memoirs: Herman Jantzen, Jacob Klaassen, and Elizabeth Unruh.

These young people have nothing to say about the end of the world. They remember the beautiful countryside, and the snowy peaks of the Tien Shan mountains that "glistened," Herman writes, "in a bluish haze." They remember how hard it was to get up on the cold mornings, when the hanging laundry froze into chunks of ice, and the growls of the stray dogs stealing meat right out of the camp. By the time he reached Kaplanbek, Jacob Klaassen could count and swear in Kyrgyz. As for Elizabeth, her memoir concentrates on food, it's as if she's starving, she describes all the fruit: apples, pears, plums, cherries, peaches, apricots, strawberries, grapes, "so many kinds we knew no names for." There were dates, she writes, figs, olives, melons. "Oh, it was lovely here," she continues, "if only a severe sickness had not befallen us." That winter was so warm, tulips bloomed on the roofs. The unseasonable heat contributed to a typhoid epidemic. Nearly a fifth of the company died that year.

The men, exhausted by overwork in the stone quarries, grew too weak to fight off illness. Instead of stopping work between midmorning and afternoon as the local workers did, the Mennonites worked through the heat of the day. "The result of this mistake," writes the historian Fred Belk, "was that many strong young men contracted what the Russians call 'climate typhus.'" When spring came and the steppe turned green and blossomed with sedge lilies, the climate typhus among the Mennonites grew worse. "In a short time," writes Herman Jantzen, "my Uncle Heinrich Jantzen had lost his two older sons, the very handsome Abram, twenty-five, and Heinrich, age twenty-one. What that meant to the stricken parents one cannot utter in words."

Instead of words, there is silence, or a howl. Some sound without shape. So Herman Jantzen documents the failure of documents. There are sounds that cannot be spelled. Yet he gives us what he can, a brief and simple phrase, *the very handsome Abram.* In this phrase, the image of a body hovers for an instant, carried through a doorway, laid out on a bed. The words are inadequate, but they make a gap. Just for a moment, they pierce a hole in time where pain slips through.

Miraculous, to make something happen in another's body. You write your poor, approximate words in German in 1950, and seventy years later, in English translation, they shift the breath of a woman on a moving bus.

Grieving, swept by fevers, the Bride Community still gathered at dusk each Sunday to share the evening meal, the love feast. Claas Epp Jr.'s letters were read aloud. He urged the group to go on, insisting that their true home lay in a valley south of Samarkand. This was fabled Shar-i-Sabs, their Valley of the Carrots: Shakhrisabz. To go there would mean crossing into Bukhara, and they had been told the emir would not let them in. But Epp quoted Revelation 3:8: *Behold, I have set before thee an open door.*

An open door, and no man can shut it. Language to shift the breath.

"Pull over, pull over!" cries Frank. The bus lurches into the shadow of a cliff. These, says Frank, ushering us eagerly outdoors, must be the mountains described in Elizabeth Unruh's memoir. *Mountains* seems a grand word for these stark and rocky mounds, black with graffiti and littered with broken glass. Higher up, a loden-green plant grows on the slopes, spiny in the hand, with a fragrance like sage. We try to identify it, trading guesses in English and Russian. Kholid says it's used in traditional medicine as an antibiotic. I think of healing, and especially of an essay stuffed in my backpack, "Pilgrimage as Healing," by Walter S. Friesen. This essay describes pilgrimage as a kind of spiritual tonic that lets the brain "reconnect and reintegrate tissues, organs, memories, and learnings of the body." I watch Micah, the youngest of our party, a college student traveling with his father, scramble up the hill until his blue shirt disappears on the other side. When it's time to return to the bus, we shout to call him back. A pilgrimage is a quest narrative: it has a clear trajectory, a shape. Its line contains the randomness of movement. "What are the likely conditions," asks Walter S. Friesen, "of pilgrimages that foster such wholeness?"

I can't answer. I feel cast adrift, like a teenager loosed on the tumbled landscape, whose brain records every hillock as a mountain. Back on the bus, Frank passes the microphone to Lois, Arnie's wife, the great-granddaughter of Elizabeth Unruh. He invites her to read aloud from Elizabeth's memoir, and she recounts stories of healing as we cruise between formal fields of summer cotton, through a greenness so entire it seems to soak into the sky, an olive haze behind the undulating lines of telephone wire. She reads of traditional medicine. Elizabeth Unruh's mother was a bonesetter and, as her role no doubt demanded, a brusque, no-nonsense type. Once, after a wagon accident, she treated an injured man by wetting his displaced eye with her spit and shoving it back in the socket. Among her cures was a stone with healing properties called a Bloodstone, with which she cured a man who had been badly crushed in the quarry: she rubbed the stone with vinegar and gave him the liquid to drink. "That made him vomit," Elizabeth explains, "and all the blood he had in his lungs was vomited up."

The reading makes us laugh and squirm: these stories of bodies brought roughly into line. But I can't help thinking that those Mennonites, as a group, were traveling outside any legitimate line, toward a Second Coming that would not come. They thought they were pilgrims, but they were wanderers. And how do you know whether you're on a pilgrimage that will foster wholeness or just aimlessly roving? Curled up in a patch of sun in the corner of my seat, I read of the Mennonite boys heading out to water the horses at the river, ambling, following no particular route. They gave in to distraction, taking every opportunity for a race, exploring the fields, the forests, the rocks where the shepherds sheltered from storms, and the steppe, the glorious steppe, "a veritable flower-carpet far into the hills," writes Jacob Klaassen, "with every kind of flower imaginable, a splendor of colors that cannot be described." I see them galloping, whooping for joy, far from any path, among the radiant patterns, the grass exhaling its pure breath toward the sun.

Usmon, scanning his cell phone, discovers the English name of our mystery plant from the hills at last. It is wormwood.

The Emir of Bukhara had told the Mennonites the East was closed. Most of them listened. A large group decided to stay in Russian Turkestan, settling in Aulie-Ata, in present-day Kazakhstan, where they were offered the option of forestry service in place of the draft. A small group, however, refused this compromise and turned toward Shar-i-Sabs, in accordance with Epp's prophecies. They sent him a telegram from Tashkent: "By faith, Abraham obeyed when he was called to go out to a place which he was to receive as an inheritance; and he went out, not knowing where he was to go."

July 28, 1881. Ninety-nine degrees Fahrenheit. "Still," writes Fred Belk, "the train of forty-eight wagons carried one hundred and fifty-three hymn-singing Mennonites resolutely forward along the dust-choked roads."

Unser Zug geht durch die Wüste. "Our Journey Leads Through the Desert." Their favorite hymn.

They entered the lunar landscape of the Hunger Steppe. "The name," writes Jacob Jantzen, "caused a feeling of horror to come over us." We're traveling through the same region, and yet a different one, transformed, a fertile basin fed by a Soviet irrigation system. Now it blossoms, all the territory between Tashkent and Samarkand, with the network of water responsible for draining the Aral Sea. When the

Mennonite travelers passed here, it was a barren place. They built fires from branches of shriveled *narthex asafoetida*, which gave off a strong, oniony smell when lit. They encountered a terrible poisonous spider, the *falange*, wide as a man's hand, covered with dirty yellow hair. They found tortoises here, too, and "cave salamanders" which, Bartsch says, "terrified our women with their screams." I have searched in vain for evidence of these screaming salamanders—I can only find references to those that hiss or squeak—but Elizabeth Unruh echoes Bartsch, describing a salamander whose screams woke shepherds in the night, and which was "the size of a native cow."

An atmosphere of wonder and terror, as in the Book of Revelation. *Behold a great red dragon.*

And then the streams, rushing, violent. They hired skilled horsemen to help them cross. In the deafening thunder, writes Bartsch, "Revelation 1:15 came to mind: 'And his voice was like the sound of many waters.'"

Large, flat rounds of bread as they drew closer to Samarkand. Canals that watered the fountains of the city. And the magnificent mausoleum of Amir Timur, its dome rising above the rooftops, engraved with delicate lines, as if stitched with a needle. Shade trees grew in the courtyards, and men pushed barrels about the city on wheels, sprinkling the streets with water to keep down the dust. The Mennonites camped, Elizabeth writes, at a palace. "One thing we girls were sorry about, the high walls surrounding the palace, where we stayed, we could not see out and no women dare go outside the wall."

My research identifies Elizabeth's "palace" as a former prison. Perhaps it was both. Certainly it was vast, decayed, abandoned for some time. One night, when they lit the lamps after supper to hold communion, the air filled instantly with hundreds of bats. The creatures swept down from the rafters, disturbed by the light. Elizabeth describes the ensuing panic: "Of course the lights were put out immediately, we were all quite stirred up, whether we had communion I do not remember."

Elizabeth is less erudite than Franz Bartsch, less eloquent perhaps, but her account has the same sense of weird, excessive experience. "So many things happened on our journey," she declares, "which I saw and heard, was witness to, that I cannot write all here for it would fill books."

Sad comedy of the border. They spoke to Russian and Bukharan officials, received conflicting orders, crossed into Bukhara, were turned back, crossed again. As the weather turned colder, some brought their samovars into the wagons for warmth; one family lost consciousness from the fumes and had to be carried out. The Bukharan side of the border looked exactly like the Russian side: November. They begged to be allowed to stop somewhere for the winter. They held up faith like a lamp against the chilly bureaucracy of the nation-state and its arbitrary lines.

This is one way of looking at it. It's possible to see these travelers loading their wagons, weeping in the cold mud, turned away from Bukhara again, as part of the family of all those who are termed *illegal people*, the ones who languish in camps, who are outcast, detained, deported, neglected, killed. It is also possible to see them as simply stubborn, fanatical. All of my sources stress that they were repeatedly told not to enter Bukhara. "When I think of it now," writes Elizabeth Unruh, "how befogged a person's mind, even a Christian's, can get, when we do not want to listen to reason, but only think of ourselves."

At last they were sent to a valley on the Bukharan side, eight miles from the town of Serabulak. There they built a village called Ebenezer, the stone of help, so named for the stone set up for remembrance by the prophet Samuel after the Lord had delivered Israel from the Philistines.

There were mulberry trees in the valley, and food and other supplies were cheap. In a sentence that bears an eerie resemblance to her earlier one about Kaplanbek, Elizabeth Unruh writes, "It really was prosperous country, if only the blackpox had not been.

"It wiped out nearly all the children. Although our youngest three had them, only my youngest brother died. Those that got well had so many pox marks on their bodies, their faces so scarred, they hardly looked like themselves."

Such losses—enough to freeze the imagination. And this seemingly boundless resilience. They built sod houses, with glass windows they had carried in the wagons. Elizabeth Unruh was strong enough to dig sod, and after working she hiked with her friends in the hills, for "even though we had some hair-raising experiences, we still wanted to see more of the country." In the gullies they encountered the salamander the size of a cow and were followed by "a type of owl-like birds." "Me being the inquisitive one," Elizabeth writes, "I spotted their nest so I crawled up the cliff to see their young." The grown birds attacked the intruders; Elizabeth almost fell, and one of the hikers was struck by a bird's wing, "hurting her back, it got all blue." Terror and wonder. In the caves, "veins of gold and silver all a-glitter with all kinds of colored stones . . . like precious stones lying on the ground."

As for the boys, they watered the horses, rode them to market for supplies, and cheered the "devils-chase," in which mounted men fought to seize the carcass of a goat. "It was very amusing for us boys," Jacob Klaassen writes in a breathless rush, "standing on the roofs, watching the chase when the whole band would come pounding into the village and roar over donkeys loaded with bags, over bags of wheat, rice, and raisins, over tables of meat, grapes, apples, and baskets of apricots, and finally become thoroughly entangled in a ball, fighting one another with whips whistling over their heads making the dust fly from the hair, until someone would, at last, extricate himself without paying any attention to the shouts and curses of the sellers who sought to rescue as much of their wares as possible and who had the damage, but no amusement out of it all." They were learning the country, its temporality, the call to prayer, the days of fasting when men sat ready for nightfall with food laid out before them and pipes in their hands, the houses, the rugs, how to sit with your legs folded, the taste of camel meat, how to eat rice neatly and easily with one hand. Jacob Jantzen was invited to the home of a local braggart, something of a bully, the tallest man in the village. He was afraid to go there alone. But in the end, he accepted, and found a little oil lamp burning, and soup, and silence. "I will never forget it," he writes.

> Here I raise my Ebenezer,
> Hither by thy help I'm come.
> And I hope by thy good pleasure
> Safely to arrive at home.

Thinking of these travelers, I recall the lines of the beloved hymn. They had built their Ebenezer in hope, but in the end, they were not safe. They had settled in defiance of the Emir of Bukhara, who sent his chieftain with a carmine tent and smartly dressed soldiers the Mennonites called "the many-colored ones." The soldiers dammed the water supply. They tore down the sod houses. "The glass windows," writes Belk, "which Mennonite housewives had painstakingly wrapped in linen before their departure and which had been brought so carefully along on their journey, were first shattered by the troops." After they broke the windows, the many-colored ones tore off the roofs. Herman Jantzen, who stood in their way, was bound and thrown onto a cart. "It was a tumult," writes Elizabeth Unruh. "Camel's cry, the children crying—So ended our Place of Peace."

Herman Jantzen writes of his journey tied up on the cart. In Bartsch's and Belk's accounts, this is a brutal moment; in Herman's own words, it's stranger and more nuanced, in fact oddly brotherly. "We had hardly begun to travel when I became numb with cold. I begged the soldier who was with me to untie me. It was obvious that I could not escape in the deep snow. He ordered a halt, untied me, and allowed me to run beside the wagon until I was out of breath and of course also warm. Then he stretched out his hand and pulled me up onto his horse beside himself. He threw his long wide fur coat over my head, which covered me completely. I stuck my head out behind his neck so that I could get air, and on the warm horse, under the warm fur, I was not cold anymore."

Later Herman describes this soldier as "my protector." Delivering the boy to the *Aksakal*, or head elder, of Serabulak, the soldier said, "This is the son of the Aksakal of the frontier-breakers." He requested that the elder take the boy in, give him a warm bed, and watch over him in a manner befitting a Muslim.

The frontier-breakers stayed in Serabulak. Several families found shelter in a mosque: the Kok Ota or Blue Grandfather Mosque, surrounded by elm and poplar trees. Their hosts let the strangers use the mosque on Sundays, for church.

In that mosque, one of the Mennonite leaders, Johannes K. Penner, preached a vehement sermon against Claas Epp and his prophecies. Penner's one-year-old son had died the previous day. Some were so disturbed by his words, they went to pray in the wilderness. Herman Jantzen spent the whole night awake in a nearby valley: "I agonized in prayer until dawn." And later, in that same mosque, Epp himself preached to the community, having arrived with the final wagon train from Russia, two years after the migration began.

He read from the Book of Daniel, Isaiah, the Gospels, and Revelation. He preached into the dome of Kok Ota, into a murk of conflicting emotions, turning the beam of his charisma toward those who were with him and those who were passionately against him. In fact, only a minority of the travelers considered him their leader; the Mennonite groups on the trek came from different settlements in Russia, temporarily united in their search for peace. In the series of calamities that dogged the trek—the Kaplanbek fever, the struggles with border officials, the destruction of Ebenezer—great swaths of the group peeled off, leaving for America, remaining in Tashkent, or moving farther north into Russian territory. Claas Epp didn't gain followers; he lost detractors. As the group dwindled, those who remained were the ones committed to his project. His influence grew as other, often more popular leaders despaired, stayed behind, emigrated to America, or died.

On the bus, Arnie remarks on Claas Epp's pride, his assumption of leadership and prophethood. He says he can just imagine the members of the third wagon train, who didn't come from Epp's settlement in Russia, who might have read his book, but didn't know him, listening to his sermon in the mosque: "Who does this guy think he is?"

Among the various leaders, Epp was the visionary, the interpreter of signs, the poet. He wrote hymns as well as sermons. His book of prophecies is a blistering tract that occasionally erupts into verse. Printed in Russia at his own expense, *The Unsealed Prophecy of the Prophet Daniel and the Meaning of the Revelation of Jesus Christ* was widely read and reprinted several times, and its tangled hermeneutics and scalding rhetoric played a significant role in drawing Mennonites eastward. Apparently, he's not a great writer: "Epp was not a learned man," his translators say; his German is often confused, his syntax hard to follow. But his images are vivid, frightening. "Already," he declares, "horrible lightning illuminates the abyss which shall swallow up everything." In the midst of his bewildering calculations, which ostensibly prove that Russia is the eagle in Revelation and Napoleon the sixth head of the beast from the sea, he groans, "Ach, Lord." He seems overcome. He bursts into song: *"Oh, let us quake before this day / Which like a snare appears."* *The Unsealed Prophecy* reveals Epp's style: it gives a hint of the sermon he delivered at Serabulak, its weight, its tone. Prophecy is all urgency; it withers irony, burns it up. *Therefore flee! flee! flee from the land of the midnight hour!*

Such pressing haste. Epp stayed in Serabulak for less than a week before he set off to meet with the Khan of Khiva. The mission was a success. Here, at last, was their open door: a friendly khan, exemption from military service, and a promise of land on the Amu Darya River.

Not everyone would follow through that door. Among those who parted ways with the Bride Community was one of my documentarists, Franz Bartsch. He and his wife joined ten families who dug in their heels at Ebenezer. Though Bukharan soldiers had destroyed the buildings, they pitched their tents on the site, led by Epp's letters to believe they must not cross back into Russian territory. The soldiers returned to force them out. "While we were singing Psalm 23 and praying, the tent poles of our worship sanctuary fell away under attacks by the 'many-colored ones.'"

This small group suffered not only the terror of a physical assault but also the pain of a reproach from Claas Epp Jr., who, when he arrived at Serabulak, instead of praising their fortitude, excommunicated them for staying behind at Ebenezer. They had misinterpreted his letters, misread the signs. How easy to do. How easy for me, I think, as I work through these memoirs, reading in translation. One of Epp's translators, Dallas Wiebe, meditates on this problem in his novel based on the trek, *Our Asian Journey*. He writes of a certain despair that arises when consulting the source material. "From the scribbled records left by the people who enacted this story, we reconstruct, we create a fiction no matter how closely we render the events as we think they happened. Even if we had been there, the writing would be in some way false. That we are writing in English is a distortion." In distorted language I write of Bartsch's misreading of Epp's letters, and of Epp's prophecies, his misreading of the Bible. Is the problem that these documents have been infected by what Epp's own father, referring to his son's millennialism, called an "unsavory fanatical imagination"? But then how to read a document without the imagination, which compensates for the poverty of the words?

"We can say with Ezekiel," writes Franz Bartsch, "'The wall is no more, nor those who daubed it.'"

The tents are fallen. A sound of weeping falters over the snow. Bartsch stumbles, collecting his scattered papers, a spoon, a dented pail. Suddenly a cry rings out: a woman collapses in what he will later call "a hysterical seizure." Other women run toward her and cradle her body. Her head flung back, her cap awry, she screams: "Turn back! But not to the mountains!" Then she begins to babble with joy. She can hear the angels sing. She sees all the children who have died on the trek, lined up and smiling, in Heaven. Weeping and laughing she recites their names. The women are wrapping her in a blanket, trying to coax her into a wagon. Soldiers watch them, the "many-colored ones," clad in the embroidered robe of the region, the *khalat*. The winter twilight turns the shadows blue.

Bartsch climbs onto the box of his wagon, muffled against the cold. He is going to Serabulak, but not to Khiva. His trek is over. "And so I left—an apostate. Lightly? Let him judge who has discarded an ideal for which he lived and which he had loved because it had melted away under his feet like softened ice."

The end. His ideal is vanished, and so he writes of shadows, of earthly things, those things that have occupied him, that make his memoir. He writes of a certain Sister Gräve, who, noticing a dark spot in her rising dough, put her hand into it and was stung by a scorpion. The sting caused "dreadful pain," he writes, but surely not more than the deaths of the children, surely not more than the ruin of Ebenezer. Yet he chooses to linger on the domestic scene. And he is not wrong. There is something powerful in the image. The bread. The sting.

Bartsch and his wife left for Tashkent alone. "We were childless again." They had lost a baby boy in Kaplanbek and another in Serabulak.

On the narrow trail to Khiva, the men were forced to ride so close together their legs rubbed against the horses, making the blood flow. They crossed the foaming Zeravshan River and its tributaries several times, where the wagons sank to their boxes in quicksand and had to be hauled out. The cliffs above the streams were dangerous too: Jacob Klaassen was walking behind his family's wagon when the vehicle toppled over into a gully. "I cried out in horror, for the wagon carried everything dear to me on earth, my mother, brother, and sister. I was sure they were all killed." Somehow, though, the horses kept their footing, hurtling down the slope to arrive at the bottom with all the passengers unhurt, and the gully proved wide enough for them to avoid the water—a miracle, Jacob writes. "Only my overcoat was lost."

Miracles and loss. At the edge of the desert, a young girl died. They mourned for two days, then took the wagons apart and loaded them onto camels. Aided by Kyrgyz and Turkmen drivers, they made boxes out of bedsteads and secured them to the camels so that the women and children could ride.

The howdah, covered with linen to shield the riders from the dust. The image is familiar to me from classical Arabic poetry: the poet Imru al-Qays leaping into the howdah with a woman, and the erotic rocking over the desert sand. In his great poem, his *Muʿallaqa*, Imru al-Qays conjures a scene of richness: he remembers women gathering around a freshly slaughtered camel, the meat so abundant they tossed it about in play. The marbled fat, he says, was like the fringes of a shawl. And now these Mennonites enter, dogged, tenacious, spurred by faith, with a certain spirit that's hard to define: a blunt practicality not without humor. Here's Belk on the Mennonite howdah: "Johann Jantzen loaded food supplies and a goat on one side and his wife and three children on the other and achieved perfect balance."

Swaying over the sand. Elizabeth Unruh: "We went real slow, what a train! What a sight!"

But the road, she remembers, was "near unbearable": their conveyances "swayed, jarred, shook and cracked. We had only gone a few days when many got sick from all that shaking. Axles and tongues broke, daily a repair job." She recalls how hard it was to stay in her seat as the camel rose: her fingers got pinched, and her head crashed against the frame "so that I nearly lost my hearing and seeing. Yes, we had troubles without end."

Amidst all the troubles, the irrepressible eagerness of this young girl. "I was so interested in everything, some had their curtains closed; but I always had mine open, so I could see all there was to see." She would have seen ruins in the desert, and dunes nearly two hundred feet high. All in a pale and ghostly light, for the travelers journeyed by night to avoid the heat. "I had rather seen the desert in the day," Jacob Jantzen writes, "but the moon was shining." And there was, as well, the Great Comet of 1882, fair as manna, so brilliant the travelers could read by its light.

They stopped to rebuild the wagons on the far side of the desert. Soon the horses smelled water and raised their heads. It was the scent of the Amu Darya, which watered the orchards of Khiva. The Mennonites reached it at the beginning of autumn.

At a village, they rented the long, shallow boats called *kayiqs* and went on by water. Some slept on the boats, others in the forest on the shore. Those in the forest kept fires going all night against tigers and leopards and the jackals that, Elizabeth writes, "cried like little children."

A child was born on the river. "Just how this could all be in such crowded boats, I do not know; but he grew up and later lived, married in Nebraska, USA."

She places a comment about women in parentheses. "(How my tiny frail mother, or any of the women could endure that long, hard journey.)"

In Khiva, the Mennonites first settled at Lausan. The location did not impress Elizabeth Unruh: "But—oh, my! What a place!" she writes. "No trees, no grass, only some small brush with thorns . . . We had come out of the land of plenty, into a desert."

Prickly country. Wild animals lived here: hyenas, wild pigs, peacocks, "jackals by the hundreds." The dirt was rust-colored and full of tough licorice roots. Elizabeth, now seventeen years old, helped make bricks and dig cellars and wells. The Mennonites built a waterwheel and planted potatoes and corn. "Yes, all these hardships that we had to go through and all for nothing," Elizabeth writes. It seems impossible, after everything the community had already endured, but Lausan, bleak Lausan of the red soil, was to be the scene of some of their worst trials. Lausan, where they whittled Christmas trees and painted them green, as there were no pines or spruce. Lausan, where half their homes flooded the first year. They moved to higher ground. And after the floods, like a series of biblical plagues, came the grasshoppers, the wild hogs, and the thieves.

Grasshoppers "like a dark thundercloud." They were nearly as big as sparrows. Haste, haste! Elizabeth runs with the others, banging two pans together. She runs in the corn, in the peas and barley, shouting and choking on the smoke that rolls over the fields, for noise and smoke are the farmers' only defense. These are agricultural people; their pride is in their farms. At Kaplanbek, it humiliated the men to work in a quarry. (And who knows, perhaps that's why they worked so hard there, pushing themselves toward death.) Now they have land at last, and this cloud rushes over them.

"The next morning early before sunrise," Elizabeth Unruh writes, "father went to see—not one green leaf was left, they had eaten all, right into the ground, the gardens were black. And at the edge of the small ditches, the grasshoppers sat in large clumps."

They burned the clumps of insects. They burned everything. They started over.

Over. And over. The green plants grew. And the wild hogs came and devoured them. They were creatures of preternatural intelligence, their movements swift and soundless, their stealthy bodies melting into the night. Jacob Jantzen, determined to stop them, sat up with a friend all night, guarding a melon field, ready to attack the hogs with a dung fork. The boys never closed their eyes, but in the morning the field was trampled, the melons gone. "Again, as often before, a little more hope and joy was buried."

They plowed and planted again. What else could they do? They started over.

The relentlessness of spring. It comes every year.

Let us recall the reason behind these struggles. The choice of Central Asia, it's true, is based on prophetic visions, but the original reason for leaving Russia is peace: the refusal of violence, even in self-defense, the refusal to enable the violence of others. In this shining absolutism lies the great honor and dignity of Anabaptist life. This is their gift to the world, and it is the reason the world needs them: these travelers are not just a quaint German-speaking cult but the stewards of a precious ethics. Back in Russia, they refused the option of forestry as a replacement for military service, because Russian foresters would become soldiers in their place.

On the bus, speaking loudly over the rattle of our progress, Kholid tells me the Mennonites of Khiva are the most interesting, their story the most appealing, because "they are the most pious." They never compromised, never accepted a government job, never cooperated with the state in any way, unlike other Central Asian Mennonites, the ones who stayed in Russian territory, those whose descendants still live in Kyrgyzstan. The Bride Community held themselves apart. They held firm. Their constancy compels the imagination. I think of one of the articles packed in my suitcase, by Jesse Nathan, written after his own Central Asian tour. "Is there anything," he asks, "for which we would, in our materialist America, give up our many things and comforts to pursue? Would we weather all sorts of hardships for God—or for anything larger or harder than our immediate lives?"

These Mennonite travelers may have been fanatical, Nathan argues, they may have been wrong-headed, completely mistaken about the end of the world, but despite their haywire reasoning they had something to admire. A core. A flame that kindled every aspect of their lives.

But at Lausan that moral certitude is given another test. Thieves come in the night. The cherished horses, bought with money from farms that were sold in Russia—the thieves take them. When no one attempts to stop them, they return in greater numbers, seizing livestock in the middle of the day. They walk into homes. They pick up clothing, utensils, whatever they like. Who are these strange folk, they must wonder, who stand so still while they're being robbed? The Mennonite farmers look at the ground, they don't raise a hand.

Fifty horses are stolen. Thirty cows. It's unbearable. The victims' submission seems to fill the thieves with cruelty. The Mennonites don't know that they have settled on the site of a Russian massacre of Turkmens, which happened only a decade ago. They don't know how that European brutality has scorched those who now shoot out the windows of these unwelcome European homes, who scream for the intruders to come outside. The Turkmens search the houses for money, slash the bedding, smash the clocks. They break the chairs and tables and set them on fire. They strike the crowd with their bayonets. "One woman was hit so bad on her back that she could not walk," writes Elizabeth Unruh. "My mother often had to set bones and massage their muscles. One old man they chopped off half his one ear, another they cracked his skull."

Through all this—no attempt to defend themselves? Not once? Were they so steadfast?

No. The younger men could not endure it. A few of the older men gave in too. They made themselves swords in self-defense. One of these was Herman Jantzen.

The pain of sin. Of betraying oneself, God, the community, the family. So much fear, rage, and shame.

"During such times," writes Herman, "the older men were on their knees with Ohm Epp in prayer. When I came home in the morning, somewhat wounded, I would have to listen to Father's reprimand."

And still it went on, to the point of death. One day some men in the town joked with Heinrich Abrams that they would like to buy his wife Elizabeth. That night, a group broke into the young couple's home. They shot Abrams dead and stabbed the body. Hearing the noise, Elizabeth Abrams escaped through a window. She took refuge in a neighbor's house, where she hid underneath the bed. She was pregnant. She must have known, from the sounds, that her child's father was dead.

According to Belk's account, she was almost too terrified to speak, and could only whisper, "Be quiet! They are coming."

It was the end of Lausan. The Khan of Khiva, hearing of the Mennonites' troubles, offered them a more secure settlement, a "big garden" surrounded by walls. Many refused to go, deciding that they were through with Claas Epp Jr. and with the East; they would move westward instead, to America. Among these were the families of Jacob Jantzen, Jacob Klaassen, and Elizabeth Unruh. A cruel separation, marked by bitterness and grief. "Especially our beloved mother," writes Jacob Klaassen, "who had been through so much hardship in the last two years in addition to the death of her husband and sister, found the parting very difficult." It was hard to bid farewell to those with whom they had suffered so much, harder still to see old friends turn against them for abandoning the true way. "But now," writes Elizabeth Unruh, "they called us, that wanted to migrate to America, 'Outcasts.' How harsh they were towards us."

Of my documentarists, only Herman Jantzen remained. He was one of those who helped dismantle the Lausan settlement, taking the logs, the door frames, and the last unbroken windows from the houses, loading them onto the wagons, and setting out.

The mother of Heinrich Abrams, the man killed in the night, had already left the community, and was in her final illness on the Russian side of the border. Before she died, she cried out, "Heinrich, come now!" Her last words. Her son had been killed two hours earlier in Lausan.

Thirty-nine families moved to the khan's "big garden." They built their houses in a square inside the wall. In the center they placed the school, the teacher's house, and the church, brushed with whitewash. This was Ak Metchet: the White Mosque.

There was not much farmland. The men found work as carpenters for the khan, the women as seamstresses and crafters of decorative boxes. They grew vegetables, melons, and rice, and harvested fruit from their peach and apricot trees. They sold their butter and fruit in the markets of Khiva. Perhaps it was painful to give up farming again, but it would not be for long. The day of Christ's return was drawing near. They built extra homes for the refugees who would surely come streaming out of the West, fleeing the fire and terror of the Last Days.

Claas Epp Jr. excommunicated one of his fellow ministers, referring to him as the dragon in Revelation.

He declared Christmas and other holidays unbiblical. In 1886, he took a trip west, claiming he was going with the prophet Elijah to confront the Antichrist.

The Bride Community had not reached fabled Shar-i-Sabs, or Shakhrisabz, but they had found a home in the East, and for many, this was enough to confirm Epp's prophecies. And so on March 8, 1889, the day Epp had marked out for Christ's return, they carried the altar out of the church. They set it up in the village square, under the open sky. They were dressed in white. They fasted and prayed all day. The Bridegroom never came. After the years of pilgrimage, the labor, the heat and cold, the sickness and terror, the deaths of the children, the world didn't end.

The steadfastness of the virgins who watch and wait, their lamps ready. This is one of the images that sustained the community. For the Kingdom of Heaven is like unto ten virgins, which took their lamps, and went forth to meet the Bridegroom. And five of them were wise, and five were foolish. They that were foolish took their lamps, and took no oil with them; but the people of Ak Metchet were like the five wise virgins, who took oil in their vessels with their lamps. They were those who, hearing the cry, *Behold, the Bridegroom cometh*, would arise and go into the wedding. I see them in their ecstasy and exhaustion. Claas Epp, in his white robe, seated on the altar he calls his throne. A wave of delirium as the sun goes down. All eyes turned upward. Surely now He will come, with the last rays! But He doesn't come. In the dark, the robes look gray. They wait there until midnight, aflame until the last instant of March 8.

This is what my history book called "a monument of warning." This wild desire for something that can't be true.

As for us, we're drawing closer to Samarkand, a busload of tourists bowling along the golden road, which does, in fact, possess an amber tinge, taking its color from the surrounding wheat fields. The tawny air is shot with flecks of red: scarlet daylilies, women selling soft drinks under a red sunshade, a crimson rug tossed over a wheelbarrow. We stop at a teahouse, where we sit on a *tapchan*, a piece of traditional Uzbek outdoor furniture. This is a raised platform, like a table covered with a thin mattress and pillows. On top of this table, another, smaller table holds the tea things. We're supposed to sit cross-legged on the tapchan, but most of us find the position too uncomfortable, so we let our legs dangle over the side.

Usmon regards us sadly. "As you age," he explains, "salt gathers in your joints. Sitting cross-legged for fifteen minutes a day will cure it." Children in bathing suits are splashing in a nearby canal, and I feel sure they can easily pick us out as tourists at this distance, with the blond ponytails sticking up among us, our hats and cameras, the way we sit wantonly allowing the salt to gather in our joints. I imagine informing them that we are Germans from the Volga. Perhaps it's the strong green tea, the bloom of heat under the awning that covers the tapchan, the surreal sensation of sitting on a table topped with another table, but suddenly we all seem preposterous to me. All of us, with our bizarre investments in the past, our naïve susceptibility to narrative. I think of

Claas Epp climbing down from his altar in the dark, chilled by the night air, stiff and clumsy in his robe.

Epp's response to the failure of his prophecy was even weirder than the prophecy itself. He had, in his house, a ship's clock, an object perhaps brought with him from Russia, or perhaps, who knows, picked up in the markets of Samarkand or Tashkent. This clock, he explained to his disappointed flock, was in the wrong position. It leaned, so that its hands, which ought to have pointed to nine and one, appeared to be pointing to eight and nine instead. The right numbers were not eight and nine, but *nine and one*. Christ would come, not in 1889, but in 1891.

I have trouble imagining the reaction to this statement. I'm thinking of people I know, of my Mennonite uncles from North Dakota, men who share certain qualities with the Bride Community: familiarity with the rituals of church and farm, a penchant for simple living, an affinity with the German language. I can't picture these men putting up with the clock story for a second—much less my aunts, who would surely have censured it with a sharp "Oh, *honestly!*" But then, these are not, perhaps, the sort of people who would have gone east, seeking Shar-i-Sabs, in the first place. Or perhaps they are, perhaps we are, all of us, the same people. Sitting on this tapchan, I probably shouldn't draw too stark a line between myself and the Bride Community. The fact is that while many people deserted Ak Metchet in 1889—including Epp's own son, Claas Epp III, who sailed for America—the majority remained. They stayed for a second disappointment in 1891. They stayed for fifty years.

Hymns on the air. They kept on singing them, all the lines they'd loved before the failure. *Es erglänzt uns von ferne ein Land.* A land gleams at us from afar.

The Bridegroom tarried. And Claas Epp Jr., undaunted by the defeats of 1889 and 1891, began to call himself a biblical prince. He opened his statements to the community with "Thus saith the Lord."

He declared himself the Son of Christ, fourth member of the Quadruple Godhead. From now on, baptisms would be made in the name of the Father, *Sons*, and Holy Ghost. He signed his letters "Elijah of the New Testament, Melchizedek of the New Earth, formerly Claas Epp." How much can a person take? "Father had sold his three farms," writes a furious Herman Jantzen, "and sacrificed it all to this '*Irrsinn*' or heresy."

It was too much. In 1900, Claas Epp Jr. was forbidden to preach. He continued to hold Sunday afternoon services in his home, addressing a handful of loyal families. He was often seen sitting outside in a white robe, staring at a chicken coop. He died on the couch in his meeting room on January 19, 1913.

The documentarists were scattered. After leaving the trek, Franz Bartsch sold Bibles for a missionary society in Tashkent. Eventually, he returned to Russia. Herman Jantzen became Chief Forester of Aulie-Ata, and then a missionary in Central Asia and Eastern Europe. Dressed like a Kyrgyz, speaking fluent Uzbek, he was told, "In spite of your blue eyes, you must be a Tartar." He was imprisoned by the Bolsheviks as a counterrevolutionary, emigrated to Germany on his release, and died in the Netherlands. The others went to America, where there were prairies as far as the eye could see, farms, churches, families, and long lives. Jacob Klaassen and Elizabeth Unruh started out in Nebraska; by the end of their lives, both had settled in Saskatchewan. Jacob Jantzen, too, began in Nebraska, but then bought a homestead in Oklahoma, a broad and dusty region, in fact a kind of steppe, a place of extreme temperatures in the middle of a continent, where the Plains Indians with their tents reminded him of the nomads of Turkestan, and where, as an old man, he decided at last to write his memoirs, beginning, "As I sit here in my little house I often feel lonely."

In 1935, the Soviet government informed the Ak Metchet community that they would be exiled to Siberia for refusing state collectivization. In the end, however, they were only moved a hundred miles south, to a barren stretch of steppe where they were expected to starve. Several survived, against the odds. But it was the end of the Bride Community. Strangely—oh, so strangely!—the place where they were deported, the final stage of their journey, was the location Claas Epp Jr. had originally designated as their refuge in his prophecies: the valley of Shakhrisabz.

THREE

Samarkand

I have set before thee an open door

Ancient versus modern

On the outskirts of Samarkand, bright plastic Disney characters stand in a garden, watching us pass with their oversized eyes. Carpets hang drying on peach-colored walls. A swing set leans in a yard where two small girls are tussling over a bent umbrella. Here is a timeworn cemetery, all domes and shades of brown; here is a mini-mart called Happy Home. Six thousand kilometers from both Europe and Asia, we are in the center of a world.

The *kand* in Samarkand, I learn, is the same as the *kent* in Tashkent: it means city. There are several glosses on the word *Samarkand*. Ruling City, Stone City, Blessed City, and Fat City, says Usmon, "because of the produce and the hospitality." There's also a story about a pair of lovers: a young gardener called Samar and a princess named Kand. When their secret love affair was discovered, the boy was killed. Their passion lives on in the name of a city.

Apartment blocks drift by, all the same warm shade of pink, surrounded by trees that grow right out of the pavement. We stop at a bakery for a huge round of Samarkand bread: salty, warm, and tough on the outside, like a giant bagel. The loaf makes its way around the bus as we tear off hunks and pass it on, scattering nigella seeds from its shiny surface. "Oh, look!" cries Evelyn, pointing out a crane perched on a transmission tower, its silhouette a question mark.

The hotel, like the one in Tashkent, is constructed in the overwhelming style, with a portico two stories tall and acres of tiled floor. It's built for groups, and the few lone men in the lobby look quite at a loss, stranded in the squares of waning evening light from the tall windows. A dark red color predominates. Dinner is served in a wine-colored restaurant fringed with coral drapes. Here we gather, freshly showered, our hair still damp, dressed in clothes that, as recommended by the tour company, conceal our shoulders and legs—most importantly those of the women—in modest folds.

These are clothes I'd never wear at home: big blouses and shapeless skirts. Tonight I'm sporting a pink and black flowered shirt, which was originally a sort of summer jumpsuit, a button-down top connected to a pair of miniscule frilly shorts. By cutting the crotch out of the shorts, and sewing the rents in front and back, I managed to make this jumpsuit into a long, weird, hip-hiding shirt. I thought myself very clever at the time. Predictably, the thread at the back is unraveling. At dinner, I sit next to Nozli, the guide in training. Nozli is wearing an incredibly small white t-shirt, skin-tight jeans, and a pair of white leather peep-toe sandals. It's hard to imagine anything much further from the tour company instructions ("Comfortable solid walking shoes with strong soles and support are a must!"). It would be funny, I think, if Nozli were dressed in an especially daring way because she's hanging out with a busload of North Americans, while we've put on these dowdy tunics and voluminous elastic-waist slacks so as not to offend her conservative Uzbek feelings.

She gives me a soft, friendly gaze, apologizing because her English is not yet as good as Usmon's. I assure her it's better than my Uzbek. We show each other pictures on our phones, mostly of our children: my kids with my husband, her little boy with her mother in Tashkent.

"Tour guide is an awesome job," she says enthusiastically. "You know lots and make money traveling all over." Still, she wouldn't live anywhere but in the capital. Tashkent is a modern city, she explains, but Samarkand, Bukhara—"Ancient! Just for tourists!"

Heroes

At Amir Timur's mausoleum, the azure dome stands out against the pearly morning sky, fluted and tiled like some magnificent beaded cap. A wealth of color and texture adorns the great arched entryway, crest upon crest of mosaic built up in a towering wave, so that it overawes the gaze both with its height and the rich detail of its decorations: a portal for giants, tessellated by elves. I take a series of photographs, first from a distance, to capture the size of the monument, the gilded effect of an illuminated manuscript, then closer and closer, until the lens is filled by a single stony flower of dark blue, orange, aquamarine, and white.

Behind me, Kholid is telling Arnie about the wheat harvest, which is taking place now, and will be followed by the cotton harvest. Uzbekistan, he says, was once the single biggest supplier of cotton to the Soviet Union. We're getting used to receiving statistics about Uzbekistan's significance: that this is the location of Central Asia's first radio and TV towers, that Tashkent's TV tower is the ninth tallest in the world, that no other capital has so many juniper trees. It reminds me of the way my father used to talk about Somalia, which, for your information, has the best cell phone network in Africa, as well as the handsomest people and greatest poets in the world. In moments of depression, he would describe his country in terms that were no less hyperbolic: it was the absolute rock-bottom of existence, cursed with the world's most bloodthirsty warlords, the stupidest extremists, the most gullible populace, and the most annoying neighbors. I think Kholid must have, like my father, a second set of epithets for his country, reserved for quiet evenings at home. Usmon leads us to Amir Timur's pomegranate juice bowl, a stone tub big enough to bathe in, now cemented to the bricks of the courtyard. Timur used this bowl to estimate his losses in battle. After each skirmish, the soldiers would line up to receive a cup of pomegranate juice, and Timur could estimate how many were dead or incapacitated by marking the height of the liquid left in the bowl.

Frank wants to know why Timur is so revered. Why, in 1994, after Uzbekistan's independence, was the central square in Tashkent named Amir Timur Square? The square had been through several changes: originally called Konstantinovsky Square, after Konstantin von Kaufmann, the first governor-general of Russian Turkestan, it became Revolution Square in 1917 and held a series of statues: Lenin, Stalin, Marx. But why, Frank asks, would the Uzbeks pick Timur as their national symbol, a man whose campaigns caused seventeen million deaths?

"Timur was the hero of the fourteenth and fifteenth centuries," Usmon explains.

"Ah!" says Frank, sending a twinkling glance around his largely Mennonite audience. "So the moral of the story is, you have to be violent to be a hero!"

"Well," Usmon falters, "he didn't start like that. He was betrayed, lamed hand and foot. Then he vowed never to forgive."

Frank seems keen to go on with this debate, but Kholid puts an end to the pacifist analysis of Amir Timur. "This is history," he declares. "Timur is the national hero of Uzbekistan. Not the USA. Not Georgia or anywhere else!"

I'm not sure how Georgia got into the conversation, but anyway, it's over. Usmon shows us the wall where Timur would stand to address his troops. There's a deep notch in the top of the wall, where the conqueror placed the heel of one boot. This brought his hips level, so he no longer looked like a man with a limp.

Turkestan Album

As for the Bride Community, there's no doubt that their hero was Konstantin Petrovich von Kaufmann, the first governor-general of Russian Turkestan. Although he died before he could sign the paperwork that would ensure their protection, he was sympathetic to the Mennonites, and his promises of land and religious freedom opened the door to Central Asia. Of Austrian extraction, a veteran of the Caucasian War, and committed to the rule of a largely Muslim populace, von Kaufmann was willing to make unusual accommodations—including exemption from both military service and taxes for fifteen years—to import these European, Christian farmers.

I see him reading their letters in his residence. This is in the European district of Tashkent, separated from the native city by the Ankhor Canal. Known as the White House, the residence gleams among its gardens on Cathedral Square, near the Church of Saints Joseph and George. The arched windows and patterned brickwork of the residence, the fine tracery of the church against the limpid summer sky, the broad green lawns of the square, and, indeed, the regular contours of the entire European quarter, testify to von Kaufmann's energy and will. When he arrived in the city, there was nothing here resembling a capital. The place was an immense wasteland without a single tree; the Russian housing had a disordered, temporary feel; there was a dismal fortress and a narrow, undistinguished church. Now, thanks to his efforts and the climate of the South, in which willows and poplars flourish with marvelous speed, the European quarter gives an impression of grace and permanence. Trees shade the long avenues, and everywhere one hears the lapping of canals.

But how hot it is! He takes out a scented handkerchief to wipe his domed, hairless brow, and wishes for a moment that he could withdraw to his summer garden in the suburbs, where freshness emanates from the square pond surrounded by rose trees. There, in the evening, the branches are hung with paper lanterns, the nightingales sing, and von Kaufmann, clad in a flowing *khalat*, smokes his pipe in a Bukharan tent. But today he will not go there; he will finish reading the Mennonite papers, then put on his coat, heavy with decorations and epaulettes, to review the troops. A weary exercise, but a necessary discipline: in summer the soldiers drink even more riotously than in winter. Last week they smashed up a tavern, broke so many bottles the street reeked like a medicine chest, and heaved all the furniture into a canal. He comforts himself with the thought that in the evening he will go to sit for an hour among the cool walls of his greatest achievement, the public library, and peruse, once again, the photographs in the huge *Turkestan Album*, in which the peoples and places of his realm are laid out like rare coins.

It is the modern age, the time of categories, of statistics, of bureaucracy, of the organization of species, of the massive European expeditions to foreign lands, of the pseudoscience of race, of imperialism, of anthropology, of the photograph. The *Turkestan Album* consists of six volumes on four subjects: archaeology, ethnography, industry, and the history of the Russian conquest. Each volume measures forty-five by sixty centimeters. There are approximately twelve hundred drawings and photographs. Seated in his library in the evening, von Kaufmann turns an enormous page. The weight of the paper, the way it falls with a series of snapping and susurrating sounds, offers a distinctive, lively pleasure, like the rippling of a clean shirt. Here is a photograph from 1868, showing Samarkand freshly conquered and in ruins. Here are representative portraits of the peoples under his command: Sarts (also known as Uzbeks), Tajiks, Kazakhs, Kyrgyz, Arabs, Jews, and the Turkmens whose massacre he recently ordered in Bukhara. Many of the photographs have captured enormous vistas that dwarf the human figures. In these images, such as one of the citadel of Khodzhent, the human inhabitants, seated on the ground beside carts piled with bales of hay, appear to have been included only as a sort of rubric by which to estimate the soaring height of the battlements. The effect is that of a doll's house or a military map. Von Kaufmann has more personal power than any other Russian governor-general. Insulated from the center of czarist government by miles of steppe, he singlehandedly determines the privileges of Russians in the region. He seals death sentences or, if he chooses, revokes them. Here is a worker in a flour mill, up to his shins in luminous white powder. Here are men going into the coal mines of Syr Darya, dressed in long robes that give them the look of penitents. Von Kaufmann commissioned the *Turkestan Album*, arranging a series of scientific expeditions to produce these magnificent tomes. He oversaw the collection of artifacts, regional costumes, human skeletons, and, on occasion, living humans, such as the three representatives of the Asian peoples belonging to the Russian Empire he sent, with his compliments, to the Congress of Orientalists in St. Petersburg.

He turns a page. He presses his handkerchief to his sweating mustache. A scene of skin stretched on poles: Tashkent's leather factory. Barefoot workers trampling the hides. And the bridge at Karabulak, a fragile grid above the darkness of the gorge. A few men stand on the bridge, tiny dots in their white turbans. The smudged trees, tossed by the wind, look like columns of smoke. Somewhere among these volumes there must be a photograph of Shakhrisabz, the Green Town, which Claas Epp Jr. named "the place of refuge." This site, so prominent in the imagination of the Mennonite travelers, was conquered by Russian forces in 1870. According to a Persian account, the *Nim-Padshah*, or half-emperor—Governor-General von Kaufmann—accomplished what no enemy had been able to do in eighty-seven years: he destroyed the independence of Shakhrisabz.

The crows

Among von Kaufmann's employees in the early years was the war artist Vasily Vereshchagin. Vereshchagin had little interest in Russian Tashkent. He preferred the old, native quarter on the other side of the Ankhor Canal: the knotty streets, the mud houses with oil-paper windows. When it rained there, the horses sank to their knees in mire. The artist had no great love for Turkestan, but he liked the feeling of freedom. "Give me a yurt," he said. He took part in the conquest of Samarkand and was awarded the Saint George Cross, which adorned his civilian coat for the rest of his life. Still, he was not an uncritical patriot. One of his most famous paintings, *The Apotheosis of War*, depicts a desert with a wrecked city in the background, where crows haunt a mound of human skulls. The pyramid of skulls might be taken simply as local color, a reference to Amir Timur, who left such grisly monuments in his wake—save that Vereshchagin dedicates the painting to "all great conquerors, past, present, and future." The painting is thus dedicated, in part, to Konstantin von Kaufmann. Crows gather on the withered trees. Shards of bone litter the sand. *The Apotheosis of War* was banned from exhibition in St. Petersburg, on the grounds that it threatened the reputation of the Russian military.

It is unlikely (though not impossible) that there were Mennonites in von Kaufmann's army. We are people of peace. An ungenerous view would claim that, in Vereshchagin's painting, people like us are represented by the crows.

How sweet you are, you bitter life!

In the evening, under a burgundy bedspread stitched with a gold design, I set aside the article on von Kaufmann for a collection of Uzbek stories in translation. Von Kaufmann appears as a character in one of them: Khayriddin Sultonov's "How Sweet You Are, You Bitter Life!" It's a winter day in 1876. The sun dispenses a feeble ray and then withdraws into the fog that covers the rooftops. Von Kaufmann has come to see his orders carried out, to witness the execution of a freedom fighter. He is accompanied by a visiting Russian prince and several dignitaries. His wife and her lady friends arrive, lifting their skirts away from the snow. As the women apologize for coming late, the crowd roars, and the condemned man is brought out. He's young, in a ragged coat, his face streaked with blood.

When the hangman places the rope about the youth's neck, von Kaufmann's wife pales. "Oh, what a pity!" she cries. *"Ach, mein Gott, das ist schlecht! Ach, mein Gott!"* Yet she recovers quickly once the man is dead, and turns to address the prince. She is sorry there is no decent music here, no theater.

White clouds cross the sky. A breeze blows a faint perfume from the Aravon Mountains. Adjusting her furs, she invites the prince to play cards. "Forgive us, Prince, this game is the only source of entertainment we have here. I suppose, in this wild country, we ourselves will soon become wild."

In Tashkent, to cross the Ankhor Canal into the native city was, for a European, to expose oneself to wildness, dirt, and disease. The Asian population, wrote one Russian administrator, "lives in unthinkable filth." The houses, stuck together with handfuls of clay, were on the verge of collapse. People drank the grayish water of the canals, becoming infected with a dreaded parasite, a wiry worm that had to be slowly drawn out of the body on a reel. Contemporary accounts suggest that most Russians hated Tashkent, the local people, and each other. The city was boring, the Russians there were all scoundrels, escaping their creditors back home or hoping to scheme their way to a quick fortune. Still, they were Europeans. They represented civilization against the deplorable squalor of the native quarter. On the Russian side, a visitor enthused, among the houses set back from the street and flanked by trees, one might almost have been in New York.

In "How Sweet You Are, You Bitter Life!" the condemned man's mother arrives on the scene just in time to bid him goodbye. She is Qurbonjon dodkhoh, herself a formidable fighter, a legendary figure of the resistance. At the sight of her, the crowd bursts into cheers. Dressed in a traditional suit of blue velvet, with a cotton shawl on her head, she rides up to the scaffold and tells her son that he has inherited martyrdom: his father and grandfather both died at the hands of the Russians.

Her son weeps. "Mother! My dear mother!"

Her aged face reflects deep silence and tranquility, as if she cannot hear him. A lock of white hair escapes her shawl, light on the wind. She turns her horse.

"Farewell, my son. I'm contented with what I have fed you."

The German sense of order

On the way to Registan Square, Frank reads to us of the *Wagenburg*, the Mennonite wagons drawn together in a circle in the evenings. "Here comes the German sense of order!" he exclaims. He describes how Herman Jantzen was tasked with ringing a bell "exactly by the clock." We all admire this consistency, the determination to preserve routine against the chaos of circumstance. I admire it, although it also gives me the creeps—a vague sense of alarm that deepens when Frank asks Lois to read her great-grandmother's account of the Chinese girl. In Tashkent, Elizabeth Unruh and her family lived across the street from the Chinese quarter. "We felt so sorry for the five- to six-year-old girls," Lois reads, "whose feet were bound, so that they would remain small for their life . . . The little girls asked us, why we had such big feet, we told them, so we could walk well, run and jump and play well. This made them sad, they wished they too could run and jump and play." I've read this story before. The way the historian Fred Belk tells it, the Mennonite girls practically instigated a revolution with their big, healthy feet. Their freedom "disturbed the Chinese girls so much that they openly criticized the custom imposed upon them by their parents." But Elizabeth only describes one girl who balks at the tradition, who asks her grandmother if she can have big feet. "Soon after we never saw her outside anymore. One morning when we went over there, we heard her whimper and moan and cry. She begged her grandmother to loosen the bandages, but she would not. Her grandmother did not want us to come anymore, so we never saw that little girl again."

The bus stops and starts again in the traffic with a lurch. The high apartment complexes block the sky. Sunlight bounces glaringly from the windows. Samarkand looks like Cairo, it looks like Nairobi, it looks like anywhere. A sense of the repetitiveness of life, its dull exhaustion, it never stops, it's something you can't get out from under. Frank describes the many advances the Mennonites brought to Khiva: the cotton gin, the sewing machine, the camera.

By the time we reach the Registan, I'm thoroughly depressed. We disembark on another massive plain of brick, a baking vista without an inch of shade that must be crossed to reach the domes and portals in their lonely splendor. Why do these monuments have to be so remote, why are we always toiling across the dust to the opulent gates of the caravanserai? And when we get there, everything's too gigantic for human use. I point my camera listlessly at the Brobdingnagian arches. Glancing at my companions, I can't tell that anyone else is particularly cast down by the recent lecture on the good fortune of the Uzbeks, especially those of Khiva, in having among them, for fifty years, punctual Mennonites with clean habits and superior strains of wheat. I'm afraid to ask. I'm sensitive to the feelings of my companions, so many of whom are descendants of Central Asian Mennonites, who may have grown up ashamed of their history, of Claas Epp Jr., who has sometimes been compared to David Koresh, the cult leader of Waco, Texas. "I can recall several times," writes the genealogist D. Frederick Dyck, "being told a person's name by a third party with a whispered follow-up and knowing nod, 'His parents (or grandparents) were on the Asian Trek,' as though it was an illness passed from one generation to the next." The shame of inherited illness, contamination, a permanent taint. I remember reading Dallas Wiebe's novel of the trek, *Our Asian Journey*, how he writes of his outrage as a young man, his sense of injury when historians and theologians made callous, sneering remarks about his ancestors. "What right does any theologian have to say anything about this world? Who gave him the right to take a cheap shot at one's grandmother?" To set the record straight, he writes this dense four-hundred-and-fifty-page novel, meticulously researched, crammed with detail, a book that's now out of print. My sympathy for Dallas Wiebe's feelings about the trek is compounded by my affinity for overambitious, unread novels, my protective literary instincts that go into high gear when I hear of some writer's obsession chucked in the dustbin of history. Like Dallas Wiebe, I want to rescue the story of the Great Trek. I want to save his novel. I daydream of writing the foreword to the new edition. I want to see the Mennonites of Khiva as more than a failure, an embarrassment. But not at any price.

The missionary effect

When Dallas Wiebe published his novel in the nineties, the history of the Great Trek was half buried, discussed in hushed tones, glanced at hurriedly and then suppressed. It was such a mortifying episode, tinged with heresy. In the twenty-first century, however, the story has been revived. In writing, a documentary film, and a series of Mennonite heritage tours to Uzbekistan, North American Mennonites are reevaluating the history of the Mennonites of Khiva, of this village, Ak Metchet, the White Mosque, a tiny Christian community in a Muslim khanate.

As the story is retold, the Mennonites of Ak Metchet have been reconfigured as, writes the scholar Dov Yaroshevski, a "modernizing diaspora." Wilhelm Penner, the Mennonite photographer, introduced the camera to Khudaybergen Divanov, the first indigenous Uzbek photographer, known as the father of Uzbek photography. The Mennonites brought sewing machines to Khiva, stimulating the textile industry. They installed and maintained the cotton gin. They imported new, more productive varieties of cotton and wheat. This is exactly the sort of thing the Russian colonizers were hoping for. "Mennonites are very important to the khanate of Khiva," one Russian observer wrote, "since the natives see the model order in the German village, value the rational, business-like intellect of its residents, esteem their industry, their entrepreneurship and their skills and thus they try to learn from and imitate the Mennonites in all these traits and values . . . No doubt, every German appears to the natives as a very clever and virtuous person."

How do we enter the stories of others? I am thinking of bodies in motion. How do we disembark in another country? For a long time it has seemed to me that, within the dominant strain of North American Mennonite culture, such an entrance takes a form I call *the missionary effect.* We long—intend—demand—to be of service. We must arrive with something to offer, if not the Bible then a language, a medical treatment, a seed. There's a structure to our arrival, a framework that operates far beyond the mission field, informing our idea of ourselves. Our capacity to give, the assumption that we possess valuable skills and qualities others lack, becomes bound up with other facets of our self-definition, including religious ones, until it's one inextricable tangle, leading John H. Redekop to ask in bewilderment in the book *Why I Am a Mennonite,* "What's particularly Christian about developing new agricultural crops and breeding first-rate cattle?" There's nothing Christian about it, it's just an aspect of our culture. I guess you could call it the German sense of order. Rhoda Janzen taps into it in her bestselling memoir *Mennonite in a Little Black Dress,* in the appendix, my favorite part of the book. In this appendix, Janzen discovers a collection of sketches and photographs called *Heritage Remembered: A Pictorial Survey of Mennonites in Prussia and Russia.* She's intrigued by a picture of a wagon with the caption "Russian wagon, compare to Mennonite wagon on page 249." It sounds, she thinks, as if the Mennonite reverend who wrote this book is on the verge of a boast, but that would be so counter to the Mennonite ideal of humility, surely it can't be true. Oh, yes it can: "I obediently turned to page 249, where I was met not with one, not with two, but with *three* Mennonite wagons, all of which clearly kicked the ass of the lesser Russian wagon." When I read this, I burst out laughing—the pained laughter of recognition. I remembered Franz Bartsch among the Kyrgyz: "Our covered wagons, already greatly admired by the Cossacks, raised the awe of these primitive people even more."

Note that Bartsch considered his own covered wagon a piece of junk. It's only in comparison to outsiders that his wagon becomes "our wagons," his personal inadequacies subsumed in the general excellence of the group, which shines so brightly against the miserable foreign

backdrop. I am familiar with this dynamic. If you're a Mennonite serving in a poor country, either in a mission or, if you're the type who respects other religions and finds church-planting kind of offensive, in
the mission's offspring, the non-governmental organization, you will
find yourself transformed overnight into a very clever and virtuous person. You'll find that you're now an extremely modern person, cutting
edge, although back in North America you may often have felt awkward when non-Mennonites assumed you had no cell phone ("I noticed
you wear a wristwatch") or asked if you were permitted to drive a car.
That's over now. In the whirling dust of Lokichogio, your cheap haircut doesn't matter. On the red roads of Yambio, your second-hand *Little
House on the Prairie* dress looks good. Here, you are modern. Nothing can
take that away from you, not your quaint diction, not your ignorance of
television shows. Moreover, you have a high purpose: to bring light to
the people who walk in darkness, either the light of Christ or the light
of Western-style development, which go hand in hand and often seem
to amount to the same thing, material and spiritual blessings seamlessly
blended. In the face of your calling, history fades like breath. Your project is futurist and idealist, nothing to do with yesterday or the day before, an orientation that makes it easy to suppose that you, yourself, are
the source of your capacity to give. And you're unlikely to encounter
many challenges to this view, either on visits home, where people gasp
over the photograph of your pit toilet, or in your place of service, where
people gasp over your contact lenses and marvel at the workings of your
solar panel. Such elegant alchemy: a simple airplane journey and you're
born again. Your wagon becomes "our wagons." Whoever you may have
been before, you now represent the highest quality of life, the most useful knowledge, the most desirable human attributes. In South Sudan, I
was white.

These two drops

Amir Timur, I am told, dug a tunnel between Samarkand and Shakhri-sabz, just wide enough for a single horseman. How narrow it is, the open door.

A photograph of a village on the outskirts of Samarkand, scanned from an article on the *Turkestan Album*. Flat roofs, winter trees, a stream. Over this still landscape, I imagine the shadow of Governor-General von Kaufmann's wrist as he reaches to turn the page. The air coils and darkens. "Although we lived in our own land," an Uzbek man said of Russian rule, "we were told by others: 'You are nothing but sheep, you are uncivilized animals!'" I remember Alexander Rempel, who visited Ak Metchet after his fellow Mennonites had been deported. "What a mess!" he wrote. "Only Asians can bring about such a state of disorder."

The citadel of Ura-Tyube, with a view of the Orthodox church. I examine the caption on this photograph, but I can't find the church. I imagine Konstantin von Kaufmann searching for it, too, bending over the page in his lamplit library. Could it be that little dome, like a gazebo, on the left, with the strange empty pavilion beside it? The rest of the picture is filled with a village that appears entirely deserted, overshadowed by a rocky hillside planted with cypress trees. But perhaps these trees are people marching in some sort of procession. Perhaps it's Sunday, and they are going to church. Is the church that gray escarpment on the summit of the hill, could it even lie concealed on the other side? The scene makes a barren, melancholy impression, but there's something compelling about it, too, and I imagine von Kaufmann returning to the White House in the evening, carrying the memory of this spare, mysterious vista against his heart, like a love letter or a passport. They are going up the hill, in the heat, in the silence, without fainting, without rest. He draws aside the curtain of his carriage, observing, with a breathless swell of hope, the identical dark houses passing behind the trees. As the carriage turns into Cathedral Square, the moonlight, freed from the branches, engulfs his vision in a glacial light. "Bury me here," he will write before going to bed, "so that all may know that here is true Russian soil, in which no Russian need be ashamed to lie."

Winter 1876. Qurbonjon dodkhoh, the warrior queen, cracks her whip and gallops away from the place of execution. She will not watch as her son is choked to death. She clatters over the bridge on the Ankhor Canal, into the native quarter. Farther, far beyond, to the air, to the mountains. Snow flies up from her horse's hooves. Her face is no longer serene but warped, like a weapon being forged. "Two hot tears dropped on the horse's hair," writes Khayriddin Sultonov, "and these two drops burned the horse's whole existence."

The place of hunger

On the high arch of the Sher-Dor Madrasa, a fantastical mosaic: twin tigers chase twin deer on a dark blue, flowered field. Each tiger has a human face embedded in its back, crowned with coppery rays that extend, as if from a sun, toward the geometric border. I've never seen anything like these hybrid creatures. Pale faces with winged black brows, their noses flanked by neat, symmetrical moles. They look startled, as if surprised by their own glory, the sunshine showering from their heads, or as if, even after four centuries, they can't get used to observing the world from inside a tiger. Usmon explains that the architect of Sher-Dor was executed for violating the Islamic prohibition against the depiction of people and animals, although he clearly did his best, trying to come up with some impossible chimera, some outlandish, composite monster. He was pleased with his own effort. "The architect has built the arch of this portal with such perfection," proclaims one of the inscriptions, "that all of heaven gnaws its fingers in astonishment, thinking it sees the rising of some new moon."

What lifts me up is astonishment, what plunges me down is the repetition of the known, the same old stories recited over and over, the strong stories, the ones that trample everything in their path, the type my graduate-school professors called a totalizing narrative. But even the term *totalizing narrative* feels like a totalizing narrative. I hate those stories where you already know the end. Explanations that come with a knowing nod have the stench of a particular kind of monotony to me, a killing and ruinous boredom. Everybody is talking about these amazing human-face tigers, whose fiery manes may be traces of the Zoroastrian sun mythos. Frank leans toward Kholid, who explains that only fish can be drawn in Islamic art, because the fish is a symbol of purification.

The light in Frank's face. How delighted he is with each new scrap of knowledge, here in this venerable place of learning, this *madrasa*, a word that means Islamic school in English but in Arabic just means school. A place of craving, of enlightenment. It's the thudding predictability of the strong stories I can't bear, the sense that there's nothing to learn, no new perspective that isn't already old, so that the sobbing of a child with broken feet is swept up at once, slotted into place, catalogued under "ancient versus modern." There is the horror of torture and then the horror of its retelling, its *application*. The numbness, the dreariness of the known. I remember a retired Mennonite missionary who boasted that he spent forty years in Africa and never changed his mind.

But this is the place of hunger. Usmon explains that the tigers in the mosaic represent the students of the madrasa, the deer their teachers.

"That's an unusually honest depiction of the teaching profession," I tell him, observing the poor deer glancing over their backs in terror.

We're all laughing now. But of course the point of the mosaic isn't the deer, it's the tigers, so ravenous for knowledge.

Usmon translates another inscription, which declares that the acrobat of thought, climbing the rope of imagination, will never reach the top of this minaret.

Star catalogue

A pilgrimage has a trajectory: the end is already known. But I'm interested in the randomness of movement. More than just interested: I'm desperate. Whenever I'm among Mennonites (that is, for most of my life), knitted into the cozy safety of the group, I find myself digging for evidence of anything outré, off-kilter, outside the norm. Talk to me of Menno Simons and I'm sure to bring up the coach story, or that other apocryphal tale about Menno preaching from the top of a molasses barrel: somebody told him the authorities were on their way, and in his haste to escape, he fell into the barrel, soaking his hose to the knee. To prevent him from leaving a sticky trail, each of the women present took a good lick at his hose, until all the molasses was gone. This story is said to explain why Mennonite children in Holland have such a sweet tooth; to me, its subdued eroticism seems to explain something much more profound about the transfer of sexual energy into the baking of shoo-fly pie. But anyway, that's only one example of my instinctive response to the feeling of being absorbed into a well-known collective narrative. What I like best about the Easter story is that after Jesus rose from the dead, he ate a piece of broiled fish and some honeycomb. And, of course, when it comes to Mennonite history, I'm most interested in the prophet who rode off to meet Christ in Central Asia.

The magpie condition, I realize suddenly, is not only about moving *toward* the apparently insignificant detail, it's also about moving *away* from the main idea. It's a mode of thought opposed to any central argument or thesis. This suggests that undertaking a pilgrimage might not be the best plan for me, that I might kick against the guiding line every step of the way, which is in fact what I've been doing, bringing my notes on colonial history and Mennonite self-regard into what feels like a deadening, overly reverent story of Mennonite achievement. However, if this were a White Privilege Tour of Uzbekistan, I guarantee you I'd find it equally dispiriting. No doubt I'd get so tired of the subject, I'd wind up hunkered in the hotel restaurant with Kholid late at night, swapping dictatorship stories or arguing about the origins of the samosa. The thought that I might be congenitally averse to the perception of wholeness, bent on finding the cracks in any position whatever, begins to seriously worry me as I trudge through the heat with my fellow pilgrims toward the statue of Ulugh Beg, the great medieval astronomer.

High noon, the light too harsh for photography, and the statue gazing away from us, exhibiting its noble profile. Ulugh Beg, the grandson of Timur, studied the sky from the top of his observatory at night, Usmon tells us, and from its underground chamber during the day. He had a library upstairs and another downstairs. Did he never sleep? He built his sextant inside a mountain, to protect it from earthquakes. We enter a door and descend into the cool artificial light where a set of curved rails drops away like the track of a roller coaster. This is all that remains of Ulugh Beg's massive sextant. "The hole in the top shone light down onto the slope," Usmon explains, "and Ulugh Beg would be on the steps observing the light." His voice echoes tinnily in this subterranean science lab, and the fluorescent bulbs drain him of color, so that he looks a bit ghostly, as if he might dissolve into the white glare and black shadows in his black trousers and white Hugo Boss t-shirt.

Here Ulugh Beg stood and mapped the stars. Two hundred years later, portions of his astronomical table and star catalogue, the *Zij-i-Sultani*, began to appear in Latin. Circles of knowledge and the desire for knowledge: these too are links. And how precious they seem, those moments when the doors are open. Upstairs in the museum hangs an engraving from the star atlas *Firmamentum Sobiescianum* by Johannes

Hevelius, published in Gdansk in 1690. Urania, the muse of astronomy, sits with the sun and moon in her hands, flanked by rows of astronomers going back to Ptolemy. Ulugh Beg stands among them, a sash knotted on his stomach, one hand raised between the folds of his ermine cloak. There is a human inheritance, but how to keep it in mind? This huge vision, all-encompassing, without end. A photograph of the night sky above the city of Samarkand, so thick with stars it looks like a mosaic.

A Latin banner hangs over Urania's head, with this English translation: "I leave my work to the deserved ancestors." This doesn't seem quite right to me; surely one leaves one's work, not to one's deserved ancestors, but to one's deserving descendants? Yet there's something striking in the idea of undertaking a project in honor of the ancestors you deserve. On the bus, we sing the Mennonite travelers' favorite hymn, "*Unser Zug geht durch die Wüste*," in the English version "Through the Desert Goes Our Journey." It's sung to a well-known tune, so I can't be the only one who knows it, but I'm the first to admit it, and so I wind up leading the hymn, forcing my voice above the rumble of the engine. *Through the desert goes our journey, to the blessed promised land.* I forgot that the hymn runs low rather than high, I've started it too low, it's not right, I want to do it again correctly, but that would mean interrupting everyone, which would be even more embarrassing, so I ignore my German sense of order and barrel on. The altos and basses follow my lead, gamely pressing their chins into their chests. I love this positive attitude toward a group project. In the collective will to harmony, personal failings are subsumed, caught up, stripped of significance, transformed into music. From the inside, this concord feels like grace. It only hurts if you're outside. I think of Elizabeth Unruh on her way to America, traveling through Berlin, a refugee, on the wrong side of the order, the German officers shoving the women and children onto the train. "And one took hold of my mother too, she looked at him, and told him, in all our travels in Asia among uncivilized people never had they been treated as roughly as here, in this so-called civilized fatherland, where the people were loaded into the train like cattle, what have we done to you, why are you doing it?"

There is a crater on the moon named Ulugh Beigh. An asteroid called Ulugbek circling the sun between the orbits of Mars and Jupiter.

The *Zij-i-Sultani* was the most comprehensive star catalogue of its time. Ulugh Beg wanted to record the whole outside. But, of course, there wasn't any "outside"; he couldn't be outside his object of study, which was the universe, and he wasn't even outside his equipment. His entire observatory was an instrument of perception. He didn't have a telescope; he was inside one. Unfortunately, his powers of perception as a leader didn't match his skills as an astronomer: he lost control of his empire and was assassinated by his own son. Down in the depths, concentrating on the vastest heights, he forfeited his place in the world between. His home was the place of hunger: not a known constellation but the darkness between the stars, where further stars come into view. And I would be like him, I think, as we leave Samarkand, passing green fields under a hot expanse of sky. I too would watch for vagrant stars. I recall the words of the poet Hafiz: "Like a great starving beast, my body is quivering, fixed on the scent of light."

PART TWO

*

Home-ache

FOUR

Kok Ota

sad comedy of the border

Blue Grandfather

Kok Ota, the Blue Grandfather, struck his staff on the ground and dragged it behind him: that was the first canal. Bearded and shimmering, he is one of the water saints of the desert, with their wonder-working sticks, their sense of wells. His mausoleum stands near the mosque in the village named after him, which the Mennonite travelers knew as Serabulak. Here there is no grand hotel. We step down from the bus into a corridor of heat between henna-colored mud-brick walls. Sparks of blue stand out against this background with striking clarity, a saturation of color that makes me blink. A blue door, an overturned blue stool. A boy on a bicycle dressed in blue, like a speeding flake of ultramarine. Blue speaks a language of coolness and relief; I long for it as if the sight of the color alone is a form of water.

A group of men come out to meet us, dressed in dazzling white shirts. Kholid translates their greetings, taking over the role of guide, while Usmon seems content to stand in the background now that we've departed from the typical Silk Road tour. As we stroll past the pea-green pond in the gardens of the mosque, the men tell stories of Kok Ota. When the mosque was being restored, the builder thought avidly of his salary, and the dome began to cave in, but when he prayed aloud, the bricks returned to their places, springing miraculously toward the sky. An exuberant man propels himself along beside us, supported by a thick cane like a young tree, underscoring Kholid's English translation with grunts of approval. He seems hugely pleased with our visit; the others clap him on the back to calm him down. He has Alzheimer's, they say. Kholid relates the story of a bus on a tour of holy places that neglected this site: it broke down outside the village but started up easily once the passengers had paid their respects to Kok Ota.

At the door of the mosque, they give us presents of little striped hand towels, the ones they make for visitors to this holy site, for mopping your brow in the summer heat, for drying your damp neck, for collecting your tears when you remember what your people received in this place: food, shelter, peace. Inside the mosque, we stand barefoot on dark red rugs beneath the bell-like curve of the dome. It's a small, austere place compared to the looming structures we've visited in the cities, like being held in the hollow of a hand. Bare bulbs hang from the ceiling on wires, unlit at this hour, catching the sun from the arched windows. In one corner a podium leans against the wall, a tangle of microphones and balled-up white cloths at its feet: a tableau with the homely air of holy things on recess, familiar to me from church basements. Our hosts watch with cordial interest as Tom, a descendant of one of the Mennonite travelers, takes the floor to read from his ancestor's journal and then from an essay by Elizabeth Stauffer, who came here on an earlier tour. Would we—we Mennonites—Elizabeth

Stauffer wants to know—would we welcome Muslim refugees to use our churches, as the Mennonite refugees were invited to use the mosque at Serabulak, to sleep there, worship there, marry there, baptize there? Tom's voice cracks and trembles, finally breaking like dry ground. We are all overwhelmed. Pressing the towels to our eyes, we sing the hymn "Take Thou My Hand, O Father," which the Mennonite travelers sang in German. Harmony quivers and fills the air, nestling into the dome. We join hands. We shake hands with a descendant of a nineteenth-century imam. Once, this man's forebear welcomed a group of desperate strangers into this place. Now he clasps our hands, he pulls us eagerly close to him, he beckons toward our dusty group, some of whom may only exist because his ancestor met theirs with the same gesture. *Come in, come in.*

The mosque has been rebuilt since those travelers stayed here; perhaps not one of the original bricks remains. But the shape it makes in space is the same. It's the shape of a womb. I think of those exiles gathered in and comforted by this space. And the other one, the alien among them, the drifter, the freak.

Eat this book

And the voice which I heard from heaven spake unto me again, and said, Go and take the little book which is open in the hand of the angel which standeth upon the sea and upon the earth. And I went unto the angel, and said unto him, Give me the little book. And he said unto me, Take it, and eat it up; and it shall make thy belly bitter, but it shall be in thy mouth sweet as honey. And I took the little book out of the angel's hand, and ate it up; and it was in my mouth sweet as honey: and as soon as I had eaten it, my belly was bitter. And he said unto me, Thou must prophesy again before many peoples, and nations, and tongues, and kings.

—REVELATION 10: 8–11

Among the Mennonites on the trek to Central Asia was a German from outside the community named Johann Drake. His life, recorded piecemeal in the memoirs of the travelers, contains some of the story's strangest episodes. Johann Drake had settled among the Mennonites in Russia to escape the German draft. When Claas Epp Jr. departed for Central Asia in the last wagon train, Drake went with him. Tall and lanky, with a tendency toward impulsive behavior, he seems to have been hounded by unhappiness. He joined the trek after a Mennonite girl in Russia rejected him, and an air of isolation continued to haunt him, a sense of being set apart from the others, despite having undertaken the journey with them. The Mennonites called him "the outsider."

It was here, at the village of Serabulak, that Drake received news of his mother's death in Germany and sank into paralyzing grief. Unable to go on with the journey, he stole a horse and several thousand rubles from a Mennonite family and headed back to Tashkent. He had reached the train station, where he intended to buy a ticket to Germany, when a stranger approached him, addressing him by name. The stranger called Drake a thief and ordered him back to Serabulak. Drake fled, not knowing whether he had met an angel or a devil.

It is possible that the mysterious figure at the station was nothing more than a figment of Drake's fevered imagination. Prevented from going home by this apparition, Drake returned to the Mennonites and became increasingly unhinged. One Sunday evening at the temporary settlement of Lausan, a group of girls saw him clapping and laughing in a field near the church. Soon afterward he marched into the church and up to the podium, where he sang the Prussian royal anthem:

> *Heilige Flamme, glüh',*
> *Glüh' und erlösche nie*
> *Für's Vaterland!*
> *Wir alle stehen dann*
> *Mutig für einen Mann*
> *Kämpfen und bluten gern*
> *Für Thron und Reich!*

> *Holy flame, glow,*
> *Glow and expire not*
> *For the fatherland!*
> *Then we all stand*
> *Valiant for one man*
> *Gladly fighting and bleeding*
> *For throne and empire!*

The strains of this patriotic battle hymn must have fallen on the church full of pacifists like a thunderclap. It took several men to carry Drake out. Yet an even stranger chapter followed, for shortly after his ejection from the church, Drake was seen on a nearby hill, holding a staff and apparently choking. He stood there "like a statue." Fixed on his work. He was attempting to swallow a small Bible. When one of the men yanked the book away, Drake's mouth bled. The Holy Spirit, he said, had told him to eat the book and preach its contents.

A play in three acts; a song for three voices. First, the voice of the stranger at the station, which might be Drake's inner voice. Drake wants to go back to Germany, to go home, but the voice commands him to go back in a different direction, back to his Mennonite hosts, to the people he has lived with for several years now, whose lives he has shared, whose money he has stolen, to whom he owes a debt. Burdened, perhaps, by the guilt of having abandoned his mother in Germany, Drake is filled with a new guilt: that of having abused and deserted his Mennonite family. He turns, aghast, observing the fractured paths of his past, the maze he has made of his life. The outsider has too many homes.

The second voice enters, brash as a trumpet: Drake belting out the royal anthem in church. This sacrilege, precisely calculated to pierce the hearts of European Mennonites, suggests that Drake understood the people he lived with, that he had absorbed their sensibility. The beautiful harmony of Mennonite singing, taken in like breath in childhood so that even small children show a wonderful ease and facility with music, forms the core of what is still, in many ways, an oral culture. The hymn provides roles for everyone, notes for every voice. For a moment, quarrels are dropped and cold wars of silence broken in a thaw as the voices of the combatants join in song. Music, that most transportable of the arts, accompanied the early persecuted Anabaptists, it murmured in their nights as they fled, it carried their stories from place to place, it sheltered their history, it bore them like an ark. And among their descendants, whose culture tends to harbor a deep suspicion of the arts, music, like quilting and needlework, like the composition of gardens, is also a refuge for the aesthetic impulse. Faith, family, history, identity, beauty: it was this potent constellation that Johann Drake dragged through the mire. His performance mocked the power of hymns by filling the church with another music, a call to arms, a form of belonging antithetical to the community's faith. I wonder if his voice broke as the words of the anthem moved him, perhaps against his will, if he thought of the community he might have had, the brothers who would have embraced him, surely, if only he'd stayed in Germany, joined the army. He might have seen his mother again.

On the crest of a hill, the third voice enters: a voice that demonstrates, with elegant precision, the primacy of speech over writing. Johann Drake is trying to swallow a Bible. *Take it, and eat it up.* Eating a book is a nonliterate response to text. Ingested and digested, the words become part of the speaker, who is then endowed with the spirit of prophecy. The image echoes the sacrament of communion, in which participants ingest the body of Christ, the Word made flesh. The vision of eating a book evokes a transcendent relationship with language, in which one is not a speaker but an instrument. The words of the Book flow from one's mouth. Pure praise, pure expression, like lark song. As the old hymn puts it, "How can I keep from singing?" Or, as Claas Epp Jr. expresses it in his book, echoing the Apostle Paul: "Woe to me if I don't witness."

Eat this book. A bleeding mouth. Poor Johann Drake! After the blasphemous singing that got him thrown out of the church, he tried to find his way back in by making himself a prophet like Claas Epp Jr., by forcing the little Bible down his throat.

The Home in the East

And what about the books that shouldn't be eaten?

At the end of the eighteenth century, a doctor called Johann Heinrich Jung-Stilling published *Das Heimweh*, a novel that influenced the course of history. Inspired by *Tristram Shandy* and *Pilgrim's Progress*, the book recounts the allegorical journey of a young Christian named Eugenius. As the Last Days draw near and Christ's return grows imminent, Eugenius and his wife, a woman he met in a Mennonite home, find refuge near Samarkand, in a valley of Stilling's invention called Oestenheim, the Home in the East. The idea for the novel, Stilling explains in his autobiography, arose from some lines he wrote in a friend's album:

> *Blessed are they that long for home,*
> *For homeward they shall surely come.*

"We have no word in use in English, corresponding with the German word 'Heimweh,' which literally means 'home-ache,'" writes Stilling's English grandson, W. H. E. Schwartz, "probably because no such disease exists in this country." Certainly Claas Epp Jr. suffered from home-ache, from the spiritual pangs Stilling describes in his book: "The afflictions of the earth awaken a homesickness [*Heimweh*] for the house of the Father." Epp was so moved by Stilling's novel that one can say *he ate it*: he absorbed and preached its contents. In his own book, Epp explains how he has determined the location of the place of refuge for believers in the end times, which he will eventually identify with Shakhrisabz. In addition to calculations matching biblical imagery to modern empires, periods, and places, he brings forward, as evidence, the vision of the future revealed to "the man of God, Stilling," in his novel:

*Concerning the detailed description of this place, which I've been
asked about, God's word points to the inner regions of Asia. An
even more precise description revealed to us, if we want to accept
it, is where the spirit of God led the man of God, Stilling. Even
though Stilling sought the place of refuge in Palestine and therefore let Eugenius take this wrong way, Stilling had to follow the
spirit which let him see the assembled peoples of the spirit in the
regions of Samarkand and Bukhara. And further how Eugenius,
already on the flight but still in Europe, married a member of a
Mennonite family and then both of them made the trip to Samarkand. After the assembling of the peoples had happened there,
Eugenius first went to the place of refuge which lay in the nearby
regions. This is how it was revealed to Stilling.*

And so the tale of Eugenius, a fictional character, became bound up
with the lives of the Mennonite travelers. The absorption of a novel
in this way seems superstitious, excessive, bizarre. After the failure of
Epp's prophecies, it appeared so to many of his followers as well: Franz
Bartsch laments their "fanaticism based not on Scripture but on fiction,
on a religious novel." Yet Epp was not the only one to receive Stilling's
book as a revelation. Next to the Bible and the revered Anabaptist history *Martyrs Mirror*, *Das Heimweh* was the most popular book in the
Russian Mennonite colonies. It had influenced Epp's father's generation, those who migrated from Prussia to Russia, seeking a refuge in
the East. In 1873—four years before the publication of Epp's *Unsealed
Prophecy*—Martin Klaassen, another Mennonite from the Russian
settlements, published a history of Anabaptism in which *Das Heimweh* forms the basis for an argument that the faithful will eventually
gather in "the lands of the rising sun." Part of the novel's appeal among
Mennonites undoubtedly stems from Stilling's sympathetic portrayal

of them, but this is not enough to explain the book's power—a power it held over the imaginations not only of Mennonites but of others anticipating the end of the world. Inspired in part by Stilling's depictions of Oestenheim, radical German separatist groups emigrated to Russia beginning in 1816, some pushing as far as Georgia to be near the place of Christ's return. When the Molokans and Doukhobors, Russian religious dissenters with millenarian leanings, were exiled to the Caucasus in the 1830s, some used Stilling's novel to read their banishment as part of a divine plan, moving joyfully toward Mount Ararat.

In his autobiography, Stilling describes letters and visits from readers who lauded his prophetic powers, who believed, among other things, that *Das Heimweh* had accurately predicted the defeat of Napoleon. One visitor kissed the author's hand and "wept almost aloud." "I know nothing at all of all this," Stilling protests, insisting that his book is "mere fable and fiction." How bewildered he must have felt, standing in his study in his home in the town of Marburg, a patch of garden visible through the window, explaining to weeping pilgrims that there was no Oestenheim. How astounded, how aghast he would have been to learn of the effect of his allegory on the Mennonites after his death, this man who, at the end of his life, was troubled by its impact on German readers, who tried to discourage them from moving east. I see him in his study, this cataract surgeon who often performed operations free for poor patients, who wanted to help people see. He has just shown his visitor out. The back of his hand still tingles from the tears that have dropped on it, the burning kisses. He stands at the window, catching his breath, fighting a feeling of doubt, wondering if, after all, his novel might have been divinely inspired, for it is true that the writing of *Das Heimweh* represents a special period in his life, a time of extraordinary tranquility and delight. During that golden season he forgot his persistent melancholy, the spasms that plagued his stomach, the ever-present menace of the

French, and the cruel convulsions of the neck and shoulders suffered by his wife, which deformed her entire upper body. In the moments between sleeping and waking, visions of Paradise rose before him, dreams that would communicate themselves powerfully to Claas Epp Jr. almost a century later. These images followed one another so swiftly and radiantly that Stilling was hard pressed to write fast enough, filling four large octavo volumes between August 1793 and December 1794. His exalted state of mind lasted only as long as he was working on the novel, after which he plunged into an even deeper dejection than usual, so that he would always treasure those days when the narrow streets and clay houses of Marburg seemed infused with celestial brightness, when the waters of the river Lahn shimmered with silvery beauty, so that even in winter they seemed to be proceeding directly to Heaven, and when, as the English version of his autobiography puts it, "ideas glistened past his soul."

The outsider comes in

The descendant of the imam insists we come to his home, drawing us in as his ancestor welcomed the Mennonite travelers long ago. Pallets covered with flowered cloth are spread on the floor and stacked up against the walls in shades of crimson, blue, and gold. Plums on the table, cherries, tea. No option here but to ease the salt in our joints by sitting on the floor, and we manage with varying degrees of effort, a knee poking up, a leg stretched out, it's crowded, awkward, hot, and we all fit, and the flaky bread is delectable, tearing in tender layers. Our hosts in the doorway, a man and a woman, beaming. They want to slaughter a sheep, but we don't have time, and nothing could please us more than the white honey drizzled on bread, the densely colored fruit echoing the vivid fabrics around us, the patterning of every possible surface. I pick up a dimpled black cherry, I put it in my mouth, thinking of Johann Drake as I bite down carefully, wary of the pit, how he entered the Mennonite story, and how it entered him in turn, a process fraught with the risk of choking.

Accounts of transformation, of how a new narrative takes up residence under the skin, often involve some physical violence. Just this morning, during the daily devotion on the bus, Frank read to us about the conversion of Paul on the road to Damascus. *And suddenly there shined round about him a light from heaven.* A stroke of pure, shattering glory. For three days, he couldn't see. Now the imam's descendant tells us, via Kholid's translation, of a man who stole a brick from the wall around the mausoleum of Kok Ota. Instantly, the thief suffered a palsy, his mouth twisting across his cheek. That was the touch of the Blue Grandfather. Another old man, standing out in the hall, as the room is so full, thrusts himself into the doorway to join the conversation: when he was a boy, he says, he stole a fish from the pond in the courtyard of the mosque. At once all the fish in the pond jumped out and turned into cats. The cats fled, disappearing into the cemetery. And he himself—he slaps his arms—by the time he got home, he was covered with eczema.

Identity is a story carried in the body. I remember Frank describing the influence of the novel *Das Heimweh* on the Mennonite travelers: "Fiction plus scripture plus history equaled their destiny." This formula, it seems to me, could describe any human life: a blend of imagination, tradition, and experience. Claas Epp Jr. was wrong about Stilling's novel, but only slightly: the story doesn't literally map the way to Oestenheim; the story itself is home. Every book I've read about Uzbekistan discusses this process of identity formation through storytelling, explaining, sometimes patiently, sometimes with perceptible exasperation, that Amir Timur wasn't Uzbek. He came from the Barlas tribe, a Mongol group assimilated into Central Asia, speaking a Turkic language. It was the Uzbeks who chased Timur's people out of the region, forcing his descendant Babur to flee to India, where he founded the Mughal Empire (and, according to some sources, introduced the—Uzbek?—samosa). But Timur, the outsider from a different tribe, has become the ultimate symbol of the Uzbek nation. In this close, bright room, as I reach for a strip of bread pulled off by other hands, I'm amazed by this shift, how someone can move suddenly from the margin to the center. How a man named Saul, a persecutor of Christians, turns into Paul, the great Christian preacher. His story is told three times in the Book of Acts, versions that don't quite match up: a common feature of stories that are told, that is, of stories that are alive. In Acts 9, the people traveling with Paul to Damascus hear a voice but don't see anyone; in Acts 22, they see a light but hear nothing. The point is not what others saw and heard, but what happened to Paul himself, the action of the story in his life. The story, too, has its book of acts, like the stories they tell us here, the man in the doorway slapping his arms, telling us of his altered life, as Paul tells his story again and again, to the Corinthians, to the Galatians. *And last of all he was seen of me also, as of one born out of due time.*

Carry the story and it will carry you. I think again of Johann Drake, with his keen intelligence, his sensitivity, his troubled relationship with an adoptive tribe that must have frustrated him bitterly at times and for whose sake he was willing to risk suffocation and even death. Yes, to die, to be martyred. In the last recorded chapter of his history, he enters a narrative of Christian sacrifice, a story of nonresistant courage in the face of violence that gleams out of his lonely life as if painted on glass. It was at Lausan, after the midnight murder of Heinrich Abrams. A group of Mennonite men rode after the killers. When their spokesman, Peter Unruh, confronted the murderers, demanding to know why they persisted in harassing the Mennonites even to the point of shooting them in their beds, the thieves' leader retorted that Unruh, too, would lose his life for his words, commanding him, "Kneel and pray before your death." It was then that Johann Drake, the outsider, stepped into the torchlight. In an act that must have impressed the would-be executioners—for they harmed no one else that night—Drake raised the kneeling Peter Unruh to his feet and embraced him, placing his body between Unruh and the guns. In this way, he entered the Mennonite story on a profound level: the core of martyrdom, where suffering defeats force and faith is triumphant in death. In that moment, the outsider, having imbibed the story to its acrid dregs, left the margin for the center.

I think of the picture of the martyr Dirk Willems on the cover of my copy of *Martyrs Mirror*, that great compendium of Anabaptist stories. The image shows an icy river and two men. One man has fallen through the ice; the other reaches down to save him. Most of the images in *Martyrs Mirror* show scourged or dying martyrs, but in this picture Willems is not suffering. It's the man chasing him, the man paid to capture him, the thief catcher, who has plunged into the deadly water. And Willems, who might have escaped, has turned back, his hands outstretched, he's going to rescue this man, his enemy, his neighbor, his brother. He saved the thief catcher's life. And he was caught. And he was burned at the stake on a windy day outside the town of Leerdam.

It's hard to express the power of this story, its centrality. It's the only story in *Martyrs Mirror* I don't remember learning. As if I've always known it. Is there a genetics of storytelling? Which is closer to me: this story or the shape of my hand?

All the accounts in *Martyrs Mirror* tell of suffering and dying for one's faith, but the Dirk Willems story adds something more: a life. A life that was saved. In giving his own life to save his persecutor, Willems becomes a mirror of Christ.

In his critique of the leading role martyr histories play in Mennonite consciousness, the writer Ross Bender argues, "The Mennonite story is not a narrative but a sort of consensual hallucination." I ask myself, What else could it be? What is any group identity but a story a whole community has swallowed? Johann Drake stands with his arms around Peter Unruh, home at last, his harsh breath loud in Unruh's ear, his heart steady, his eyes closing in a fierce serenity. "Brother," he murmurs, "I will die for you."

The insider goes out

She was a grande dame, a leading lady of the London stage. Critics praised her commanding presence, her mesmerizing contralto voice, her energy, her intelligence, her wit. She was known as the intellectuals' actress, electrifying in the plays of Eliot and Beckett. But though she loved the avant-garde, seeking out innovative directors like Peter Brook and creating one-woman shows from the works of Joyce and Woolf, she was equally successful in the classics, "a matchless exponent," one critic wrote, of the plays of Shakespeare, Chekhov, and Ibsen. According to another, she was "the most heartrending Desdemona of her generation." She won three Tony awards. Noel Coward wrote his last play for her. After seeing her as Hedda Gabler, the critic Walter Kerr declared her "just possibly the best actress in the world."

Her background was murky. After her death in 2002, obituaries reported her birthplace variously as Fairbury, Lincoln, and Omaha, Nebraska. Part of the confusion came from that marvelous voice, which, after her decades in England, the director Peter Gill observed, "betrayed no hint of her American upbringing: it was based on the great speaking traditions of the English theater." Many regarded her as a British actress, and *Vanity Fair* reported in parentheses in a 1988 feature, as if whispering a bit of gossip, that the title she received from the queen was only "(Honorary Commander of the British Empire—she's American)." The artist's behavior did as much to obscure her history as her voice. She kept her origins "as misty as possible," wrote Gill, "if not positively foggy." She rarely discussed her private life, evading even seemingly innocuous questions, such as whether her father had been a musician. She would never write her memoirs. "I couldn't bear a book tour," she said. "I couldn't bear being interviewed by these terrible people." When pressed, she occasionally skipped over her roots in Nebraska altogether, hinting that she had been born in Los Angeles.

June 21, 1883. The village of Lausan in the Khanate of Khiva. Heinrich Abrams is murdered, dying from one bullet and thirty-one saber wounds. It's the night of Johann Drake's heroic act, his acceptance of sacrifice, when he delivers himself up to the threat of death. Meanwhile, the murdered man's young wife, Elizabeth, has escaped through a back window. She is at the neighbors' house, hiding under a bed. "Be quiet!" she whispers. "They are coming!" And, a moment later—"Oh my Henry, they are killing him, go get him!" She is pregnant. She emigrates to America, to Nebraska. Her little boy is called Henry, after his father. And he becomes the father of Harriet Elizabeth Abrams, named partly after her grandmother, who will take the stage name Irene Worth.

After Irene Worth's death, the *Los Angeles Times* spoke with her brother, Luke Evans (he, too, had dropped the family name). A biographical sketch emerged. Harriet Elizabeth Abrams was born in Fairbury, Nebraska, in 1916. In 1920, her family moved to California, to a Mennonite community in the San Joaquin Valley, but in 1928 they left that group, and Mennonite culture, for the Central Coast and a mainstream Protestant church. Young Harriet would recite *Romeo and Juliet* while she washed the dishes. (I realize she must have attended Ventura Junior High, now Cabrillo Middle School, where my daughter went for two years, though I didn't know that then; I missed the chance to think of Harriet when I lived in California, to conjure her image against the white wall of the school, a place now removed from my life, only its name remaining, peeling and frail, in a bumper sticker on my car.) She longed for art, poetry, painting. In one of her interviews, she makes an uncharacteristic reference to her childhood, revealing that her father was a school superintendent and describing California as "a place of unspeakable horror. There was nothing to see."

She would get out. She would become an international star. But, writes Peter Gill, "she had one disadvantage: she came late to the theater." She would never play Juliet, making her name instead with "ladies of a certain age": Hedda Gabler, Madame Ranevskaya in *The Cherry Orchard*. Getting out takes time. Even though her parents had left the Mennonites, it was too great a stretch for them to support the idea of a career on the stage, perhaps the worldliest of professions, with its ostentatious displays of wealth, its links to a demimonde of prostitution and crime, its ceaseless demand for the spotlight, its vanity, its faking. An actor makes a living by showing off and telling lies. There was the tiny role in a film when she was at UCLA, a courtroom drama in which she played a witness, speaking only one line. After that, an acting career forbidden, she became a kindergarten teacher, a job she hated so much it made her physically ill.

During her brief brush with Hollywood, a studio executive suggested she change her name if she wanted to stay in the business. He gave her a list of options, including a name both mobile and stately, keen and rounded, like a golden boat with a silver oar, in which she finally rowed herself to New York, and then to London. Always original, she pronounced her first name with three syllables: *I-ree-nee*.

I see her inquisitive face, her chestnut hair, her beauty that will be described as unconventional, dominated by the large, hooded eyes now turning their sweeping gaze on the dark and bombed-out specter of postwar London. Grim, frozen, shabby, offering nothing for sale but drab utility goods and drab utility food to be purchased with ration cards, London is starved for joy, and people flock to the comedy *Love Goes to Press* by Virginia Cowles and Martha Gellhorn, Irene Worth's first venture in a starring role. In contrast to gloomy London, Cowles and Gellhorn are in a madcap mood, still tottering from the nightmare they observed as war correspondents, desperate for any kind of fun,

Gellhorn delirious with relief following her divorce from the "loath-some" Ernest Hemingway. *Love Goes to Press* is written in ten days; Cowles and Gellhorn each write half of it, then stick it together with sellotape. The director is a former prisoner of war, seasoned by years of amateur theatricals in a German camp. Costumes cost nothing (the men wear their old uniforms), tickets are cheap, the theater warm, Irene Worth in her element, impish, canny, effervescent, she's determined to make it in London, she wants to play Shakespeare. "I thought it the daftest ambition I had ever heard," Gellhorn wrote later, "but look what happened."

There were the shows in small theaters like Bolton's, a members-only club housed in the square building that had once been the Radium Picture Playhouse, then the breakout role as Celia in Eliot's *The Cocktail Party* (the author's only specific direction to the cast: "The wife should be harder"), and at last, at the Old Vic, that devastating Desdemona. Her ambition achieved, she never stopped, she stayed hungry, quickly tiring of the West End's "horrendous banality." She wanted the feel-ing of *Richard III* in a tent in Stratford, Ontario, where the rain poured down, and no critics came, and the audience was captivated. In Paris she holed up with Peter Brook and his international theater group at the former Gobelins tapestry factory on the Left Bank. For props, they used sticks of bamboo, in homage to Japanese theater and the pursuit of "Zen calm." Language barriers among the diverse cast were considered ir-relevant, as Brook was interested in universal communication through the sonorous qualities of speech and would have them rehearse in a made-up language called Bashtahondo. These experiments culminated in a journey to Iran, to test the power of universal communication in Ted Hughes's play *Orghast*, written in an invented language also called Orghast and performed among the ruins of Persepolis. This was the closest Irene Worth came to the place where her grandfather died. Did she think of him there? Did she know? I can't tell, there's no record of her feelings, only this photograph, her moonstone face emerging like a ceremonial chalice from the crypt of Artaxerxes, from the tomb.

That carven face, so empty, all identity poured out. As Jocasta in *Oedipus* she was "completely mask-like."

She knew the power of masks. How to free herself from herself, until her face became pure and hollow as an alabaster lamp. Then how to fill the lamp with oil. She swallowed the language of others, always seeking, she said, "to understand the mentality of the author." It was a matter of consuming the diction, the rhythms of another. And the lamp would burn. This was her sorcery. In the classical Arabic tradition, poetry is known as *sihr halal*, lawful magic—an oxymoron, as magic is by nature unlawful, forbidden. The ambivalence of the term sihr halal has always seemed to me to characterize the attitude toward poetry, not only in Islam but in the wider heritage of which Islam is a part, the Abrahamic tradition that includes Jews and Christians, the People of the Book. When I read about Irene Worth's one-woman show, how she "caught fire" from the words of Joyce, how her reading of Woolf "cast a bewitching spell," I think that in a curious way she was close to Claas Epp Jr., who was so filled, so ignited by Stilling's novel *Das Heimweh*. In the eldritch light of Epp's bibliomancy, the fear of poetry in the text-centered, monotheistic tradition appears quite reasonable, based not on distaste for imaginative literature but on respect for its power. After all, Epp took Stilling at his word. He was a bad reader, but he was also the ultimate reader, embodying the words of another. I wonder if his extreme reaction to what was essentially a fantasy novel would have been tempered by a bit of education in the fantastic, if exposure to what Irene Worth understood so well, the nature of play, would have alleviated his dogged literal-mindedness. And I wonder if she, who took herself so far away from the world of her grandparents, ever considered that they, too, were devoted eaters of books, people who memorized verses, who filled themselves with sacred songs, seeking to understand the mentality of the Author.

She made her home in language, that fleet, mercurial country. Working with her was as unpredictable as jamming with a great jazz musician. Her favorite story was about a little boy who went to see *Peter Pan*: when the play ended, he stood up on his seat and cried, "Oh curtain, curtain, please don't come down!" Let it never end, never close. At eighty she hopped across the room, mimicking a kangaroo "eating a piece of cake and playing with himself at the same time." She exhausted her friend Cecil Beaton, who suffered from headaches and was a few days away from a stroke. "God, the vitality!" he wrote in his journal. "She is a blockbuster. Reading, late into the night, all morning, reciting Shakespeare, as if that was not enough, she asks advice from Smallpeice on herbs, how to prune, how to cultivate, how to tell one rose from another, one bird. She is lifting heavy weights across the lawn . . . She leans out of my window till she is in danger, to spy on the newborn birds. She says, 'You must read Tennyson, George Eliot . . . You must go to Persia again, to Kashmir. You must go to Spain!' I am whacked. Her voice rises like a little girl's. She laughs, giggles, looks a hundred, but the spirit is undimmed. She is a remarkable girl-hag."

What remains once one has left the tribe? Nothing, perhaps, but those wide cheekbones, described by Gill as "almost middle European." I think of my friend from college who has made her home in the world of the theater, acting, writing, directing, who gets so fed up with telling people she's Mennonite. It always brings on the same host of annoying questions, the same eager interest—a Mennonite on the stage!—the type of interest that makes you want to defend yourself, because it's not directed toward you as a person but as a sample, a case, an object, a fetish. Sometimes she just doesn't mention it. Irene Worth never mentioned it, ever. She made herself over in a completely different mold, the English accent, the aristocratic bearing, allowing nothing to give her away in the elegant clothes, cashmere and wool, the few choice brooches and bracelets, or her perfume, "Knowing" by Estée Lauder. What remains, once one has left? I think of her last great role, as Grandma Kurnitz, the Jewish immigrant matriarch in *Lost in Yonkers*. Speaking in an interview of how she approached the play, she explained that Grandma Kurnitz came from a poor, rough background. "I wanted the audience to feel that this woman's hands had scrubbed floors and washed out ice cream cans and done plenty of hard work. She came to this country without a husband, and she had four children to raise, and by God, she did it." The impoverished, widowed, immigrant mother: it was Elizabeth Abrams. (So many parallels between certain Jewish and Mennonite communities: the blend of religion and ethnicity, the German-based vernaculars, the names. I wonder if the Abrams descendants changed their name to seem less Mennonite, less German, or less Jewish.) Neil Simon, author of *Lost in Yonkers*, remembers how he went with the director to meet Irene Worth for lunch in London. They wanted her for the role, but they were worried that, with her refined elocution, she wouldn't be able to manage the character's German accent. When they hinted at their concerns, Irene Worth fixed them with "a cold, chilling stare" and told them she hadn't auditioned in forty-two years. Then she asked the waiter for the dessert cart, and began musing out loud, in a German accent, "Shall I haff ze strudel, or perhaps ze apple tart?" She thanked the waiter: "*Danke schön.*" Neil Simon wrote admiringly, "She never looked at us or smiled. She was smarter than all of us." He saw her skill, her shrewdness. But I see the ghost of Elizabeth Abrams, her spirit undimmed, her voice conducted across the years.

The taste of love

We sit at the low table among our ghosts. Shadows flutter against the blinds, cast by the little flags that dance in the wind, on the other side of the wall, at the cemetery gate. In the heat and emotion, everything radiates: pit of plum, a china bowl. Our hosts go on deprecating everything they've given us: it's too early for the best apples, there's no *plov* on the table, no meat. "Come back when the fruit is ripe," says the old man descended from the imam, "and I'll kill twenty, thirty sheep!" His face flushed with determination between the white beard and the broidered cap. And although I'm relieved to escape the prospect of being served a whole flock of sheep, I'm moved by his extravagance, this declaration through which he tries to express the passion of his generosity. *Take, and eat.* I think of Irene Worth at the Istanbul Festival in 1986, reading a poem Süleyman the Magnificent wrote for his queen, who was raised a Christian and converted to Islam. "My orange, my pomegranate," said Irene Worth in her beautifully modulated voice, "the flaming candle that lights up my pavilion." Images of the beloved as sweet food and inner light, and then as city, as home. "My Istanbul," she murmured, "my Baghdad and my Khorasan . . . my love from a different religion." Such openness. This room feels suddenly like a dream of entering and leaving at will, a porous place of crossing. As if, here on the old trade route, all the outsiders might come in, without violence or punishment, no hard-edged books crammed roughly down their throats, and no need for hiding, either, no names abandoned along the way, they'd simply sit down, Irene Worth and Johann Drake, and eat these bright cherries, this bread.

And the honey, above all, like condensed light. How greedy we are for the little bowl of pale translucent stuff. It's full of white specks, as if whipped with milk. Sun through the blinds, so brilliant my hand disappears when passing through it, transformed into a phantom hand, while the glass bowl of honey gives off sudden fire, like a diadem, like a ring of Ulugh Beg's stars, like the Great Comet of 1882. *Pass the honey. Pass the honey!* Someone's hoarding the bowl, and we laugh, we're sympathetic, we all have this desire to hoard the honey, its creamy weight, its slight graininess on the tongue, its alchemical power that transforms a morsel of bread into gold. When I eat this honey, I'm not thinking about the Mennonite travelers. Only later, on the bus, do I wonder if they tasted it too. Eating this honey requires everything of you. I think of the Sufi philosophers who compared spiritual experience to the taste of honey. Honey is sweet and sugar is sweet, but their tastes are not the same. Is it possible to explain the difference in words? No: you can only *know* the taste of honey with your body. And only through feeling can you know the taste of love. When we leave this place with a bag of apples, one more gift for the road, I will think, There is so much goodwill in the world. And that one sentence will seem to weigh as much as a whole book. That's it, I'll think, that one sentence, that's all I have to write. But by the next day it will look worn, its sheen dissipated, it will have turned back into an ordinary glass bowl, and I'll think, what's wrong with me, why are my ideas so simplistic, so insipid, why do I think like a greeting card? How can a sentence like *we are all one* be so true and so false at the same time? I don't know, I tell Frank in the courtyard, if we can ever relate this experience, if we can ever express it without the tight grip of a handshake, the tang of cherries, the thickness of honey, and he says, "That's why we have writers."

Who we are

After lunch, in the courtyard, one last tale. An elderly man brings out a gift from an earlier group of North American pilgrims, an old calendar from Mennonite Central Committee, the volunteer organization I worked with in South Sudan and Egypt. He singles me out, excited, pointing from the calendar to my face. My face, we are to understand, is in the Mennonite calendar. Everyone gathers around, and look, a photograph, the month of April, it's an Ethiopian woman, it's my face. It's true. She has the look of the Horn of Africa, and so do I, the narrow throat, the high forehead, so yes, she has my face. We're all laughing, the old man with the calendar exultant. He can't read the caption, of course, he doesn't know that the woman in the photograph is a beneficiary of an MCC project. He just sees someone who, from the look of her, might be a cousin of mine, smiling among banana leaves.

This morning, when Frank read the story of Paul on the road to Damascus, he told us that Kholid had asked him who the Mennonites are. "We might reflect on our Damascus moments," Frank suggested, "to tell us who we are." The moment of shock, of contact, of feeling the story through one's skin, through the soles of one's bare feet at the door of the mosque. The moment of transformation, when history wells up suddenly, the ghostly accent spilling from one's lips. The moment of the gesture, the beckoning, protective hand. *And immediately there fell from his eyes as it had been scales.* The moment of realization, that this Ethiopian woman's face—for this old man, in this courtyard—this is who we are.

FIVE

Bukhara

safely to arrive at home

Halfway

At the midpoint of our journey, we enter the glossy shade of the groves of Bukhara. "Of this valley," declared Herman Jantzen, "Jung-Stilling must have written." The visionary must have seen this place in a dream, ringed with poplars that flicker with every breath of wind, leaves sparkling like festival lights. Here they make silk paper. It's not made from silk, but from the bark of the mulberry tree. "It's brown in color," Usmon explains, "and if you read on it your eyes will never be tired." Here are the walls of Bukhara, light brown like a piece of silk paper, hazy in places with clouds of blossoming trees. Priceless Bukhara, sacred Bukhara, the religious capital of Uzbekistan. We enter another gargantuan hotel, this time through a side door, as the main portico, with its faux-Timurid mosaics, presents the obstacle of a splendid but impractical flight of steps striped with red carpet. I have read that while

Samarkand is the city of Timur and Genghis Khan, Bukhara is the city of Ibn Sina, the influential medieval philosopher, known in the West as Avicenna. This is a city of thinkers and theologians. Yet as we haul our suitcases down the garish tiled corridors common to the chain hotels of the region, then visit a series of mosques and madrasas where artisans ply their trade in the cool of the arches, I'm reminded that this is also a place of commerce, its long history blending intellectual, spiritual, and material exchange.

Here are ceramics collected from all over the country. Dishes etched and colored, and tea bowls in which, as the tea recedes, you can see banks of coral, tulips, cotton bolls, suns. Pottery from Bukhara, we are told, sounds like metal if struck with a fingernail. If it's from Khiva it sounds like plastic, because of all the salt in the soil there. If it's from Samarkand it makes a heavy clanging noise, and if it's from the Ferghana Valley it rings like a gong. So energy awakens in the mud, waves of sound in the glancing air, waves of embroidered cloth in the courtyard of the madrasa, billowing like a steppe in bloom, unfurling the colors of morning skies, evening skies, and quivering banks of wildflowers. Here Babur, the maker of musical instruments, plays the *chang*, striking it like a dulcimer. The *dutar* has two strings, the *tambur* four. The best instruments are of mulberry wood, inlaid with mother-of-pearl. For a mellow sound, construct the belly from the membrane of a bull's heart.

At the end of his demonstration, he plays Beethoven's *Für Elise*, liquid notes running out into the courtyard, our gasps of recognition and delight following, lighter, breathier, dissolving in the dusk. A tour group passes the doorway, guided in German, another conducted in Japanese, and all at once the idea of a divided world seems ludicrous. "No one knows anything about Uzbekistan," Usmon says, rueful. But ignorance doesn't mean lack of connection, it just means we don't see the links.

Kids whiz past on rollerblades. A man wheels a bicycle labeled

UKRAINA. Under a streetlamp, two men are selling a cage of doves. As we wait for a table outside a restaurant, I ask Kholid how to spell his name, but he doesn't want to use the Latin alphabet. "Neither *K* nor *H* can express it," he says.

At last he writes it in my notebook in Arabic. As we make our way to our table, where little bowls of eggplants and peppers are already glistening, Diane says she once told someone she's half Mennonite, just on her father's side, and the person said, "How can you be half a religion?"

Over the plov, Usmon tells us Uzbekistan is full of "half Muslims." He quotes Omar Khayyam: "Their right hand is on the Qur'an, their left hand on the bottle." Nozli giggles at this, but Kholid looks severe.

For dessert, a Rice Krispie treat stuffed with dried fruit.

The ethnic ghost

How can you be half a religion? The Wikipedia entry for *Mennonite* has some answers. Today it reads, "In contemporary twenty-first-century society, Mennonites are described either only as a religious denomination with members of different ethnic origins or as both an ethnic group and a religious denomination." *Either only*, or *both and*. In case this is unclear, the entry adds helpfully, "There is controversy among Mennonites about this issue, with some insisting that they are simply a religious group while others argue that they form a distinct ethnic group." Back at the hotel, seated on a shiny buff-colored bedspread, I try to explain this to Diane, who very reasonably throws her hands in the air. "What kind of religion is this?" she exclaims. "You can't even get everybody on the same page!"

She's right. We can't even get everybody on the same Wikipedia page without contradictory sentences that have to be read over two or three times. Shaking her head, Diane hangs up her shirt for tomorrow in the closet, while I stretch out with my photocopies, my notes. (I plan to hang my shirt up, too, but I'll forget, I'll be wrinkled.) I find a phrase from the sociologist Calvin Redekop: "the ethnic ghost of Mennonitism"—a reference to the fact that while the word *Mennonite* connotes a religious denomination, it also means (underneath, secretly, in a spectral manner) a group of white people with roots in Central Europe. It's in this second, ghostly sense that you can be half a religion, that Diane and I are both half Mennonite. I review my notes on the various proposals for new names that would separate religion from ethnicity and make everyone less confused. Maybe, some say, the white ethnic group should be Mennonites, while members of the religious denomination should be called Anabaptists. Or maybe members of the church should be

Mennonites, while the ethnic group gets some qualifier attached, like ethnic Mennonites, Swiss and Dutch-Prussian-Russian Mennonites (a hearty mouthful!), or, my personal least favorite, cradle Mennonites, which not only sounds like an infant's disease but suggests that nobody who is not white is born into this church, thereby excluding large numbers of Mennonites in Africa, Asia, and Latin America, as well as many in North America. And I would not be thinking or writing about this, forgetting to hang up my shirt, nearly setting a scarf on fire by draping it over the lamp to dim the light (though Diane, an experienced traveler, tells me she can easily sleep with the light on, rolls on her side, and promptly goes to sleep)—I would not be spending my time on this subject, believe me, if I thought it only pertained to a certain offshoot of the Radical Reformation, if I didn't perceive a world full of ethnic ghosts: the ghosts of modernity, of travel, of romance, of writing.

The photograph

In 1932, the Swiss athlete and photographer Ella Maillart travels through Russian Turkestan. Restless, disgusted with city life and industrial society, she seeks places and people untouched by modernity. She longs for the life of a nomad, of her own remote, prehistoric ancestors who roamed the immensity of barren soil under implacable skies, and of the wanderers of Europe with their caravans, people she admires as untamable, whose life enthralls her. She boards the train in Moscow. It's July, so hot the bacon melts in her rucksack. She passes Samara and the naphtha reservoirs of Emba. Then come the deserts of Turkestan: horizontal infinities of sand, the Aral Sea, the steppe, the rails fading into the distance. Her Leica camera around her neck, she is going to photograph the ancient world before the future overtakes it. She is also becoming a writer. She writes, "To learn how to deal with life! And above all, make it real."

Her way leads toward desolate lands, treeless and empty of habitations. She is one of the malcontents of technological civilization, the ones who become anthropologists, missionaries, and photographers, who long for something else, a something forever receding. The ones Frantz Fanon will describe twenty years later, writing, "When the whites feel they have become too mechanized, they turn to the men of color." Ella Maillart turns to the men of color. She writes, "In contact with primitive, simple peoples, mountain-dwellers, nomads, and sailors, it is impossible to ignore the elemental laws."

She gets off the train at Frunze, the end of the line. In the company of some Russian travelers, she goes on by truck across the plain of Tokmak. Rain falls in torrents, smelling of new-mown hay. An imposing string of camels passes, moving so deliberately it makes one think of a film in slow motion. The atmosphere, as evening falls, is translucent, almost as though it had been varnished. At the lake of Issik-Köl, a Kyr-gyz woman leans against a schooner, her Mongolian eyes startling in this Mediterranean landscape. Nearby, some astonishingly fair children bathe in the water. Ella Maillart speaks to one of them, but he only gives her a bored stare.

She tries again.

"*Ich verstehe kein Russisch,*" says the child.

As it turns out, they are not Russian at all. They are German children, Ella Maillart discovers, belonging to the Mennonite colony in Aulie-Ata.

The blond child, the first Mennonite to appear in Ella Maillart's travel book, is part of the community that split off from Claas Epp Jr.'s group on the journey east. Later on her trip, she meets the remains of the group that followed their prophet all the way to Khiva, the city of nightingales. She finds a German with a pointed beard at the post office in Khiva, who tells her he lives in the Mennonite village of Ak Metchet. Marveling, she rides out to the village on a bicycle, through the sand that glitters with a crust of salt.

By this time, she has been to Tashkent, Samarkand, and Bukhara. She has slept in a yurt and crested mountains on horseback. She has eaten sheep livers and fat with her hands, dipping the meat in salt and using the leftover fat on her fingers to oil her boots. The country, she has reflected, sometimes with satisfaction and sometimes with dismay, seems marooned in the Middle Ages. She arrives at Ak Metchet bathed in sweat, rejoicing at the thought that in a few moments she will be talking to Europeans.

Prosperous farms surrounded by yellowing poplars. White curtains in the windows. A voice calls, "*Maria, wer kommt dort?*"

Cows drink from a roofed-in spring, watched by an Uzbek herdsman.

Two young girls bring Ella Maillart a white hand basin, soap, and a towel. Inside the house, a pair of old aunts in spectacles knit by the earthen stove, upright in a pair of straight-backed chairs.

They speak to her of their journey, their trials still vivid after half a century. They show her their doors, constructed from cart shafts. At the supper of boiled eggs, buttered rusks, and coffee, the younger people converse in whispers, and only the older ones take honey. How poor we were when we arrived, they say. We made little lanterns to sell in the market. We sold socks and blouses. We repaired the khan's phonograph. Ella Maillart is amazed at their neatness and discipline. "Doesn't the excellent way in which you run your colony set an example to your neighbors, the Uzbeks?"

Not at all. "It makes no difference to them: they don't need any of the things that are so indispensable to us. There was a Turkmen who lived with us here for two years, an intelligent lad, and in the end he was talking our 'Platt-Deutsch' like one of us. Do you know what he said some days before he left? 'You are a strange and complicated lot of people: why does a person have to waste his time three times a day, washing fifteen plates, and knives and forks, when only one dish is necessary!'"

Ella Maillart sympathizes with the fastidious Germans, their disapproval of the unhygienic sharing of dishes, their complaints about the local custom of blowing air into a dead sheep's skin to separate it from the flesh—surely a way of spreading microbes. And yet, though the Ak Metchet Mennonites are certainly more advanced than their neighbors, there's something undeniably backward about them. On a side table lies a German newspaper, the *Vossische Zeitung*, which takes eighteen days to arrive. The Mennonites refer to it affectionately as "Aunt Voss." They are disturbed by the news from Germany, but only, the way Ella Maillart tells it, to distance themselves from it with rather sanctimonious pronouncements: "Every day we praise God that we have not forgotten His precepts." The women regard their visitor's bicycle with unease. As for them, they are using a spinning wheel, a machine that stays in place. The textbooks in the schoolroom are twenty years old. A girl sidles up to the stranger and asks her what Christian names are popular in Germany now; they are so tired of the old ones.

Ella Maillart suggests Brigitte and Marlene. She visits the quiet village square, with its two cubes of white clay, the church and the school. "The church," she writes, "set thus in the middle of a Soviet republic, is touching in its sun-bathed simplicity." She lifts the camera to her eye and takes a photograph. Yes, she takes the photograph of the church at Ak Metchet, the one I hold in my hand, the one that drew me toward this story. She takes the photograph of the White Mosque.

Cultural show

In Bukhara, our itinerary includes "dinner and a cultural show in an ancient caravanserai." Seated outside in a courtyard with a plate of steaming kababs, I ask Kholid about the people who so inspired Ella Maillart. My approach is clumsy, as I'm not sure of the right word to use. I try *Roma* and *Romany*, but he doesn't know what I mean, so I fall back on *gypsies*. "Ah!" he says. Yes, they have some communities in Uzbekistan. I ask if they're marginalized, and he tells me they marginalize themselves. "The Soviets tried to collectivize them, but it was a waste of effort and money." He puts down his kabab, which he's been consuming very neatly, while I look as if I'm not just eating but also cooking this dinner. "Their *kolkhoz* wasn't productive," he says. "They had no ideology toward the labor." I've never heard him sound so Soviet.

As the sun sets, the lights come on, and women in matching outfits perform decorous dances on a carpet spread under the sky. The evening ends with a fashion show. Emaciated models stride through colored light to the crackling sound of music from the speakers. They wear sweeping trench coats and elegant hats, all embroidered with traditional motifs, a meeting of local craft and haute couture. Nozli is in ecstasies. "Look, look!" she whispers, squeezing my arm. "It's Irina Sharipova!" She nods toward a nearby table where, wreathed in rotating light and smoke from the grill, a large woman with cropped hair sits before a bowl of ice cream, wearing an expression of ineffable world-weariness. This is the designer, Irina Sharipova herself! She's Russian, Nozli tells me, and an artistic genius. More interested in the designer than the models, we watch as a waiter, bent almost double with respect, serves the great woman a cup of tea. Irina Sharipova accepts the cup but doesn't drink it. She lights a cigarette and sighs out a plume of smoke, creating an impression that works equally well for "temperamental artist" and "woman contemplating burning down this ancient caravanserai."

Of course, this might not be a case of either/or. It could be both/ and. I'm not sure whether I'm too caught up in imagining the thoughts of the fashion designer, or whether the crowds in the courtyard and streets force me away from the group, but somehow I wind up trailing behind on the way to the bus. And so I'm the one who responds to three women who call out, "Are y'all from the States?" They're from Texas, these women, they wear sleek dresses, yellow, pink, and white. We're hurrying toward the bus. Afraid of slowing the others down, I give my fellow Americans the briefest possible sketch of our tour, our story. They're amazed to hear of these Mennonites who traveled to Central Asia. "Did they kill 'em," one cries, "because they wouldn't convert to Islam?" "Quite the opposite!" I yell back, my language becoming pompous, a nervous reaction. "They were very hospitable!"

No time for more than these few flung words. It's not enough, I know.

On the bus, I sit beside Kholid. As the lights of the caravanserai recede behind us, red and green swallowed by the darkening streets, he returns to the subject of the Roma. "They are children of nature," he says.

Alphabet of bone

At Ak Metchet, Ella Maillart makes notes on the Mennonite faces, especially their heads. She believes you can tell almost everything from a face, particularly the shape of the cranium. Years from now, on a trip to Afghanistan, she will bring calipers to measure people's skulls. Today, narrowing her eyes, she reads a stolid resistance in the block-like heads of these Germans, over which, in the case of the women, the hair is parted and tied in a bun. Their frank and guileless faces, she decides, match their low Prussian houses set with level window frames, while their square foreheads reveal the obstinacy that saved the band from perishing fifty years earlier.

Racial iconography, alphabet of bone. At the hotel, I set my pages on Ella Maillart beside a quote from Franz Bartsch: "Slanted eyes and small indented noses, accentuated by strong protruding cheek bones, lend a flat appearance to the Kirghiz countenance, in which natural instinct rather than intelligence seems to be reflected." Everything is visible. In the shape of a head, of an eye, one can read character, social organization, culture. It's an allegorical worldview, akin to the act of prophecy that reads the future in the Book of Daniel. This way of reading bodies has influenced Mennonite self-understanding. I underline a quote by the scholar Al Reimer, who explains that for many Mennonite thinkers in the mid-twentieth century, "the concept of ethnic identity was to a large extent modeled on the German concept of *Volk* and *Kultur*, and was tinged with the notion of racial purity and 'Germanness' that prevailed in the Nazi Germany of the 1930s." The Mennonite writer Arnold Dyck, for example, would have liked to organize a Mennonite migration to South Africa, "to establish our own state in proximity to our ethnic cousins, the Boers, in order to make manifest—especially to ourselves—that we are truly capable of the utmost accomplishments."

A Mennonite state, a homeland. In 1933, J. J. Hildebrand tries to establish a white settlement of Mennonites in Australia. In Canada, the *Mennonite Racial Observer* publishes articles intended "to strengthen our racial group-consciousness and to fortify the desire to remain what we are: Mennonites." In Paraguay, Mennonites create the white colony of Friesland, named in honor of their Dutch ancestry. In Ukraine, the colony of Friesendorf, named for this same origin story, replaces the formerly Jewish and Mennonite village of Stalindorf. Some Mennonites participate in the Nazi death squads that exterminate their Jewish neighbors. Many more receive the clothes, shoes, and homes of murdered Jews. Nazi organizers are fascinated by Mennonites: these racially pure, German-speaking farmers. They measure their faces. They take photographs.

37   38

It happens at the same time: the expansion, the contraction. As Mennonites reach out, planting churches and gaining converts all over the world, the idea of white Mennonite identity grows firm. The decade of the 1930s, when Ella Maillart rides her bicycle to Khiva, a time of intense racial consolidation for white Mennonites, is also a time of missionary growth. Mennonite Central Committee, an organization that will eventually send volunteers all over the world, that will one day take me to Egypt and South Sudan, begins as a relief agency serving European Mennonites, and, in the 1940s, helps confirm the notion of ethnic Mennonite identity. MCC deploys this identity to secure the emigration of thousands of Mennonite refugees from the ruins of war-torn Europe. These refugees, MCC argues, are neither Russian nor German. They are a unique ethnic group, a people. They are Mennonites.

I remember, after my father's death, going into his basement office and finding the papers recording his sponsorship of my uncles' visa applications: the documents that brought our family out of a Somalia wracked by war, out of the holding pens of the refugee camps. The grainy paper in my hands, under fluorescent light. The stamps, the signatures, the official look that evokes a distinct variety of fear, the silent panic of people in waiting rooms, squatting in hallways, pressed in long lines at fences, who find themselves at the mercy of obscure laws. Death behind, and before them someone just doing a job, maybe tired today, maybe bored. The photographs of my uncles stapled through the forehead, hair, or throat. I can understand those MCC workers in the 1940s who worked desperately to save other Mennonites from execution or labor camps. But the gains came at a cost. Peter Dyck, an MCC worker who played a central role in the process, later worried about the ethnic distinction he helped authorize. "[T]oo frequently," he wrote, "we consider the 'real' and 'good' Mennonites to be those named Janzen, Klassen, Dyck, Wall, and so on."

I've often wondered why it's so difficult, when speaking of Mennonites, to remember that most of us don't have those European names. Due to the missionary project begun a century ago, most Mennonites now live outside North America and Europe, while North America contains Black, Latino, and other ethnically diverse Mennonite communities. Our fastest-growing church is in Ethiopia. As the poet Julia Spicher Kasdorf has observed, "the most representative Mennonite is an African woman." And yet, if you pick up a book on Mennonite history, identity, or literature, if you seek out a Mennonite periodical or blog, you're unlikely to find much participation by the majority. How can so many people be so consistently overlooked?

The answer I've developed is that Mennonites are something that seems very odd, at least at first: an evangelizing tribe. A tribe that travels the world to spread the universal love of God, and at the same time maintains the occult power of its family names, its language, its traditions, its alphabet of bone.

1939: Mennonite Nazi sympathizer Benjamin Unruh extols the "religious-racial defense system" that has preserved Mennonites from contamination by foreign bloodlines.

1959: Black scholar, activist, and Mennonite pastor Vincent Harding calls on the Mennonite Church to "break down the wall of German-Swiss-Dutch backgrounds."

2016: At a meeting to discuss the racial climate at my alma mater, Goshen College, a Mennonite institution, students of color describe their isolation, how they are shut out by an exclusive, white group identity. They call this group consciousness "the Mennonite wall."

And when I heard this, I wanted to write something for those young people who came from the world where most Mennonites live. They were something that seemed very odd, at least at first: a minoritized majority. Among my notes, a scribbled line: *Write something to answer their confusion.*

Writing coming home

To be a Mennonite poet, writes Di Brandt, is to be a hybrid. It's 2004. The anthology *A Cappella: Mennonite Voices in Poetry* has just been released, and writing in the journal *Mennonite Life*, Brandt declares that in becoming a poet she died to her Mennonite self. She couldn't have imagined, back in the 1980s when she began writing and publishing, that there would be anthologies of Mennonite poems or poetry readings at Mennonite colleges. "And so I became a Mennonite poet but with a lot of deep knowledge about identity and loss and the hybridities we make out of our losses if we are lucky enough to survive them, a cultural halfbreed, with enough scars and experience to prove it."

The artist as fringe-dweller, one foot in and one foot out. It's a common trope, but one with serious weight for Mennonite writers, a true ur-narrative. In more than one essay on Mennonite literature, I've read that the term *Mennonite writer* is a contradiction, that to write anything other than prayers and sermons is to transgress, that writers are, as the title of Hildi Froese Tiessen's 1989 anthology of Mennonite fiction puts it, *Liars and Rascals*, formed by an act of crime. Di Brandt, who broke painfully with her home community, knows this story well. "And how lovely," she concludes her piece on the *A Cappella* anthology, "that the hybrids, the halfbreeds, are being invited back in now, with their stranger knowledge: it is perhaps what will save the community from atrophy or irrelevance (or plain deceit) as we figure out who we are all over again in this new age, this century with its great terrors and great hopes, and it's very nice for the hybrids too, gasping for water from those great old half-severed roots."

This image of the wounded hybrid whose knowledge saves the community is familiar from a certain racial fantasy. Brandt's poet is a sort of tragic mulatto, homeless and suffering, whose split self paradoxically carries the promise of harmony. How often I've been told I'm false, impossible, unreal. Somali and Swiss Mennonite: no one can make it work. How often I've been told that everybody will look like me once time has ushered in the blessed, postracial kingdom.

If to be a Mennonite writer is to be a cultural hybrid, and to be Somali and Swiss is to be an ethnic hybrid, and to be a Mennonite granddaughter of a Muslim sheikh is to be a religious hybrid, then I am not so much a hybrid as a Rubik's cube. Akron, Pennsylvania, 2001. I've taken my puzzle of a self to a Mennonite Central Committee orientation, preparing for three years of volunteer teaching in Egypt. It's time for the antiracism training, part of a project called Damascus Road established to address institutional racism in MCC and the church. The project's name refers to that dramatic moment of Paul's conversion, a theme that will flash like quicksilver through my trip to Uzbekistan fifteen years later. During the training, we watch a video that shows us race is a construct. Then we divide into groups at round tables to talk about our experience of white privilege.

A hitch, a pause, a prickle of dismay, a frozen moment. The leader is quick: he remembers that not all the volunteers are white. And so a handful of us, perhaps four or five, are seated together and instructed to discuss how we do *not* experience white privilege. My husband and I exchange a rueful glance before walking to our different tables. Already I have a vague sense of having failed the assignment. At my table I sit between a Sudanese man and a Black woman from Philadelphia. I remember us talking about food. It's all too weird, our sudden isolation, our separate circle. Our experiences are so varied we don't know where to start, and even if we could, we don't understand what's supposed to happen. So we talk about church potlucks. We talk about chicken.

At my first Mennonite writing conference, in 2012, I was struck by how similar the discussions were to those I'd heard at the African Literature Association Conference the previous year, those urgent and perpetual questions of writers from groups on the literary margins: who are we, how do we represent ourselves and our communities, where are we going? Every statement begins with a definition. Continual emergence. Discussions of Mennonite writing, like those around writing from Africa and the Diaspora, reveal a minority consciousness, concerned with authenticity, memory, survival, and the challenges of interacting with a dominant culture. "'Black is beautiful,' our black brothers and sisters have learned to say," declares John L. Ruth in his influential 1976 lectures *Mennonite Identity and Literary Art.* "Who can deny it? But do we ever hear, 'Plain is beautiful'?" He extends this line of thought:

> Mennonites don't need . . . evidence that we, too, can be packaged and sold in the marketplace of literary sensation. We don't need the equivalent of an *Ebony* magazine to show us ourselves in expensive clothes and staggeringly over-powered automobiles, so that we can feel real, while hucksters persuade us, figuratively speaking, to buy hair-oil to straighten out our cultural kinks and make us normal Americans.

Whatever *Ebony*'s role in African American culture, in the seventies or today, Ruth's comparison is a rich one. The visual marker of plain dress, a marker adopted by choice, corresponds here to the naturally occurring visual markers of Black skin and hair. The effect, despite the claim of figurative language, is to locate plainness in the body. Mennonite identity is detached from the spiritual process of believer's baptism, where choice is essential, and bonded to the genes. These "cultural kinks" are as involuntary, as threatened, as potentially beautiful and political as an Afro. I love Ruth's passion here, his recognition of the power of Black radicalism, the way he seizes on it, holds it up to himself like a mirror. But at the same time, it's clear how the metaphor works: Mennonites are *like* Black people because they are not Black. The comparison depends on separation: Mennonite "kinks" do not include actual kinky hair. This has a strange ring to me, since even in the seventies there were a considerable number of Black Mennonites, including my father. But if my study of Mennonite literature has convinced me of anything, it's that numbers don't matter. Anyone who is waiting for a critical mass of people of color to transform a white space will wait until Judgment Day. This is because identity is not a question of numbers. It's a question of storytelling. When I want to find stories of Mennonites like my father, I don't go to books about writing but to books about missionary work, because most of the world's Mennonites are framed as receivers, rather than creators, of Mennonite stories.

And yet this music, this labor, this creative work goes on. Consider the Somali Canadian poet Mohamud Siad Togane, whose poem "The Gullet" appears in the anthology *Fifty Years, Fifty Stories: The Mennonite Mission in Somalia, 1953–2003*. Part lament, part folktale, "The Gullet" begins with a generalized sorrow for Somalia's political failures and devastating civil war, as well as a particular sorrow for Merlin Russell Grove, the Mennonite missionary killed in Mogadishu in 1962. Somalis have failed, Togane writes, to absorb the Mennonite "lesson" of peace. However, the poem refuses a strict division between peaceful Mennonites and warring Somalis, asserting that "the message of Jesus . . . is no different / from the message / Weel-waal too tried to teach us Somalis / ages ago." An account of the legendary Somali king Weel-waal follows, in which the wise ruler points out to his followers that the gullet, a despised part of the animal, is in fact noble, for it delivers nourishment to the rest of the body: "The gullet is the symbol of selflessness." In offering this Somali counterpart to the Mennonite lesson, Togane brings together two traditions of self-sacrifice and peace. "The Gullet" also links two modes of religious experience by finding "the best definition of Islam there is" in the Mennonite hymnal:

> Perfect submission, all is at rest,
> I in my Savior am happy and blest.

"The Gullet" is a selfless poem; good will flows through it; it extends a message of fellowship to the Mennonites who are expected to read it. Yet its claim that Somali and Muslim peace traditions are no different from North American Anabaptist ones suggests that something about the Mennonite lesson is hard to swallow. We, too, are teachers, the poem insists, we have our own wisdom, we understand sacrifice and submission as well as you. Togane dedicates the poem to his Mennonite English teacher Mary Gehman, "who taught this Caliban in the benighted bush of Mahaddei."

The red plague rid you for learning me your language. Caliban is hardly a comfortable model of cross-cultural interaction. And it is the voice of Caliban that crackles through Togane's book *The Bottle and the Bushman*, published in Canada in 1986. Subtitled *Poems of the Prodigal Son*, the book contains a poem called "Caliban" with the Shakespearean character's most famous line for an epigraph: *You taught me your language, and my profit on't / Is, I know how to curse.* Mary Gehman also appears in this poem: the poet recalls how "Miss Gehman, the Mennonite missionary teacher, meowed: / HOW OLD ARE YOU?" He remembers repeating the words and being drowned in the "shaming laughter of the class," for his attempt at English sounded like the Somali for "Who farted?" "But now," concludes this acerbic and exuberant latter-day Caliban, "right white through the nose I babble pray and bray."

From the lower body to the upper, from the anus to the nose, from what creates odor to what is disgusted by the smell. The poem represents education as a method of transition from the anal zone of shame to the "right white" realm of the nose. This transition is effected through language: the body must transform itself in order to shape the unfamiliar nasal sounds. The poet succeeds, acquiring the ability not just to speak English, but to write poetry in the language.

And yet the body can only do so much. The physical alteration that makes room for the sounds of a foreign language gestures toward a second, impossible metamorphosis: the transition to a white body. *The Bottle and the Bushman* is the chronicle of a body that has failed, both through an inability to fit into a racist, Christian West, and through a struggle with alcoholism. For this poet, the two are inseparable: "I bought the best their world peddled," he writes in the opening poem, "the Bible and the bottle." In the worldview that comes with his new language, delivered through the Bible, he is Queequeg and Friday as well as Caliban, he inhabits all the great savages of English literature. And having given himself over to the intoxicants of alcohol and the English language, he can't go back. In "The Return of the Bushman," we see a man transformed by his western sojourn into "the second fattest man in Mogadishu" (a sign of corruption, for we must assume the fattest man is Mohamed Siad Barre, the dictator against whom Togane railed for decades). The prodigal stands out among the "hunger-pinched Somalis," no longer one of them. Nor is he at home among African Americans, to whom he complains in "A Letter to Harlem": "I am no savage / I don't swing from trees like a monkey / I am not afraid of Tarzan like whitey show you on TV."

If the poet is homeless in Harlem, he is even more bitterly alienated from white Mennonites. In "White Man's God," he remembers a blond, pale-skinned image of Jesus, and the missionaries' question: "Would you be white / whiter / much whiter than snow?" "Call me DHU-HU-LOW," he retorts, referring to his nickname, "'cause I am black as CHARCOAL!" The shouts and curses in these poems, the scatological humor, confront a culture and religion barricaded in whiteness. The poet's cramped "Bushman's feet" suffer in European shoes, so that he "stagger[s] through white civilization / like a camel in a *Fata Morgana*."

Dysfunctional, broken, gross. These are poems of the unhomed body. *The Bottle and the Bushman* is a necessary companion to Togane's piece in *Fifty Years, Fifty Stories*. These poems reveal another side of Somali Mennonite experience. They are fiercely critical and, in their frankness, deeply generous. Poems of the gullet.

And I remember, when I was a child, the poet Togane, whom I knew as Uncle Togane, coming to the house. His ringing laugh at the back door. The way he stamped the snow from his shoes, scoffing at our New Jersey winter, so meager compared to the icebound glitter of his Montreal. Uncle Togane was big, he had a big voice, a big beard, a big belly, he filled the house with the smell of spaghetti sauce he'd simmer for hours in the kitchen, using my mother's biggest pot, making more than we could possibly eat, cracking jokes about the culinary benefits of Italian colonialism. Spaghetti sauce was the reason the Italians were better than the British, who left you nothing but an inferiority complex and a tin of peas. Shouting with laughter, he made my brother and me come taste the end of the spoon, and his tomato sauce really was the best in the world. Uncle Togane was different from the rest of our extended family on both sides, a family which, when I was very young, seemed like a single cloud of vague benevolence and formal manners, with a thin yet implacable undercurrent of judgment. Whether the representatives of this family on a given day were Swiss Mennonite or Somali Muslim, I went upstairs when they came over and exchanged my shorts for a skirt. Family was this group of elders who didn't listen to hip-hop and whose sole dissipations were sugar and caffeine. None of the men in this group took over our kitchen, except Uncle Togane. They didn't have his boisterous gestures, his heavy tread, they didn't make my father laugh the way he did, or make him so angry either, they didn't get into the terrible screaming fights. Only later, once I began to look more closely at my family, the ones who sang before meals, the ones who unrolled their prayer rugs in front of the fireplace, the ones who were blood relations and the ones, like Uncle Togane, who were not, did I begin to sense the tenor of his friendship with my father. I saw then that they were bound together by a love of poetry and the experience of a Mennonite life. Both had been converts. Both had been young men in Mennonite schools. Years later, when I interviewed Togane, he told me that being Mennonite deeply informed his poetic practice, that he called himself Moslem-Mennonite or MoMennonite. Present in the book on missionaries, absent from the books on poetry, he is caught between *both/and* and *either/or*. And yet he is one of us. Arnie knew him in Somalia. When I played the Mennonite game in that restaurant, I used Togane's name too.

Desire for Mennonite writing. I am writing a book called *Anabaptist Visions*. I am editing a volume called *Mennonite/s Writing Now*. I have developed a book proposal based on an international colloquium for writers at the next Mennonite World Conference. I am editing an anthology of Mennonite writing in which you will find the poetry of Mohamud Siad Togane, in which Mennonites of color are not referred to in parentheses, in which the global majority is not a special issue. In this book "truly international" does not mean American and Canadian. This book realizes the potential of *Three Mennonite Poets*, a small anthology published in 1986, which includes the American poet Jean Janzen, the Japanese poet Yorifumi Yaguchi, and the Canadian poet David Waltner-Toews. *Three Mennonite Poets*, of which a reviewer for a Mennonite publication wrote that "sandwiching Yorifumi Yaguchi into the collection is forced at best," that "We're told that Yaguchi is a Mennonite pastor, and several of his poems allude to pacifism, but it is never apparent in the poems themselves that Yaguchi is *being* Mennonite." I am editing an anthology called *Being Mennonite*. I am preparing a book called *Three Thousand Mennonite Poets*. In this book, "incredible diversity" does not mean Amish, Evangelical Mennonite Brethren, and General Conference Mennonite. Reading this book, you will not wonder whether all the Mennonites of color have disappeared from the face of the earth. You will not pause as you realize that all the "new Mennonites" in the collection, those without the traditional names, are white. You will not experience that nausea, that chill. You will hear the voice of Mohamud Siad Togane speaking the language of the Bible:

> *No, I don't want to write.*
> *I can't write.*
> *How can I write*
> > *of life's song*
> > *its sorrow*
> > *its beauty*

its beastliness
its passion
its vanity
in the language of an alien tribe?

No, I don't want to write. I can't write. How can I write? So much home-ache. When I think of Mennonite writing I think of this hymn of diaspora, the pulse-beat of a wandering, displaced, and scattered people, a song about the impossibility of singing. I think of Mennonite writing as a longing for the house of the Father that has burst the bonds of discipline. I sense a desire for Heaven that has become a desire for a language that can make itself heard and a people who are still there. This is a need for shelter that is a shelter. You weep for home and in the end your weeping becomes your house. "While I still had my zither," wrote Herman Jantzen of Ak Metchet, "I loved to sing the 'Song of Home'":

Ich möchte heim, mich zieht's dem Vaterhause,
Dem Vaterherzen Gottes zu;
Fort aus der Welt verworrenem Gebrause
Zur stillen, sanften tiefen Ruh'.
Mit tausend Wünschen bin ich ausgegangen,
Heim kehr' ich mit bescheidenem Verlangen,
Noch hegt mein Herz nur einer Hoffnung Keim:
Ich möchte heim, ich möchte heim!

I long for Home! My Father's Home up yonder!
His loving heart will welcome me,
Out of this weary sin-warped world around me,
Into His rest eternally.
A thousand wishes once beguiled, enthralled me,

Now coming Home, only one thing I long for—
For in my heart one hope alone is growing:
I long for Home, I long for Home!

Herman Jantzen and his zither among the white walls of Ak Metchet. Such harsh shadows. His shirt is buttoned to the chin. And Togane mourns *Now it is the seventh season of sorrow since I ran away from home.* This note of loss reverberates through Mennonite poetry. Jeff Gundy confesses *I am a native but not exactly at home,* Sarah Klassen murmurs *Evenings you will dream of the Lost Paradise,* Jean Janzen watches her father weeping *not for home but for lack of it,* Patrick Friesen's tormented hero asks *but how do I come back?* I will tell you how to come back. You will come back through writing. As Di Brandt puts it: *writing coming home.* I am thinking these thoughts in my car on the drive to Fresno, California, to attend the seventh Mennonite/s Writing Conference. Around me the flat and thirsty golden land. Enormous trucks. A sparkling dust. I am thinking, I hope we don't miss it. I hope we don't miss the chance to see how much is shared by Mennonites across the most frightening border, the border of skin. I am pulling into the parking lot of a Best Western hotel, I am coming home, I am picking up my laminated nametag, I am entering at last a place where I won't have to tell anybody who Mennonites are, where I can relax among those who believe we are important, and look, here's someone who knows who I am, although I don't recall meeting him, and perhaps I've never met him before, perhaps he just knows my parents, and he's smiling, kind, you must not forget the kindness, that is the crucial part, and smiling kindly he asks, "Are you a runner?"

"No," I say, confused, glancing down at my dress, my shoes.

"No?" he says. "I thought you might have got some of those East African genes."

No, I'm not a runner. I'm a writer. That's why I'm here.

Ich möchte heim, ich möchte heim!

The supplicants

The Ark, a walled citadel raised on an artificial hill, is the highest point in Bukhara, where the emir once lived. "They called it the *Ark*," Frank confirms with Usmon. "The place of refuge!" Yes, says Usmon. Here Mennonite leaders came in search of their Oestenheim, their Home in the East, petitioning the emir for a place to stay. They must have gone down this corridor, past the grille with a glimpse of a prisoner's cell. The long, sloping passage gives me a sense of displacement, as if we really are inside a ship, walking through the dimness cut at intervals by shafts of powdery light from the porthole-like windows. Two girls skitter by, glancing at us and exchanging whispers, dressed in outfits reminiscent of Irina Sharipova's designs: gorgeous silk sleeves, high heels, and embroidered pillbox hats. We emerge into the emir's reception hall, an open court where sunlight pounds down on the bricks. "The heat makes you feel what it must have been like," says Evelyn, panting. We all sit down on the stone steps. There's no shelter anywhere from the sun, except in the emir's porch where he would have sat enthroned to receive the supplicants. And this is what I would like to hold, from the history of the trek to Central Asia: these moments of vulnerability, when they had nothing. I want to hold such moments in their rawness, in this pure sunlight, without rushing to hide them with sewing machines or the German sense of order. Here they stood, sweating in their hats. I picture them shuffling slightly on the stones, black and white in the wings of their coats like dark alien birds, like the mynahs we watch here, the only signs of life in the silent enclosure, migrants themselves from Afghanistan, nesting in the doorways.

When I gave a friend a stack of these notes to read before coming on this trip, he criticized my attitude toward Mennonite service abroad. "So what if Mennonites think they're literally God's gift to humankind?" he argued. "If they teach someone English or build a dam, that's what matters." I couldn't explain to him what I recognize now, in this sweltering court: the link between the service narrative and what students at my alma mater call the Mennonite wall. I couldn't explain that the notion of white generosity to a dark and undeveloped world not only affects us abroad, it affects us at home, it infuses our schools and churches, it makes those kids of color at my former college feel like interlopers, like charity cases, it made us feel the same way when we were there, the classmates I used to meet at the Black Student Union, the International Student Union, where we tried, awkwardly, amid quarrels and laughter, to make ourselves at home. Those student unions gathered the flotsam and jetsam of Mennonite history, young people cast into the college by waves of chance. Somewhere, in Belize, in Chicago, in India, in Zimbabwe, someone in each student's family had met a Mennonite. Even if this first meeting had taken place generations ago, it remained an origin story, explaining how such a student came to the Mennonite school, to receive the boon of increased knowledge and prospects. I remember photographs of my father at this same college, smiling and holding me, his newborn child.

It's hard for me to step outside this frame. At my house, the drama of North American aid to poor countries is a family dinner. It's often been indicated to me, by one side of the family, represented by friends, relatives, teachers, or fellow churchgoers, that the other side of my family, represented by my father, is extremely fortunate to have found the Mennonites. This stroke of luck transformed him from an illiterate herdsman into an American professor! I remember his stiffness if he ever overheard these comments, the anger I could feel pulsing from his forehead, his tense eyebrows, his flat voice as he said, "I would have found my way." I remember he never told me why he left the Mennonite Church, why he refused to step inside a church or attend those family

reunions, the ones on my mother's side, at sunny campgrounds, with all
the four-part singing, pancakes, board games, and devotions. I remember, later, working for Mennonite Central Committee myself, in South
Sudan, in Egypt, being trained in the right way to speak of my work,
learning never to call it charity but to portray an exchange in which we,
the volunteers, received much more than we gave. "We're surrounded by
amazingly friendly, helpful, and hospitable people twenty-four hours a
day!" I chirped in an interview for a Mennonite magazine. It wasn't a
lie. But the exchange was clearly not equal—and this, I think, is why
it was necessary *not* to claim equality, to take the lower position, to
say we were receiving "much more." As English teachers, we brought a
global language, a modern tool; elsewhere, MCC volunteers delivered
medicine, sutured wounds, dug wells. We were giving development, the
grand universal of our time, the great world religion, and receiving experience in return. In our efforts to conceal our power, to minimize our
discomfort, we achieved lyrical flights of praise for the social habits of
the poor, completely forgetting about our own material development,
the mention of which seemed, in any case, to be somehow taboo. No
one has ever told me how fortunate my mother was to receive, during
her seven years as an English teacher in Somalia, the training that allowed her, on her return to the US, to build a successful career teaching
English as a foreign language. Nor have I ever been congratulated on
the years of voluntary service that landed me, just like my father, in a
professor's office. But those twelve years in Egypt and South Sudan gave
me the facility in Arabic I needed for a doctorate in Arabic literature.
My MCC service puts food on my family's table. It pays for our health
insurance. In South Sudan, with no internet and few distractions, my
husband and I both wrote novels. Mine won awards; the advance on his
covered a down payment on a house. In the most concrete ways, our
service developed us.

In the museum of the Ark, among the arrows and rare coins, I stand for a time in front of the attendant's abandoned chair. A pink scarf hangs over the back, and a red teacup stands on the floor nearby, steaming in the climate-controlled room. The owner must have just left, must be coming back at any moment. I linger beside these things, which still seem filled with a human presence. The only other object that speaks to me here is the battered iron padlock, which someone removed from the gates long ago to let the strangers in.

La vie immédiate

Ella Maillart leaves Ak Metchet. She rides her bicycle toward the city, swooping past a band of schoolboys, her tires skidding in the sand. There are only three bicycles in all of Khiva; she's borrowed this one from a Russian postal employee. She flies, she exults, pedaling madly through the market, almost knocking into the hammering tinsmiths, terrifying the children. "The crowd looks on admiringly, and I am as proud as though I were the genius who had invented this form of locomotion." How she irritates me, Ella Maillart, with her speed, her arrogance, her fake science, the knowing air with which she evaluates people's heads, her conviction that the world exists for her pleasure. I want to shake her. I want to ride on the back of her bicycle, to grip her around the waist. It's fun to shriek on a bicycle, to go fast, to be the winner, I want to go. I don't want to have these churlish feelings. It is a lovely day. Huge sunflowers, their centers packed black with seeds, stand to attention, and tractors throb among lush fields of rye. Enormous antlers of mountain sheep, black and grooved like the undersurface of a motor steering wheel, are nailed to the walls of some of the cottages. In the fields the delicate tints of the giant poppies seem fresher than ever. Some of their seeds are so dry they taste like dust; others have a subtle flavor of groundnuts.

Who is Ella Maillart? In her sailcloth sack she carries her clothes, climbing boots, four kilograms of bread, two kilograms of sugar, two kilograms of rice, some underclothes, and a dictionary, in addition to her lined sleeping bag. In her rucksack she bears the cooking stove, spirit flask, films and camera, waterproof, medicine box, socks, linen, butter, tea, honey, a kilogram of oatmeal, two kilograms of apples, her inseparable frying pan, and her pipe for lonely vigils. She's healthy, fresh, and strong. She always eats as much as she can. One of her female traveling companions complains, "It's frightful. Ella eats more than the men!" Ella Maillart laughs. She sings Swiss songs at the top of her voice. They are the only ones she knows, and this is how, at times, she gives expression to her delight. She strips to bathe. "It is purest joy, in the great heat, to feel the icy, limpid water from the nearby peaks flow over my body." She's spirited, dashing, like a knight in a ballad, fearing nothing but visa problems and running out of money. She's not afraid of falling off cliffs or being raped in the fields. She has prepared for the worst, she remarks, by stocking her medicine box with neosalvarsan, a treatment for syphilis. That's the worst that could happen, one could contract syphilis from a rape, as one might break a leg in a gully or catch TB on the overnight train to Frunze.

"Joy! We take the descent at a gallop, landing at every bound on tufts of edelweiss springing out of the black earth."

Ella Maillart is a bolt, a force. A modern. A modern woman. Though she often travels with others, she calls her book *Turkestan Solo*.

But take me, take me with you, don't leave me behind. I imagine traveling through Turkestan with Ella Maillart, crossing a valley beneath a snowy ridge, chewing the young needles of the pines that fill the evening with their penetrating scent. To say *I want to be modern* is also to say: I want to go camping, I want to have adventures, I want to be happy. Let me go with you, Ella Maillart. I'll call you by your nickname, "Kini." Together we'll watch the camels graze, white and unreal, as if covered with hoarfrost. We'll spend the night in a yurt, admiring the stars through the hole in the roof, collecting impressions for your photography book *La Vie immédiate*. Immediate life, direct and present, startling in its clarity. The night is cold. Only the embers of the fire remain. The stars glitter remotely, as if at the bottom of some fabulous well. You speculate sadly on the future of Soviet Asia, where the Bolsheviks are collectivizing the nomads. I want to go with you, but I can't share your splendid distance, the way you cast a sorrowful eye over history as if from the top of a peak. I can't turn to the men of color the way you do, with your refined, delicious, patronizing nostalgia, because the men of color are Dad and Uncle Togane boiling tea on the kitchen stove. To turn to the men of color is to see the kitchen of my childhood, the kerosene heater squatting on the pale green linoleum. If only I could persuade you to glance into this mirror! For Dad and Uncle Togane are much like you, Kini: they belong to your tribe of wanderers, poets, and voluntary exiles, people who long for something else, a something forever receding, who live bold, undisciplined, experimental lives. They are the kind of people who, against all expectations, turn into Christian converts, history professors, and experts in Italian cuisine. They share your passion for the poignant gleam of the unforeseen, the way a new experience can shake the heart. But they don't, they can't share your hope that the men of color will never change, that the women of color will go on picking cotton in the valley between Samarkand and Bukhara, laughing as you photograph them, their faded gowns held above the knees, full to bursting with great balls of snow. My father and uncle don't share your wish that the people of color maintain, for the benefit of the white moderns, a reservoir of timeless, elemental life. How could they? By the time I get home from school, they've already gone out for a drive, their dried-out teabags abandoned on the stove.

Dear Kini. Drowsing in starlight, you are writing your first book. Years from now, at Begum, north of Kabul, you will write slowly, in a different book: "I have ceased to be proud of having, by my own efforts, turned the world into a playground."

The dreamers

In the Ismail Samani Mausoleum, a ninth-century building whose bricks are laid in a pattern as intricate as basketry, I talk with Kholid of utopias and dreams. A network of symbols decorates the walls: Muslim, Christian, Jewish, Zoroastrian. Stars and crosses linked, protected. Hint of light. When I ask, Kholid confirms that yes, right up to the collapse of the Soviet Union, Tajikistan was calling for the return of the great cities Samarkand and Bukhara, which had wound up in Uzbekistan. Before the division into Soviet republics with ethnic designations, this region was crisscrossed by multiple groups, speaking a variety of Persian and Turkic tongues, "so many different languages," as Herman Jantzen wrote in amazement. Although the Turkic-speaking people who would eventually be called Uzbeks formed the majority in what is now Uzbekistan, they were primarily rural, while Samarkand and Bukhara were Persianate cities, inhabited mostly by Persian-speaking Tajiks. How strange that this region should have been cut up and named along ethnic lines in the Soviet era, precisely during the ambitious dream of belonging beyond ethnicity, of dissolving the boundary of skin. I have read that it was a strategy of both Lenin and Stalin to ward off potential nationalist insurgencies by granting certain forms of nationhood, such as borders and languages, to the ethnic minorities of the Soviet Union. So two styles of homeland, ethnic and Soviet, developed in the same place.

I tell Kholid about Somalia's flag, the five-pointed star representing a dream of unity among the five Somali regions, now hopelessly divided.

"You said *we!*" he exclaims.

Apparently I have described this problem in the first person plural.

Kholid is twinkling, exultant, he's caught me out. "Somali first, American second!" he says, wagging a finger. I laugh too, I tell him I'm always saying *we*. I'm never sure how people will react, whether they're going to accept it or not, but yes, I did say *we*. I do.

Delicate piercings in the walls shed light shaped like moons and crosses. Kholid wants to know if my name is the Arabic *Safiyya*, pure, or the Greek *Sophia*, wisdom. This is also a way of asking if I have a Muslim or Christian name. I tell him, "Neither Safiyya nor Sophia can express it." And as if this reminds him of others who found themselves on a border between different visions, he describes the days before the Soviets, and the brief flowering of the *Jadid* or Reformist school of Central Asian intellectuals. By the turn of the twentieth century, these youths, most of them born during the reign of Governor-General von Kaufmann, were meeting in tea houses, publishing newspapers, and transforming the primary schools, teaching the alphabet phonetically rather than through memorization. Indigenous reformers, they assumed modernity was for them, that the future was theirs. They wore western-style suits and bow ties, wide robes, astrakhan hats. They were poets, teachers, philosophers, historians, photographers, cartographers. Most of them perished in Stalin's purges.

I remember one who survived: the poet Faizallah Ravnaqi Makhdum Khodjaev Shakhrisabzi, born at Shakhrisabz in 1892. As a young man, he was appointed a *qadi*, or judge, of the city, but after the Muslim courts were dissolved, he bounced from job to job in the new Soviet administration. During the Great Terror, he hid his marvelous library, which contained books of theology, Sufi treatises, and collections of poetry, many copied out in his own calligraphy, as well as hundreds of lithographs from Russia, India, and the Middle East. He fled to Tajikistan, where he supported himself by doing odd jobs and practicing traditional healing. In the 1950s, he returned to Shakhrisabz, where he spent the rest of his life writing essays on Sufism, teaching poetry, Qur'an reading, and calligraphy, and maintaining, with great success, a private medical practice based on the knowledge contained in medieval manuscripts.

In this space, which seems to hold so much in its graphic immobility, I feel there should be room for everything, for the symbols of a thousand creeds, for the preservers and the reformers, for all the living and even all the dead. Usmon points out the holes pierced at either end of the brick monument at the center of the mausoleum. Samanid rulers were said to reign for forty days after their death, and during this time you could send them messages through the holes. I think of the Swahili words *sasa* and *zamani*, loosely translatable as *now* and *then*, and the idea that for a certain period the dead remain with us in the sasa, the now, before fading into the zamani. If only we could keep them with us longer. I'd tear out this page of my notebook, crumple it up, and stuff it between the bricks. And the Samanid kings, poised between life and death, would read that I tasted *sunflower oil*. That I felt *a film of dust*.

We walk outside to admire the building's ornate heather-gray molding and the salt that makes it look lightly sprinkled with snow. There used to be an ancient cemetery here, but the Soviets razed it to build an amusement park. Now the Ferris wheel carves the sky, like the Zoroastrian symbol for sun.

SIX

The Desert

the wall is no more, nor those who daubed it

Claas Epp syndrome

"I hope we don't get Claas Epp syndrome in Khiva," Micah says. We're at a rest stop in the desert, regrouping after visiting the bathrooms, unwilling to get back on the bus before we must, stretching our legs in sun, wind, and the roar of the highway. Micah, the college student, took a school trip to Jerusalem last year, where he learned about Jerusalem syndrome, which causes tourists to the city to suffer from delusions, believing they're prophets or even Jesus Christ. A search on Tom's phone yields a photograph of a long-haired man in a robe sitting on a sidewalk, labeled "Man who claims to be a Messiah in Tel Aviv, 2010." We're laughing, although I, at least, am a little bit horrified by the image, the pathos of the sidewalk prophet on the busy street. He's so isolated, conviction surrounding him like a wall of flame. And yet, of course, he's deeply connected to others, enmeshed in a well-known story, a story that was waiting for him and caught him in some hotel, maybe even right off the plane, as soon as his feet touched earth.

The end is near. In 1530, Martin Luther hurried to publish his translation of the Book of Daniel; he was afraid the world would end before it was finished. The radical Anabaptists Hans Hut and Leonhard Schiemer, working independently, both set the date of Christ's return at Pentecost 1528. A Hessian Anabaptist predicted three end dates one after the other: September 11, November 11, and Christmas 1530. Melchior Hoffmann, whose teachings inspired the infamous Münster Rebellion, said the Lord would return in 1533. From that date until his death a decade later, Hoffmann languished in prison, feverishly reworking his eschatology, trying to make the numbers come out right. His disciples declared the town of Münster in Westphalia the site of the new Jerusalem, and took the city by force to prepare it for the Second Coming.

Older prophecies. "The last times are come upon us," wrote Ignatius of Antioch in the second century. The Joachites, who expected the world to end in 1260, roamed the Italian countryside, wailing and striking themselves with iron-studded whips. In medieval times, prophecies focused less on the coming of Christ than on the Antichrist, who was to arrive in 1184, 1229, 1260, 1300, 1325, 1335, 1346, 1387, 1396, and 1400. A tradition of ceaseless urgency, a message for the whole world. "If you do not do what I tell you," Savonarola warned, "woe to Florence, woe to the people, woe to the poor, woe to the rich!"

In the fearsome year of 1666—1,000 plus 666, the mark of the Beast—every thunderstorm was seen as the beginning of the end. In 1795, claimed Richard Brothers, the end times would arrive, and he himself would lead the lost tribes back to Israel. 1814, said Joanna Southcott: at this time Christ would return through her, a sixty-four-year-old woman, in a second virgin birth. "I am fully convinced," wrote William Miller, "that somewhere between March 21st, 1843, and March 21st, 1844, according to the Jewish mode of computation, Christ will come." A century later, the establishment of the state of Israel spurred a wave of prophecies historians call the "doom boom," led by fundamentalist Christians in the United States. The possibility of nuclear war also colored these visions. Edgar Whisenant found an audience of two million for his book *88 Reasons Why the Rapture Will Be in 1988*. Mary Stewart Relfe received in a dream a miraculous timeline that charted the end of the world, from World War III, which was to begin in 1989, to the return of Christ in 1997.

1992: members of the Dami sect in South Korea quit their jobs, abandon their families, and undergo abortions, convinced the world will perish that October. 1994: mass murders and suicides in Switzerland by members of the apocalyptic Order of the Solar Temple. 1995: attacks in a Tokyo subway by the Supreme Truth, a cult intending to set off the final world war. 1997: members of the Heaven's Gate cult in California commit suicide to reach God's kingdom by UFO, expecting planet Earth to be destroyed and "recycled."

Such acts are extreme, the most uncompromising rejections of the world. They are visions of terror, but always accompanied by longing. Let it all end. Let it burn. There's rage against the world as it is, anticipation, desire for transcendence, a passion for the heavenly home. Apocalyptic prophecies created the horrors of Jonestown and Waco, Texas; they underlie the fanaticism of the Islamic State. They also carry a heroism, a revolutionary spirit. If utopia is *perfect space*, writes Martin Buber, the millennium is *perfect time*. It can be a time to come, as in the Abrahamic traditions, or a return to time past, as in the Ghost Dance of 1890, which was to bring back the spirits of the dead, eject the white colonists, and renew the world for Indigenous people. Around the same time, in New Guinea, the prophet Tokerua predicted a series of floods, earthquakes, and volcanic eruptions, which would usher in a true New Year, during which the wind would change, the trees grow heavy with fruit, and the dead return in boats. In the later Melanesian "cargo cults," people slaughtered their animals, spent their savings to get rid of European money, and awaited the dead at banquet tables. The harshness of doomsday prophecies is also a form of hope. The end of time is its perfection. Yet, though apocalyptic movements are stimulated by persecution, suffering, and poverty, they cannot be attributed entirely to these factors. Such ideas are always mutating, always with us. The historian Richard Kyle identifies two essential characteristics of end times thinking: elasticity and persistence.

But of that day and that hour knoweth no man. We know we don't know and can't know the future; still, we can't stop guessing. A certain type of imagination, at any rate, can't stop peering into that smoky mirror, pressing an eye to the glass. This vision compulsion might be called disease. "My dear brother," warned a friend of William Ramsey, after the publication of Ramsey's 1841 book on the Second Coming, "do let me advise you to stop your studies of the prophecies. I never knew a man who began to study them and to write on them who did not ultimately go crazy." As we board the bus, joking about the dangers of Claas Epp syndrome, of our whole group running amok when we reach our destination in Khiva, I think of Claas Epp Jr. toward the end of his life, sitting by the chicken coop, dressed in his white robe and staring into space. Maybe he was sick, but it's true that his world was about to end. Since the 1870s, he had been preaching that revolution was the biblical "beast from the sea," that the uprisings of people overthrowing their God-given rulers formed a darkness rolling over the whole earth. Had he lived long enough, he would have seen revolution come to Russia. He would have seen, at last, what he had predicted: a wave of refugees from Russian territory coming to Khiva, which by 1920 looked like a true place of refuge from Bolshevism. And in 1935, he would have seen this refuge, too, stamped out. He would have been deported to the steppe with all his people, marooned in a distant dump where, forbidden to worship together, they would cease to exist as a church community. This was his vision: *Woe, woe, woe!* His prophecies would have come true, but only the part about the tribulation, which is always true, always coming true somewhere. Taken together, predictions of the end times add up to a vast cry, less like prophecy than recognition: the world is ending every day.

All or none

How did it end at Ak Metchet?

In 1935, the Ak Metchet Mennonites refused the collectivization required by the new Bolshevik government, and ten of their leaders were
arrested. The ten men were sentenced to death by firing squad; their
belongings were to be confiscated and their families sent to Siberia.
When the authorities arrived to arrest the ten families, the women and
children of Ak Metchet crowded around their vehicles. "Take all of
us or none!" they cried. "All or none! All or none!" They forced their
way into the cars, climbed on top of them, lay down under the wheels.
Shocked by the action, the officials departed, leaving their cars behind.
A few days later, the people of Ak Metchet were told, "All or none it
shall be!" The entire Mennonite community was to be exiled to Siberia;
their leaders would not be shot but sentenced to hard labor. Alexander
Rempel, who tells this story, writes that instead of Siberia, the exiles
were sent south of Samarkand, dropped in the desert at Shakhrisabz.
They had nothing but a few tools. With these they built sod houses and,
taking turns, yoked themselves to the plow.

Revisions

Skimming along right beside the bus, a bird with black-tipped wings.

"What is truth?" asks Frank. "What happened, and how did we remember it?" Today he reads to us from the Book of Luke. "Forasmuch as many have taken in hand to set forth in order a declaration of those things which are most surely believed among us, even as they delivered them unto us, which from the beginning were eyewitnesses, and ministers of the word; it seemed good to me also, having had perfect understanding of all things from the very first, to write." The writer of Luke knows that others have also told this story, and believes it needs to be told again. One of the best gifts of the early church, says Frank, is that it gives us four gospels, four versions of the story. I completely agree. I remember reading all the gospels in a row in high school, how it seemed like some fantastic postmodern novel: events repeated with uncanny shifts in detail, anonymous characters suddenly identified with virtuosic flair.

"The writer of Luke has a bias," says Frank. "He wants us to believe. He must decide what to include and what to leave out. Does this change the nature of the truth?" I think of this story we're in, made of diaries and memoirs of the Great Trek, history books and academic articles. This story is agglutinative, like a Turkic language. It is formed by the addition of new parts. Kholid's father is still researching the Ak Metchet Mennonites, as is Frank, through these tours of Uzbekistan and trips to Germany to interview the Mennonites' descendants. Something new is always being added, and something is always being forgotten or neglected, which is why we need each other. Grit strikes the windows of the bus with a light pinging sound as we enter the Kyzyl Kum, the Red Sand, the desert. In the memoirs of the trek, I read that the Mennonites crossed both the Kyzyl Kum and the Kara Kum, Red Sand and Black Sand, but now I learn that no, they were mistaken, they never crossed the Kara Kum, which lies on the other side of Khiva. Someone was misinformed, or something was garbled, misremembered. Finally, Kholid solves the mystery, explaining that the Mennonites crossed the *Aral Kara Kum*, the Black Sand to the north, on the border with Kazakhstan, and not the larger Black Sand to the southwest.

And where is the place of refuge? When they were deported, where did the Ak Metchet Mennonites go? The valley of Shar-i-Sabs, says Alexander Rempel—but does that mean the city of Shakhrisabz? I discuss this problem with Frank and Kholid, the three of us talking loud over the drone of the engine. I'm twisted around so that I can see Kholid, who sits behind me; Frank stands in the aisle, bending over us, swaying with every bump. All of us possessed by this story. Rempel describes Shar-i-Sabs as a valley one hundred and seventy kilometers southeast of Samarkand, but Shakhrisabz is only eighty kilometers south. Rempel's distance would put the deported Mennonites in Tajikistan. People in Ak Metchet say the Mennonites were exiled to *three* places: some to Tajikistan, some to Bukhara, and some to Uzbekistan's Ferghana Valley. The scholar Dilaram Inoyatova also mentions three locations: Tajikistan, Kazakhstan, and Kyrgyzstan. These are threads, faint tracks that have not been fully mapped. But the Tajikistan direction seems the most promising: Frank finds the historian Walter Ratliff's blog on his phone, which places the Ak Metchet Mennonites there. In addition, Kholid's father has written of a man named Otto Toews, who visited Ak Metchet in the 1970s from the Vaksh Valley in Tajikistan. Toews, a child of the Ak Metchet Mennonites, had been told by his father to return to the village, cook *plov*, and share it with their former neighbors. In the school at Ak Metchet he found a desk inscribed—probably by a relative—"Otto Toews's desk." He offered $100,000 for this desk, but people were too afraid of the secret police to sell it.

So it seems everything must be revised. Or that there is another Shakhrisabz, a Shakhrisabz of the mind. Ever beyond us, green. A place that exists only in the abstract, where we can never go, for there is no refuge on earth. In Germany, Frank interviewed a man named Traugott Quiring, who was three years old when his family was deported from Ak Metchet. Traugott Quiring grew up in Tajikistan and emigrated to Germany, as many Mennonites did, after the dissolution of the Soviet Union. By this time they were not practicing Mennonites; they had become Baptists. In his childhood, Traugott said, they had no active religion at all. Devotions were forbidden. They lived in a place called Village Number Seven. He remembers the barrenness when they arrived, the desolation. He was one of those who survived that trial. There was nothing. People plowed by day and built their homes by night. In his youth, he told Frank, he was sustained only by the name his father gave him. Traugott: *Trust God.* His place of refuge was a word.

Elementary German homework

We move through a flat immensity covered with *saxaul*, the dusty green plant the Mennonites burned for fuel more than a century ago, its pale branches twisting weirdly above the sand. In the light from the window, I am doing some elementary German homework. Using a dictionary downloaded to my phone, I make my way laboriously through the first page of *Das Heimweh*, the novel that so inspired Claas Epp Jr. My tools are new, but what I enter is old, both language and landscape.

Blessed are they that long for Home, for homeward they shall surely come—said the Parson, and when I told my Father, he looked at me, as a Mother looks at her eighteen-year-old Son, when he with Feeling praises a pretty Girl.

It begins this way, with feeling. With the specter of a bride.

And my Mother looked at my Father as if to say, it will soon be Time; I looked them both in the Eyes—I felt at once as if my Vest were too tight, so that I actually unbuttoned it.

Silence for half a Minute.

This is the hero, Eugenius, with his parents. The young man has just witnessed an act of intolerance: the parson has been disciplined for burying a Mennonite woman, a body from a different faith, in the churchyard. The dead woman has caused a problem: she has been smuggled across a line, settled in the wrong earth. In response to the heartless authorities who would keep the border closed, Eugenius's heart expands, it threatens to burst his buttons.

Father—it cramps my Chest—I must have Air.

I must give vent to / vent my anger / feelings / frustration / emotions. The parents react to this outburst with a deep, covert, half-frightened joy that gives the scene the weight of a rite of passage. Father looks as if he wants to ask, *Have I really won a great Fortune?* And Mother looks at Eugenius still more longingly, but without saying a word, until she exclaims, *Good! It is enough to give you Home-ache! You are right!*

Eugenius catches the home-ache. He comes down with it, as with a cold. He breaks out with the home-ache as with a rash. All in a tableau laced with feminine imagery: Father looking at him like a mother, the imaginary girl, the dead Mennonite woman. Eugenius gasps. His body swells. It is time: he has come of age. It's a sexual awakening expressed in a spiritual register. It is also a moment of ethical maturity. For the first time, he has perceived injustice: a shock, like falling in love.

Heimweh can be translated as both *homesickness* and *nostalgia*.

In this condition, Eugenius leaves the family home.

The thicket of Gothic script. I can barely read it. But there is, at this time, no English translation of *Das Heimweh*.

Czeslaw Milosz writes, "Language is the only homeland." Yet for so many of us, home lies on the other side of a language barrier. Archives document your history in letters you can't read. Your elders converse in the next room, softly, in foreign tongues.

All right, then: make your home in the language where you are.

Perhaps—but Eugenius is looking for something else. He leaves in pursuit of the ultimate Home, where all meet, where there are no exiles, no language barriers, where the grave opens its borderless embrace.

Adorno: "It is part of morality not to be at home in one's home."

Eugenius is looking for a place beyond language. The world hurts him. Existence cramps him. He must get some air. He has caught the philosopher's feeling: what Heidegger calls *Heimweh*.

I notice at once that in order to do the most elementary German homework, I have quoted Theodor Adorno, a half-Jewish exile, and also Martin Heidegger, a member of the Nazi party. I am returned to the question of *whose body* and *whose earth*. Lunch interrupts me, sandwiches passed back along the aisle of the bus, miniature green apples whose wintry flesh darkens with the first bite, and outside the window the plain of *saxaul* drains away slowly into the pinkish, corrugated dunes of the Kyzyl Kum. Streaks of saxaul still mark the sand here and there, narrow inlets from the sea we've left behind. The shadows blur, the air becoming gauzy in the wind that lifts a haze of fine sand toward the bleached sky. And I think of the ones who find no home on earth, the imprisoned, the exiled, the deported. I think of Shakhrisabz, the dream of Shakhrisabz, and the historical Shakhrisabz, a place on earth, like any other, where the Yiddish poet Leyzer Volf died in 1943. Born in Vilna, Leyzer Volf was a founding member of the literary group Yung-Vilne; he earned his living sewing the fingers on gloves. His debut was a poem called "Green Joy." In 1930, he attempted to break a world record by writing a thousand and one lyrics in a month. In 1941, he was among the Polish Jews deported to Shakhrisabz, where, after two years of starvation, he collapsed while braiding rope. Shortly before his death he wrote, "And I set off in the tracks of Leyzer Volf, the greatest nothing of the twentieth century."

It cramps my chest. I must have air. I can't stand these murderous borders. I want the unity, the courage of the women and children of Ak Metchet, that rallying cry of *All or none!* Let it expand, like the desert, let that fervent shout grow over the whole earth. The final exile of the Ak Metchet Mennonites is such an apocalyptic scene, their world crumbling before their eyes, and this is what sparks the moment of *all or none*. With survival at stake, the community works like a single organism. Is that what it takes? I think of the scholar Dipesh Chakrabarty, whose essay "The Climate of History: Four Theses" describes the potential for solidarity under the threat of environmental ruin, "a universal that arises from a shared sense of catastrophe." A planetary crisis, he reflects, might give us a common ground at last. I don't know if he's right, but I recognize the desire, a longing that animates dystopian fiction as well as doomsday cults, the yearning for a force to bring people together. It's not that we crave disaster, it's that we don't know how to join hands. If only the whole world would catch fire! Then we could drop the problem of *whose body* and *whose earth*, forget inequality, give up the gruelling struggle of working for justice. So Eugenius turns away from the dead Mennonite woman, the dilemma before him, and sets his gaze on the higher Homeland, which some call the Kingdom of Heaven and Chakrabarty calls "negative universal history."

Like Lightning it went through all my Limbs: the Fever of Home-ache.

Other deserts, other endings

This is how I was born: in 1953, the first American Mennonite missionaries arrived in Mogadishu, Somalia. Fifteen years later, the mission had expanded to five locations and more than thirty missionaries. They ran schools, a clinic, a hospital, a bookstore. They were cautious yet determined in sharing their faith with local Muslims. At the Mennonite school, students who wanted Bible classes had to sign a paper declaring that they had requested the classes themselves, that no one had coerced them. After independence, in accordance with the new laws, the missionaries hired Muslim scholars to give classes on the Qur'an. Still, things became more difficult for these foreign, Christian, mostly American workers during the Cold War. In 1976 they were asked to leave. In 1981 they were invited back, and some worked in health and education until civil war reached Mogadishu in 1990. In 1992, two nurses returned, but spent less than a year in the capital: they were withdrawn after their building was attacked while they sat on the roof. After that, Mennonites concentrated on their work with ethnic Somalis in neighboring Kenya and Djibouti. Somalia had become too dangerous.

It was the end of a project that can be seen as either a success or a failure. On the one hand, Mennonites managed to make a name for themselves in Somalia, to build a reputation as good people, despite being non-Muslims, and excellent teachers who educated a generation of intellectuals. One of Somalia's presidents, Hassan Sheikh Mohamud, studied at Eastern Mennonite University. The name *Mennonite* retains a certain strength in the Somali territories, serving to open doors, as Mennonite visitors found when they received a warm welcome in Hargeisa in 2008. The unexpected durability of this relationship shines out of history. On the other hand, for those Mennonites who dreamed of a flourishing Somali church, the project must be seen as a failure. Islam is so intimately bound up with Somali identity, it's almost impossible to separate the two. We might say "ethnic Muslims," as we say "ethnic Mennonites." "So, if you then become a Christian," one convert explained, "you are totally not Somali. You are out." The extreme dislocation caused by conversion made it a rare occurrence even in the early years, under the Italians, who legalized freedom of religion. One Mennonite missionary quit in 1954, depressed by the overwhelming difficulty of getting Somalis to hear the Christian message. Over the years, the handful of Somali Christians faced increasing persecution; during the civil war they became one of the most vulnerable populations. By today's estimates, they number less than a thousand. The church couldn't graft itself onto Somali culture, it didn't take. Nor did the foreigners, as a group, cross over into that culture. Two American missionary women who married Somali Muslims were disciplined by the mission board. But there was a wedding between a Somali and an American missionary that was sanctioned by the church in those days, celebrated by Muslim and Mennonite friends and relatives, on a school basketball court, the young couple bending together to cut the cake, gleaming, pliant, beautiful. These were my parents.

Those Somali students who took Bible classes, students like my father, those who absorbed the new faith, became convinced, and asked to join the church, engaged in a process of deep learning about others that eventually became a personal discovery. A spiritual experience—yet it is also true that this process took place in conditions of inequality. The Mennonites with their hospital, their schools, their modern agricultural methods; the Somalis just coming out from under colonial rule. It is true that these unequal conditions made the missionary presence possible, that the mission's roots were planted in the colonial system. This is why the poet Patrick Friesen calls missionaries "the soft armies," their pith helmets and safari shirts a uniform. It's easy to forget this element of spiritual and cultural warfare, reading now of Mennonite support for Muslim peace-building practices and traditions, reading of the Somali Muslims who attend the Center for Justice and Peace-building at Eastern Mennonite University, their studies geared toward conflict resolution, not Bible class or conversion. It is easy to forget, considering this Mennonite emphasis on peace, that in the beginning this was war. In the words of the 1956 booklet *God Led Us to Somalia*: "The greatest opportunity of all is for men and women who love the Lord Jesus supremely and are ready to go for Him to one of the earth's hardest battlegrounds to live and die for Him." It's easy to forget. But look at the websites devoted to Somali Christians: Somalis for Jesus, SomaliMission.org. Observe, if you can bear it, their lists of Christians killed by extremists, the blurred photographs of bodies, blood soaking into the ground. Observe how these photographs circulate as an argument against Islam, as an incitement to further violence. There are times when the missionary effort in Somalia, the Mennonite mission included, seems to me like a machine for the creation of martyrs. And I ask myself, if there is a tradition of peacemaking in the Somali territories, and if Mennonites have managed to connect with these ideas, if they have such respect for Islam and Somali structures of social healing, then why did anyone, ever, have to be converted, why did even one have to be subjected to that alienation and danger? Why did a single person have to begin to worship in secret? The answer is that the respect for Islam is new. There has been a shift in Mennonite attitudes toward other faiths, causing a change in practice, from battling Islam to working with Muslims for peace. This is why, when you examine the history of Mennonite work abroad, a kind of split personality appears.

This split is actualized in the programs of the two major Mennonite organizations at work in the world: Eastern Mennonite Missions, which emphasizes evangelism, and Mennonite Central Committee, which pursues relief and development work. It took me a long time to figure this out, and I still find it confusing. What I understand is that many Mennonites have moved away from proselytizing and church-planting, have become supporters of all the world's religions, Islam included, have become advocates for peace in all places, Muslim Somalia included, to the extent that at peace conferences in Somalia supported by Mennonite Central Committee, where various Somali factions were brought together to draft a new constitution, the drafts all stated that Islam would be the only religion permitted in Somalia, prompting Chantal Logan, a worker with Eastern Mennonite Missions, to worry that Mennonites were completely forgetting Somali Christians, that the focus on peace above all else had resulted in Mennonite support for a constitution that denied Somali Christians the right to exist. This reminds me of the Mennonite theologian J. Denny Weaver, who wrote, "Somalia has placed Mennonites in a difficult position, and our theological response is indeed messy. With Somalia, we are caught, no matter what we do." I understand that part: being caught no matter what you do. It comes from feeling like an error, an error of history.

Interviews with converts

On the bus, in the desert, I page through my notes. I read interviews with converts.

I feel sometimes I am an outcast.

If I died today my family will have the worst experience ever, because nobody will come to my funeral.

One time even stoning happened. Even people . . . a man slapped me . . . They were three . . . One tried to beat me up, and the other two held me back. So he hit me . . . They came to me. They harassed me. They tried to threaten me . . . because I had disowned or left Islam. "The consequence is that you have to be killed. You know that," and so on . . . Especially there is a man who is very close to where we live and always he says: "Are you still alive?"

They can insult you. They can say to you that you are even a dog or a donkey. They make you very . . . like dead. They call you a dead person.

I met danger, great, great danger, really, God protected me, but I was near to die. They shot me with a bullet. They tried to stab me with a knife. They beat me many times with a stone. They boxed me. They insulted me. They spat on my face. They kicked me. They did whatever they could . . . I thank the Lord whenever I remember this.

Even if I want to work with the Somalis they refuse. They say, "No. If you want to work with us you must repent back to Islam." Since I became a Christian I have not worked anymore.

One thing is that you should never encourage believers to run. You should encourage them to stay . . . to stay in their locality. Like when Jesus healed a demon-possessed man, the man said, "I will follow you everywhere." Jesus said, "No, no. Go back to your father and mother, and declare what I have done to you."

I know someone who also has been killed. I remember last year, 2007, one who was among the leaders . . . He used to come to this fellowship. He went back to Somalia and immediately he was killed. He was called Farah. And I remember that . . . he was . . . yeah.

A few conclusions

Mennonites should never have interfered with Somali Muslims through their Bible classes. Having given such classes, having baptized people, they should never have left Somalia, they should have died there like Somali Christians rather than abandon the church. None of this bloodshed would have happened if not for Muslim extremists who refused to practice religious tolerance. Mennonites would never have tried to bring Somalis to Christ had they been capable of true religious tolerance. Today, Mennonites have learned religious tolerance, and work together with Muslims for peace, rather than trying to convert them. Today, Mennonites use subtler conversion techniques—for example, peace-building workshops—to infiltrate Muslim culture without getting caught. There is no point in Mennonites working with Muslims unless, eventually, they manage to bring at least one Muslim to Christ. The point of Mennonite work with Muslims is to increase understanding across religions and cultures, thereby promoting world peace. If enough Muslims became Mennonite pacifists, there would be world peace. Religious conversion of the disempowered by the powerful is a form of violence. Mennonites have done a great deal of good in Somalia, but only to themselves. Mennonites have done a great deal of good in Somalia, but only by accident.

Your stories, my elders

And I read your stories, my elders. I read the missionary adventures. How you were lowered from the boat in a basket toward the turquoise Indian Ocean. The noise of the dock, the road, the little goats standing on their hind legs among the thorn trees, and the monstrous baobabs trailing their arms in the dust. I read, skipping over your aims, your convictions, your mortifying self-righteousness, I enter the grand old rooms of Mogadishu, where every sound echoes against the tiled floors, I slip into the remnants of Italian colonial gardens, among the stunted pines, the throbbing shade of the flame trees against the terrace. Torpid evenings, games of chess in the light of a kerosene lamp. As night comes on, the soil breathes a faint, fresh scent. Such deep silence when the generator dies. The Southern Cross a pendant you could flick with a fingernail. Through you, I sense the donkeys braying at dawn, the camels silent, dignified, only the low and rounded notes of their wooden bells, the way they seem to glide above the dust, and the sound of children chanting at *dugsi*, studying the Qur'an. Remember the piece of painted Masonite set up as a chalkboard, the students playing tag in the courtyard, fast on the hot concrete, the weaver birds hanging upside down to build their nests, their twittering calls, and the mission's night guard who says that English sounds like the language of birds. Remember the sow bugs climbing down the curtains, the snakes in the kitchen. The misunderstandings, the conflicts, the children shouting "*Gaal!*" and throwing stones, the missionary nurse who was sued for striking a cow, the missionary doctor accused of murder when a patient died under his care. The missionary deaths, too: the couple who lost their baby boy, the young man who died in a motorcycle accident, and the terrible murder of the American teacher who was stabbed in his office, his wife who was also stabbed, who survived, who never pressed charges, who forgave. Is this a record of failure? Pale photographs of Lido Beach. Postage stamps of a vanished era, vivid under clear plastic. The leopard on a branch, the overflowing basket of bananas, and my childhood favorite, the woman robed in pink. What remains of your grandiose plan, your dream of a Christian planet? Only the purr of the Vespa winding north through the silvery scrub desert, turning to cross the Shebelle River, passing the sugarcane fields of Johar, the old Italian refinery, the processing plant for coconut oil, the full moon on the way to Jamama and having to swerve so as not to hit people seated calmly on the road to gather the warmth of the tarmac, the glint of cook fires in tiny ephemeral villages, five or ten houses that spring up like grass and then fade until even their garbage is seized by the marabou storks, they are gone, disappeared, snuffed out like the hippo you shot in the gardens of Mahaddei, a massive beast like a Land Rover that roared and slobbered its way to death, it's memory, that's all, only memory buried in obscure books almost nobody reads, and it's only like this, as memory, that these images have any value for me: the densely packed sand with its delicate blush, the great coral reefs, the dim jade of the pools, the sharp sea urchins that sliced at your feet, the cowrie shells domed like cathedrals. So if this is a record of failure, then it's also the only success you can have now, with me at least, for I don't read your books to congratulate you or mourn your defeat, but only to catch for an instant the parching heat, the torrid rays of the setting sun through December grass so dry it crackles as if subtly aflame, the harsh wind whipping the laundry in knots and the rain, the rain, the first drops so slight, you breathe them in, try to fill your lungs, then the crash as it hits the tin roof with its promise of flowers and floods and everyone stops, the young men get up, they open the door, lift their arms so their shirts draw away from the skin, before them the pound and rush of the rain and behind them the lamps in the empty school where, after hours, they have been studying the Bible.

Apocalyptic

The Gospel of Matthew, Chapter 24. Shortly before his crucifixion, Jesus prophesies: *And this gospel of the kingdom will be preached in the whole world as a testimony to all nations, and then the end will come.* The missionary David W. Shenk, who officiated at my parents' wedding in Somalia and is now my uncle by marriage, writes that "the church has the astonishing responsibility of cooperating with the Holy Spirit in preparing the whole earth for the second coming of Jesus Christ. Preaching the gospel to all nations is at the core of that responsibility."

A responsibility to help usher in the Last Days. A desire for an ending as strong as that which led the Mennonites into Central Asia. Like the children born at Ak Metchet, I have a dream of the end at my beginning. My origins are apocalyptic.

Mirror

Precious in the sight of the Lord is the death of His saints.

—PSALM 116: 15

At one point, in order to grasp, if I could, the apocalyptic strain in Mennonite culture, I took to studying *Martyrs Mirror*, the enormous compendium of martyr stories that, after the Bible, is the most influential book in the history of Mennonites. I had not grown up with this book in my house. By asserting this fact, I immediately identify myself as a person with something at stake here, someone who stands in the shadow of this book. I've noticed this reaction, which so often springs up immediately, like a reflex, when I mention *Martyrs Mirror* to other Mennonites. "We didn't have that book," my interlocuters rush to inform me. "I haven't read it." "I've never even seen it!" The rapid disavowal reveals the book's towering, ambivalent status, the attraction and repulsion it radiates at once, like some infinitely twisted magnet. Those of us who distance ourselves know that there are other Mennonites who read it regularly; one of my friends grew up with these tales of torture for bedtime stories. And many of us, without having read the book, have imbibed it in other ways. We've heard the stories, we've seen copies of the marvelous engravings, we've absorbed the weight of this text, so that its title can never be neutral for us but awakens nebulous feelings, such as the awe that filled me, when I was young, whenever I thought of this tome whose mysterious power seemed concentrated in the absence of an apostrophe I felt certain should be in its title somewhere, but which everyone assured me did not belong there, as if, through its spiritual ascendancy, the book had escaped the laws of punctuation.

I ordered *Martyrs Mirror* in the mail. It arrived: huge. I'd read that it was the largest book produced in colonial America, when German-speaking Mennonites in Pennsylvania decided to translate the original Dutch text into their language. It looked like the biggest book ever printed anywhere, at any time. If you happen to have one, or get one, I advise you not to try carrying it in your backpack. Its cover was yellow, with a chocolate-brown reproduction of the famous etching of Dirk Willems, who turned back to save his pursuer from the ice.

Dirk Willemſz. 1569.

The picture is by Jan Luyken, an engraver and author of devotional poetry, whose illustrations for the 1685 edition of Thieleman van Braght's *The Bloody Theater, or Martyrs Mirror of the Defenseless Christians* made the book immensely successful, and helped embed it in the consciousness of its readers. *Martyrs Mirror* connects stories of biblical and early Christian martyrdom to the persecution of Anabaptists in the sixteenth and seventeenth centuries. The idea is to reveal an unbroken narrative of sacrifice and faith, which, van Braght hopes, will jolt the Dutch Mennonites out of their complacency, as he's disgusted by the way they've embraced the consumerism of the Golden Age, acquiring splendid homes and throwing extravagant parties. "But most beloved," he says in his coaxing-yet-threatening introduction, "do not expect that we shall bring you into Grecian theaters, to gaze on merry comedies or gay performances. Here shall not be opened to you the pleasant arbors and pleasure gardens of Atlas, Adonis or Semiramis, which are said to have been built in the air, and of which the ancients used to sing their merry lays." His theater is the proscenium of horror. He is going to bring you into dark valleys strewn with bones, among broken, drowned, burned, and beheaded bodies, and among others who, escaping, still bear in their flesh the marks of torture as they wander through the mountains and forests, forsaken, stripped, dispossessed.

I photocopied several images from *Martyrs Mirror*, hauling the book into the copy room at work. I couldn't close the cover properly over the massive thing, and kept shutting my eyes, scared of retinal damage from the flashing light. Now these pictures accompany me in my notebook, secured by transparent tape. The longer this trip goes on, the more I feel I belong to the Ak Metchet Mennonites. Not only because they represent a link between Mennonites and Muslims, not only because, like missionaries, they were inspired by apocalyptic dreams, and not only because I'm here, like them, moving through what Herman Jantzen called "the desolate, awful, silent desert." I feel I am theirs, and they are mine, because the same stories formed us: first the Bible, and then *Martyrs Mirror*. I think of the long poem "The Community of Christ," written by Gustav Toews and performed by the Ak Metchet youth choir in 1934. Commemorating the community's fiftieth anniversary, the poem records their history without a single mention of Claas Epp Jr. Instead, Toews traces their origin to the "beloved ancients," the sixteenth-century martyrs who were "pierced, mocked, and burned alive." The story was there, so close, available for use, ready to explain all the losses, the ravages of the journey, a story made for outcasts, filling misery with grace. "They had no shelter and no tent," wrote Toews, "but they sang wonderful songs."

This story has been there for many Anabaptists in times of uncertainty, when questions of identity become urgent. Julia Spicher Kasdorf traces the publication history of *Martyrs Mirror* in the United States, noting how it tends to be reprinted under the threat of war. From that first printing in Pennsylvania in the years before the Seven Years' War to my own 2002 edition on the eve of the Iraq War, *Martyrs Mirror* has served to inform and strengthen a small community committed to nonviolence in times of government and popular support for military action. The martyr history has also helped answer questions about identity for Mennonite missionaries, especially in the early days, when people raised with the idea of being separate from the world found justification for entering it, for traveling its length and breadth, in the image of the mission as a mirror for—in the words of Orie O. Miller, a founder of Mennonite Central Committee—"the pilgrim life of scattering and suffering." And I turned to *Martyrs Mirror* in much the same way. If you wake up one day and wonder, What defines my community? Who are we?—and if your community happens to have been carrying around a gigantic illustrated volume for three hundred years, it only makes sense to look inside.

Sight

And when I looked inside, I found the catalogue of pain. They were placed in stocks, stretched on racks, rubbed between millstones, scourged with rods, slashed with razors, dragged through the streets, immersed in boiling water. Wooden gags and tongue screws were put in their mouths, hot tar poured over them, red-hot slippers placed on their feet, their old wounds scraped open with potsherds. Burning candles were held underneath their arms. Their hands were squeezed until the blood flowed. Their nostrils were flooded with vinegar and salt, their mouths with urine. They were suspended by an arm or a leg, imprisoned in dungeons full of vermin, in total darkness, in total isolation. All this because they were outsiders, heretics, convicts through their convictions. Adriaenken Jansdochter, silent, exhausted, and docile, standing at the stake, dressed in her red petticoat. And Ursel, who asked her torturers, "And may I not sing a little?" She who was stripped and scourged with rods, who "was also tender of body, so that before her imprisonment, she had to turn her stockings inside out, and put them on and wear them thus, because she could not bear the seams of the stockings inside on her limbs."

A wave of suffering seemed to emanate from this book, unmoored from time. Time, in fact, is an important subject for Thieleman van Braght, and as he concludes his history of the first fifteen centuries of Christian martyrdom, as he moves into the more urgent part of his project, his account of the Anabaptist martyrs, he pauses to address it. "It is true," he writes, "that fifteen hundred years extend over a longer period of time than about a hundred and fifty of like years; and that the persecutions which occurred during this long time, when put in the balance, would be heavier than this last one, as well as the number of persons who were persecuted; but never in the preceding fifteen centuries did any persecution continue for so long a time without alleviation; never was there in so short (though actually long) a time so much innocent blood shed; never were there in so small a space so many dark prisons, deadly tribunals, scaffolds, fiery stakes, and other instruments of death erected and made use of as were at this time in Germany and the Netherlands."

A glut of blood. Time bulges to accommodate so much torment. This time doesn't end. It produces inherited trauma, an ongoing experience van Braght describes succinctly with the words "so short (though actually long) a time." Trauma is a form of time travel, and the time machine is *Martyrs Mirror*, especially its illustrations, which enter the eye in a flash. It's a powerful process, capable of generating many things: reverence, grief, commitment to one's beliefs, solidarity with the dead. Anger, too, at least in my case, outrage at the injustice, at their helplessness, at my helplessness because I couldn't go back and save them.

The pity of it. The wrenching fact: for insisting on believers' baptism, nonresistance, and separation from the state, my people were ground like wheat.

Yet, as many have noted, there is something disturbingly ambiguous, perhaps even morally objectionable, about looking at such images. The Mennonite writer Stephanie Krehbiel recalls how her graduate advisor, not a Mennonite, remarked that *Martyrs Mirror* "sounded pornographic." Krehbiel agrees that it might be easier for men to draw inspiration from this book. "As a young woman in this misogynist, pornography-drenched culture, though, I'm at no loss for narratives that depict splayed, exploited bodies that look like mine. The *Martyrs Mirror* offers me no refuge." Krehbiel recognizes how the book itself, so large, so lavish, invites a violent visual consumption. This is bloody theater, a spectacle that endures. Dwelling on these scenes can feel dangerous, morbid, an act contrary to life. As close as I felt to the martyr history, almost overwhelmed at times, I also recognized that I was part of the audience. I remembered the dictum of Ibn Sina of Bukhara: distance is a key component of sight.

Voice

Amsterdam, 1571. Anneken Hendriks flies toward Heaven on a ladder. She's fifty-three years old. They have filled her mouth with gunpowder. "The Anabaptists," writes Emily Ralph, "had a bad reputation—they couldn't hold their tongues." Anneken Hendriks is launched toward fire. She cannot hold her tongue. Soft black night. Light from a streetlamp coming in the window. Shadows of trees. I wake up convinced I can't hear anything. Bounce out of bed, heart pounding. Pace. This happens for several nights, perhaps a week, while I am studying the martyrs. I can't hear, I'm going deaf, I've gone deaf. I don't want to wake my husband, I know I'm having some kind of panic attack, I'm not really deaf, I just have to convince myself that everything's fine, I have to do it without making noise, so I pace the floor and tap my ears. When you tap your ears, it makes a small but unmistakable sound. *Tap tap tap.* I can hear it perfectly, yet I'm sure I'm going deaf. Listen, idiot. You're not deaf. Listen to the taps. It's as if gunpowder has exploded too close to my face.

I'm not sure why I had this reaction to *Martyrs Mirror*. I don't even know what to call it. Is it an auditory hallucination when you think you can't hear? Maybe it was the obverse of the experience of reading, which was primarily an encounter with voices. The pictures struck me, fascinated me, moved me, but they were also immobile, frozen in stark lines, while the voices unspooled across the page. These words, carried by collective memory, sprang from the poor and working classes, people who weren't associated with eloquence. "Cobblers in their bench," one angry friar called the Anabaptists, "bellow-menders, lantern-tinkers, scissors-grinders, broom makers, thatchers, and all sorts of riff-raff, and poor, filthy, and lousy beggars." Story after story in *Martyrs Mirror* shows this conflict between learned ecclesiastics and Anabaptist "riff-raff." Reading about the friar who scoffed, "At what university did you study? At the loom, I suppose," I thought of Peter Glück, a weaver, my first ancestor to come to America, who arrived in 1748, just as Mennonites in Pennsylvania were publishing *Martyrs Mirror* in his language.

Antwerp, 1577. Hans Bret, a youth in his twenties, sits on a block in chains, his hands quiet in his lap. Patiently he endures the torturer's work. No appearance of strain. There is a light on his face. There is a vise in his mouth. "And when he put out his tongue, the executioner fastened it with a piece of iron, and screwed it very tight with a vise or screw, and then touched the end of the tongue with a hot iron, that swelling, the screw might not slip off or become loose. O bitter cruelty and great tyranny."

The executioner holds the iron in the fire. His other hand steadies Hans Bret's mouth. It's like a visit to the dentist. A soldier looks on, leaning on his halberd; others chat in the background. This is the prelude to a strangled scream. Bret is the only bareheaded figure in the

scene: this allows him to catch the light like no one else. Light, like silence, will intensify for him, becoming a conflagration, but unlike silence, the light of the fire will eventually go out. So I think of light here not as silence but as the voice, the dying voice, the last light of it shining on him, or from him. A voice he could not stifle any more than a firefly can snuff out the luminescence that allows a child to capture it in a jar.

I read Hans Bret's letters, preserved in *Martyrs Mirror.* "Affectionately beloved sister in Christ Jesus, whom I love from the heart," he wrote to a friend, "*I cannot refrain* from writing you this brief letter, here in this pit into which I have been cast, without any light except the light of the candle." The words, *I cannot refrain*, in italics, must have been underlined. *Martyrs Mirror* brims with the letters of the dead. Long missives to friends and family, exhortations to fellow believers, urgent outpourings by candlelight. Mennonites, in my experience, just as in these stories from the sixteenth century, are not associated with eloquence; Anabaptist communities have been slow to produce literature, for a variety of reasons, many of which can be gleaned from *Martyrs Mirror.*

There is the distrust of learning and the educated classes. There is the rejection of idleness, untruthfulness, self-indulgence, and pride—sins that cling easily to writers, especially imaginative ones. And there is the need, among those who survived the persecutions, not to draw attention, to keep their heads down, to be "the quiet in the land," a phrase from Psalm 35 I heard very often growing up, which warns against publicity, making publishing a suspect practice at best. And yet how the martyrs wrote! Fluidly, lengthily, passionately. In her essay "Writing Like a Mennonite," Julia Spicher Kasdorf calls *Martyrs Mirror* "the first, and by far the most important work by Mennonite authors," a work that made trauma itself "a means of articulation and inscription." The scholar Ervin Beck locates the well of all Mennonite artistic expression, including but not limited to writing, in this compendium of stories and pictures that "stands," he writes, "at the beginning of Mennonite literary and visual art." It's the art, the writing, of those who cannot refrain. The word *martyr* comes from the Greek word for witness; the verb form means to bear witness. A martyr is one who bears witness, who speaks, who must, at any cost, in any form, on any available surface, transmit the voice. I read of Lourens Janssen, killed in 1577, who, since he "could obtain no writing materials . . . wrote and made known to his beloved friends, his affectionate mind, upon two tin spoons, with a pin."

I grew up feeling that the old Anabaptist vocalism was lost, that we were no longer speakers or writers. A kind of Mennonite melancholy. Now, on this bus in the desert, I think of my conversation with Diane last night, as we stretched out on matching fuchsia bedspreads in a Bukhara hotel.

"Most of the Mennonites I know went to these Mennonite colleges," she said. "Did you?"

Yes, I told her, I went to Goshen.

"And have you written a book?"

"Yes," I admitted.

"I knew it!" she exclaimed. "I've never met a Mennonite that hasn't written a book."

Paradoxes of martyrdom

This heavy heritage can feel so light. I remember my trip to Europe last year for a literary festival, how I traveled afterward with my family, spending one night in Zurich in a squeaky-clean rental apartment with track lighting. It happened to be Swiss National Day, which, according to our travel guide, is the only day the Swiss are allowed to make noise after ten at night. The fireworks ended precisely at eleven. We got an email from my father-in-law: "Make sure you visit the square where your ancestor Hans Landis was beheaded!" Some tourists have more to do in Switzerland than eat chocolate. In the morning, we found a plaque on the Limmat River, an engraved stone shimmering greenish gray, like a condensed square of river water, telling of the deaths by drowning of several Anabaptists, as well as the execution of Landis. My husband and I impressed on our children that this was where their ancestor got his head chopped off. The kids were like, "Okay." Then I made my husband take my picture by the statue of Ulrich Zwingli, a tall bronze figure, his shoulders green with age. Zwingli, I knew, was somebody super-important in Anabaptist history, whose contributions to theology made, at some point, some critical difference, a personage of such status in my high school Mennonite history book that you knew he was going to show up on the test. In fact, he made such an impression that, although I soon forgot what he did or said, and even exactly when he did or said it, he made his way into a song I composed in high school, with a friend, in honor of our favorite beverage, Mountain Dew.

Everybody loves it
Shakespeare drank a Mountain Dew
Ulrich Zwingli liked it too

I would like one, wouldn't you?
Oh! What am I going to do?

What, indeed? Zwingli towered above me. He held . . . a sword? Probably a metaphor. We crossed several streets, where cars stopped scrupulously at the crosswalks, and lunched in a very crowded and profoundly silent café, where my twelve-year-old son was thrilled to receive his apple juice in a wineglass. And this is how the story goes on, fragmented and jumbled, incoherent at times, but still retaining its power, because stories don't function through accuracy, they live through even the worst retellings, soaring above the laws of punctuation. They live because we keep them, well or badly. We conserve. I think of Adriaen Wens, a teenager in 1573, who searched through his mother's ashes after she had been burned at the stake and found "the screw with which her tongue had been screwed fast, which he kept in remembrance of her." I have read that this tongue screw was preserved by the family, and that the Mennonites of Amsterdam still possess a certain pear, given by the martyr Maeyken Boosers to her son before she died in 1564. How this pear has lasted for so long, I cannot say. I know that the poet Jean Janzen has touched it. This relic of our weighty heritage, having traveled through time, is now, she writes, "a brown oval, light as ash."

The martyr legacy can be borne casually, in tourist trips and comic songs. But it is also haunted by the ethnic ghost. The gray and icy skies of *Martyrs Mirror*, etched in memory as in the original copper plates, hold a history so devastating it demands primacy. I think of the efforts to expand this European story, like the Bearing Witness Stories Project, a collaborative online effort to record narratives of "costly discipleship to Jesus within the global Anabaptist family." The website represents

a critique of the blinkered, backward-looking gaze that would restrict the story of martyrdom to sixteenth-century Europe. Here I
read of Katherine Wu, a Mennonite pastor in Taiwan, beaten unconscious in 1993 for her work with child prostitutes. I read of Salvador
Alcántara, a Mennonite pastor in Colombia, threatened with death in
2003 for refusing to give up community land to paramilitary groups.
And SangMin Lee, a young Mennonite in South Korea, who went to
prison in 2014 for refusing military service. There is an ongoing story
of Anabaptist nonviolent resistance, a mirror outside the book, all over
the world. And this mirror outside the book is also outside the European Anabaptist heritage, reflecting people of color. Paradox of martyrdom: that those linked to this history by birth, but now living in
comfort, feel as if the story is theirs, while others continue to live it.
Paradox, that the accident of birth has come to play such a strong role in
defining Anabaptism, a faith that emphasizes choice. "Your dad was a
real Anabaptist radical!" a Mennonite friend once told me. "He was like
Felix Manz and all those guys!" Those guys were bold, my friend said
admiringly, they wouldn't baptize their kids, they ate sausages during
Lent and died miserable deaths. (The death of Felix Manz is commem-
orated on the same plaque that names my husband's ancestor. When
I looked all this up, I found out that Manz's execution was supported
by none other than Ulrich Zwingli, the hero of my paean to Mountain
Dew. Apparently Zwingli was not exactly on our side. He also died in
battle; this explains the sword.) I appreciate my friend's words, and the
crucial intervention of the Bearing Witness Stories Project. Yet I wonder if such comparisons work to shift the focus from the European past,
or whether they consolidate the power of that origin story by making it
the measure of the present.

An unfinished structure passes outside the window, cement and
brick, apparently abandoned. Some enormous, dusty machine on treads

at the side of the road. The desert goes on and on. It is the ninth largest
in the world. It extends in uniform folds, like collective memory, which
forgets so much. Of Mennonite history in Canada, the scholar Elaine
Enns writes, "In most cases, indigenous inhabitants are simply not a
part of our settler Mennonite narrative." She wonders why this should
be: surely the Mennonite experience of persecution should prepare us
to empathize readily with victims of violence in the Americas. I think
of the times when this has, in fact, happened, when these vital connections have been made, as in Germantown, Pennsylvania, in 1688, when
Mennonite immigrants who had joined the Quakers wrote the first
antislavery petition on American soil. "There is a saying," they wrote,
"that we shall doe to all men licke as we will be done ourselves; mack-
ing no difference of what generation, descent or Colour they are." They
were able to see, to reason from experience, to draw a parallel between
those oppressed on religious grounds in Europe and those oppressed in
America for their "Black Colour."

A jewel of insight—one we should seize and hold. But these Mennonite and Quaker activists were also part of a great invasion. My ancestor Peter Glück, the weaver, settled in the colony a generation after the
Germantown antislavery petition. He purchased land in Berks County,
Pennsylvania, in the shadow of Blue Mountain. Before he could begin farming, he was killed in a raid during the French and Indian War,
along with his wife and all but one of his children. The survivor was a
boy named John Glick, just old enough to talk. According to one version of the story, his father hid him under a bench. He was so little that
when he was rescued and asked how many brothers and sisters he had,
he could not give a number, but held up both hands and said "*Viele,
viele!*"—"Many, many!"

The boy became known as "Indian John." My great-grandfather's
great-grandfather. Paradox of martyrdom: that the children of victims

become victimizers. The Drift Prairie of northwestern North Dakota once supported thriving Mandan, Hidatsa, and Arikara or Sahnish communities. Decimated by smallpox in the nineteenth century, these groups joined together to form the Three Affiliated Tribes. In 1870, they were forced to settle on the Fort Berthold Reservation, a fraction of the lands they had once called home. In 1886, the town of Minot, North Dakota was built on the Drift Prairie. In 1906, my great-grandfather bought a farm there. I grew up visiting this farm, chasing cats in the hayloft, drinking fresh milk in the downy air.

Elaine Enns considers the power of family stories. The centrality Mennonites grant the history preserved in *Martyrs Mirror*, she writes, "may contribute to a phenomenon that social psychologist John Mack calls 'egotism of victimization,' in which communities that have survived significant violence are only able to see their pain, but not that of others."

Well, it is customary to say, we are peaceful people, we raised no weapons, we came along later, after the violence. We purchased land and entered without force the difficult places where the state desired a white and quiet presence. Thus we found a refuge after hardship: we who had suffered. I think of the way the figure of the martyr, inspired by another martyrology, John Foxe's *Actes and Monuments*, was used by early American colonists to eulogize the settlers who died fighting the Algonquians as holy soldiers:

> Whoea lost there Blud not much unlike to marters
> by disadvantage with these helish Tarters.

Tartars, savages, beasts on horseback, butchers of Christians, the Golden Horde—so much in that word, such a useful shorthand for mounted heathen barbarians, a word that has leaped outside its original meaning to take in a mishmash of others, but which still refers primarily to Turkic-speaking Muslims of Central Asia, such as the Nogai, the people Catherine the Great cleared out in various ways, burning their tents, restricting their movement, and massacring them in thousands, in order to make room for more desirable, agrarian, European immigrants, including a significant number of Mennonites.

And so once again I meet the Mennonites of Ak Metchet: this time as a settler, as a colonist. Again the question of *whose body* and *whose earth*. I remember the story of a young girl on the Great Trek, who, one dark night when the travelers were camped near the town of Chimkent, stepped on a fragile patch of ground and suddenly found herself plunged to her armpits in soil. She had fallen into a grave.

And what does it all mean? When I show my notes on *Martyrs Mirror* to friends, they press me for more, they want to know how I've been shaped by these stories, my non-Mennonite friends intrigued and curious, my Mennonite friends more insistent, anxious, they want to know what it means for themselves as well as me. But it's hard for me to answer. I have no standard of comparison; I don't know what it's like *not* to grow up with these stories. And I also know that the Anabaptist history of martyrdom is far from unique, not even unusual in this vale of tears.

What I can say for sure is this: the story doesn't work magic. It hasn't purified me of personal coldness and cruelty, any more than it has extinguished violence in Anabaptist communities, where domestic abuse and sexual assault are well known. But it does connect me to traditions of antiwar activism, voluntary community, and simple living, wherever and whenever they appear in the history of the world. This aspect of it is most precious to me. Beyond that, I can't say, because one of the paradoxes of martyrdom, perhaps the one that enables all the others, is how ordinary, how utterly everyday a story becomes when you really inhabit it, no matter how baleful or terrifying its content. Dirk Willems bends in this picture taped in my notebook, his arms outstretched, as I've seen him so often, on posters, on church bulletins, on the cover of a Sunday School coloring book, tacked to a wall in the church basement where they keep the extra chairs, in the halls of my school, in my friends' and relatives' houses, framed or affixed to the fridge. I have lived this lowering sky, this dirty ice, these wintry trees, these open hands. Not always with reverence, but while snacking or sweeping the floor. At the church retreat, we divide into groups and pick martyr stories out of a hat: each group will act out a story while the others guess what it is. The Dirk Willems story is so easy to guess, everybody groans. I'm not in that group: my group gets Gerrit Hazenpoet the tailor, who, as he was being burned at the stake, kicked off his slippers, saying, "It were a pity to burn them for they can be of service to some poor person." We can't use props, and we're not allowed to talk. One of us plays Gerrit Hazenpoet; another plays the stake. The children get on their knees and wave their arms in the air, wriggling their fingers around our Hazenpoet, in the role of flames. It's winter, at a Wisconsin campsite, beat-up couches around us, fluorescent light, and we're all laughing, and it occurs to me that this is a little bit ghoulish, that there's something macabre about the whole game, especially the children convulsed with giggles. Our martyr kicks off his shoes. "Gerrit Hazenpoet!" somebody yells.

The coziness of it. Martyrology as comfort food. The history that nourished the Ak Metchet Mennonites warms me just as well. Bitter in the belly, it tastes like honey in the mouth. Harrowing, heartrending, brutal, the story is home.

Elizabeth's dragon

On the bus, Kholid tells Frank and me about an article he read recently, an interview with a Mennonite woman published in a Soviet paper in the 1970s. This woman lived on a collective farm in Siberia, where she milked cows. What's the English word for that job? Frank and I look at each other—*dairymaid*? "A milker," Frank says at last. Right, so this Mennonite milker was interviewed by a journalist, who asked her if she was happy. Yes, she was happy, she said, but her eyes were sad. "Why do you look sad?" the journalist asked. He wanted to know if she had a normal life. Did she go to dances, nightclubs? No, the Mennonite milker replied. She said, "I'm happy to be useful to society." Now Frank and I are confused, because this Mennonite milker sounds like our idea of a perfect Soviet worker, but Kholid says the feature was written to show that this woman was backward and exploited, that the Soviet government was better than religion. They chose the milker because she was young and beautiful. They wanted to show that her primitive religious views were making her waste her life. "Why don't you go to the Black Sea beaches?" the journalist demanded. Why didn't she put on a bikini and sun herself with the other healthy Soviet youth? You see, she was brainwashed, with her cracked hands, mortifying her flesh, interring her beauty in a Siberian dairy. "I am satisfied with the life I lead," she said. I imagine her formal gaze, opaque, cloaked in a stubborn withdrawal. She reminds me of the hero's Mennonite bride in Jung-Stilling's *Heimweh*, who conceals her lambent beauty behind a death mask.

Now Lois takes the microphone to read from her great-grandmother Elizabeth Unruh's memoir. She reads Elizabeth's crossing of the Kyzyl

Kum, the desert that surrounds us. "Some read books, some slept," Elizabeth remembers, "but I knit during the day, and looked about; the sand was like sparkling silver, and rippled like water on the sea."

Lois pauses to note how rare Elizabeth's memoir is, this woman's writing. "Didn't any of the women on the trek keep diaries?" she asks. Nobody knows, so Lois answers the question herself: "Maybe they did, but people didn't think they were important, so they didn't save them." I think of all the women who lay in the street at Ak Metchet, who climbed on the cars, who carried their children onto the cars. Such women generally leave few records. Their letters, if preserved, are considered to have little meaning outside the family. These women leave behind quilts, embroidery, recipes, planting schedules. Perhaps a knack for languages. The shape of an elbow or a nose. Their legacy consists of objects and children. To seek these women, who treated their bodies so recklessly, is to be stuck with the body.

Stuck with the body, or gifted with the body. Maybe this is why, among the many extant pages of men's writing, Elizabeth Unruh's memoir glows with a near-unbearable intensity, a radiance so strong it's almost black. Precious Elizabeth! The only one to tell us of the bats in the ancient prison of Samarkand, the giant birds in the mountains of Bukhara, the caves where colored stones lay strewn like gems. The only one who tried to record the name of every fruit. As the sole woman to take her place in the history of the Great Trek, she makes me long for the lost stories of women, the diaries that might have recorded more of what I most want to know, and what Elizabeth captures best: the texture of experience.

This is the trouble with monoculture: it chokes variety out. The desert expands outside the window, rivers sacrificed for cotton, that crop the writer Colin Thubron calls "the hope and bane" of Uzbekistan, whose production, I recall, the Mennonites helped stimulate in Khiva.

The Soviet Union made Central Asia the largest producer of cotton in the world. Still later, under Karimov's regime, Uzbek activists would protest the use of forced labor in the cotton fields, while the Aral Sea subsided into salt. It seems to me that there is a fine line between *all* and *none*, and that in the realm of culture, just as in our physical environment, undisputed dominance spells annihilation. I remember reading about al-Muqanna, the Veiled Prophet of Shakhrisabz, who, like some eighth-century Claas Epp Jr., claimed to incarnate Adam, Abraham, Moses, Jesus, Mohammed, and God, uniting them in his person. "Beside me there is no God," he said. His followers dressed in white, while al-Muqanna covered his face with a green veil or a golden mask. This was to protect his disciples from his radiance. "To behold me," he said, "is death to the earth-born." In a courtyard, he drew a shining body from a well; those closest to him declared it was the moon. When his followers surrendered to the ruler of Khorasan, he poisoned his wives, decapitated his page, and leaped into a furnace.

Every universal history is negative universal history. This idea is eloquently expressed in the belief that once the whole world has heard the same gospel, it will end. In this view, monoculture is desire. In other contexts, it's fear. Either way, it's apocalypse. *All* is *none*.

Hours later, Frank is still wondering about the Mennonite milker—a woman who, even when interviewed, was hemmed in by the ruling culture of her time and place, cornered by the journalist's questions, framed inside his angle, until she retreated into sullen curtness. Unbending as ice she sat with her hands crossed. "What did *Mennonite* mean in Siberia during the 1970s?" Frank wonders. How did the milker practice her faith, what kind of church did she have, what kind of community? "You can't be Mennonite alone."

———

You can't be a pilgrim alone, either. Pilgrimage is a group project, its paths worn down by others. Even if I'd come to Uzbekistan by myself, I'd be treading in the footsteps of my documentarists, using my notes to trace their route. At this moment, I'm gazing out at the sand in a happy trance, feeling so close to those ghostly others, so filled up with the past, because Usmon, taking the microphone to describe the animals of the Kyzyl Kum, has mentioned the steppe eagle, the Russian tortoise, and the transcaspian desert monitor. This last creature is a lizard that can grow up to two meters long. Hearing these words, I almost shouted with delight. This must be the "salamander" the size of a native cow, the one that screamed in the night. I have found Elizabeth's dragon.

A swollen book

I'm terrified of monoculture, for obvious reasons: mixed people are likely to shrink from the idea of ethnic or cultural homogeneity, because if the world gets carved up into neat, monolithic boxes, where are we supposed to go? But there's more to this feeling than just self-preservation. It extends to the earth, to thought, to language, to experience, to the bus moving through the desert, to the notebook on my knee, the pen, the tension in my hands, one holding the paper steady, the other moving, writing. I don't want to leave anything out, so I write constantly. *Plastic bag in the wind. Tin foil. Chalky-looking sand.* I want to be able to tell you everything. I want to tell you about *saxaul*, the plant that threads the Kyzyl Kum like dull green lace. Saxaul produces more energy than ordinary timber. People here prefer its fire to that of coal. When you cook with saxaul, the food tastes better because of the scent, so people like making desert treks, cooking over campfires, breathing the fragrance. They will talk about such journeys for years afterward. Listen, I'll tell you a funny story about Brezhnev. Brezhnev learned some Uzbek to impress people on one of his visits, but he confused the word *aksakal*, which means elder—literally *white beard*—with *saxaul*. So out of respect he addressed a gathering as "Dear Saxauls!" And look: because saxaul is mentioned in Mennonite diaries, and because aksakal appears once as well—Herman Jantzen being referred to as "the son of the Aksakal of the Germans"—if all the Uzbek you know has been gathered from researching a tiny Mennonite village that existed here for fifty years, you can still get this joke! Isn't that wonderful? Isn't something happening inside you right now? I want to tell you about it, the dust storm arriving suddenly, in seconds, erasing all color, coming down like a white night. Sitting cross-legged with Nozli at a *tapchan*, an outdoor tea table, cups pinning napkins against the wind. We're smiling, sand in our teeth, we take a selfie with my phone, I call it our Ugly Photo, we can't stop laughing. I write everything. Kholid points out the shrubs planted by the Soviets to protect the road from the sand: "The desert is alive, it's a body, it moves." The question is how to allow the desert to move, to avoid killing it, and at the same time preserve the road, the map. At a basic level this is a question of what to include and what to omit and it presses me hard, this central question of the writer of Luke. An essential question for any writer, but I am kicking against it. I am extraordinarily committed to these notes. I have to tell you how close we felt, we and our Uzbek companions, drawn together by ethnic and religious persecution suffered, as they put it, "during the Soviets." The Ak Metchet Mennonites thrown out for their refusal to collectivize, their suspect Germanness, and their faith: this speaks to our Muslim hosts in post-Soviet Uzbekistan, whose religion was also forbidden, it fuels their interest, it ignites them. Enormous sympathy as we rush back to the bus in the stinging wind. Yet I worry, I'm concerned by the demonization of "the Soviets" in these notes, how often they appear as tyrannical aliens, so I have to add more, Usmon's gratitude to them for finding marble, minerals, and oil in the desert, and more, I have to express somehow that the Soviets were not some force from outer space, that they were also Uzbeks, Tajiks, Kazakhs, so I write that too in my notes, so I don't forget, I write the reminders, I write the window, the ashen sun, I write the noon. Pages and pages of notes in my little book. Everyone notices it, they observe my handwriting in the straight black lines. Sometimes one calls another over to look, not to pry but to admire how neatly Sofia can write, even on a moving bus. The German sense of order again! *It seemed good to me also,* says the writer of Luke, *having had perfect understanding of all things from the very first, to write unto thee in order, most excellent Theophilus.* I want to write to you like that, in order, but I have a lot of trouble with order, which is the reason, I've always thought, for my regular handwriting, it's just an attempt to cage the force, a futile one, obviously, because things keep swelling, each saxaul branch connected to an underground network of roots, and I don't know where to cut it, where to end, I'm afraid of stopping, afraid I'll miss the essential metaphor or sentence, the one capable of communicating the brokenness that has brought us here, the way we are heartbroken every one. Heartbroken over the state of our world. Micah's father explains that he decided to come on this trip not because he's descended from the travelers on the Great Trek, but because his church was hosting Palestinian refugees from Iraq and he wanted to understand hospitality. Not some idea of Mennonite modernity, not what we gave, but what we received. To understand ourselves as recipients. To see ourselves as *helplessly* connected to the world, linked not because we chose it but because we were thirsty. Abraham was a "wandering Aramean," Frank has reminded us. In my Bible, the translation reads: *a Syrian ready to perish.* A Syrian ready to perish was my father. To understand this, the link of suffering, vulnerability as inheritance. And then to give out of that, out of that knowledge of total brokenness and collapse. I am afraid that only someone like the writer of Luke, someone with perfect understanding of all things, should be trusted with this story in a world convulsed by violence. Lacking perfect understanding, I tell you everything. I see that I will write a swollen book. I am returned to the dread I felt in a high school chapel, holding a red-backed hymnal, when I was young and beginning to be a writer.

> *Could we with ink the ocean fill*
> *And were the skies of parchment made*
> *Were every stalk on earth a quill*
> *And every man a scribe by trade*
> > *To write the love*

Of God above
Would drain the ocean dry
Nor could the scroll
Contain the whole
Though stretched from sky to sky.

The words of departure

News reaches us as we near the city of Khiva. It comes through phones, to those with local plans or international data. There has been a shooting in Orlando, Florida. A man has attacked people at a gay bar with assault weapons. We learn his name: Omar Mateen. Usmon tells us the gunman's ex-wife was Uzbek. She divorced him for abuse, she ran away to her parents in New Jersey. Now he has slaughtered people at a nightclub. Fifty-three injured, forty-nine dead. And he's dead himself, shot by the police. The incident rises among us, fades away, then returns, like a wave of nausea. Kholid asks me what Mennonites think about queer people, what our position is, saying the acronym slowly: LGBTQ. In the question already Mennonites are removed from the subject of inquiry, not queer themselves. I have to tell him we have no position. We can't agree. It's wounding us, splitting us up, churches leaving conferences, pastors stripped of their offices. It's one of our biggest problems. He asks what I think myself, do I think queer and trans people should be admitted to churches, married there. I say absolutely, yes. He doesn't agree. A long, circuitous argument begins, on the bus, over the sound of the bus, on the bridge across the river, the Amu Darya. He has his convictions and I have mine. We can't converge. Tom is reading from his great-grandfather's journals: his great-grandfather Johann Jantzen, who never went to Khiva, who left the Bride Community, like most of my documentarists, for America. Tom reads of the pain of separation, the way those who had decided to leave were treated by the others, with "no esteem or respect." They had traveled so far together, suffered and shared so much, yet those who were leaving became enemies overnight. The wheat so lush, almost rosy as we come out of the desert, the deep green rice. My conversation with Kholid remains gentle, and I'm grateful for that, the effort we make not to hurt one another. Still, it has to end, it can't go on. There's something here that can't be crossed.

Kholid and I stop talking. Tom reads his great-grandfather's words, the words of departure. "There was a sadness between us. The Lord grant that this is not for eternity, but only temporary."

As we reach Khiva, it begins to rain.

PART THREE

*

The Place of Refuge

SEVEN

Khiva

all in a pale and ghostly light

Algorithm

Khiva, the city of nightingales, at last.

A steady rain whitens the surface of the pond outside the hotel. We rush through the courtyard, wheeled suitcases banging across the stones. This hotel is more modest than the ones where we stayed in Samarkand and Bukhara: the walls are white, unadorned by tiles, the furniture of plain, yellowish wood. As if to make up for this relative simplicity, the lobby boasts a giant chess set with toddler-sized pieces, watched over by a pair of adult-sized dolls. It's impossible to ignore this tableau, which dominates the lobby, dreamlike and faintly sinister, like something out of *Alice's Adventures in Wonderland*, the female figure standing, a veiled pillar of embroidery, and the man seated on an *arba*, a two-wheeled cart. Both mannequins are dressed in the style of pre-Soviet Central Asia, when the arbas with their rumbling wheels rolled up and down the Silk Road. The man, crowned with a sheepskin hat, sits with one boot propped jauntily on his knee. They've paused on their journey; perhaps they've just loosed their bullock to graze. The woman seems to be staring at the chess set, but the man regards our party sardonically with thickly painted eyes like a pair of black olives.

Thunder and lightning all night. I dream I'm moving the chess pieces downstairs, each one landing on its square with a crashing sound—a dream that seems appropriate here, in the province of the great mathematician al-Khwarizmi, known as the Father of Algebra. I have no reason to venerate al-Khwarizmi, whose innovations wrecked my high school GPA, but I'm touched by the expression of concentration on the bronze face of his statue, which we visit after breakfast, near the gates of the old town. Kholid meets us in front of the statue, cheerful after a night at his parents' house, with the air of having enjoyed an excellent breakfast. Though he lives in Tashkent with his wife and children, Khiva is his city, his family home. He calls al-Khwarizmi "Mr. Zero," as if they're old friends. He says the mathematician was known as a *Mugh*, which means fire-worshiper: the origin of the English word *magi*. Mr. Zero gazes down at his scroll, one hand raised to his chin, absorbed in the contemplation of the absolute, the pigeon perched on his turban seeming charmed into the same stillness until it suddenly takes off into the rain-washed sky. And if it's going to happen anywhere, I think, it will be here. If I'm going to experience the integration Walter S. Friesen writes of in "Pilgrimage as Healing," the relief as the parts of my life ease into place, the borders melting, it will be here, where the last of the rain evaporates, wreathing the walls in mist. It will happen in the extraordinary softness of this atmosphere, under the silken, oyster-colored sky, where Kholid takes my notebook, removes a pen from his shirt pocket, and teaches me al-Khwarizmi's formula for the perfect person.

Imagine a person blessed with a good character and manners. This person receives one point:

1

Now imagine this person is also granted health. Health adds a zero; now the person has ten points:

10

Imagine this person is also granted beauty, another zero:

100

Now imagine this person comes of an excellent lineage:

1000

Such a person is perfect—one thousand points! Yet, if one is granted health, beauty, and family, without a good character, we must remove the 1:

000

The person will end with zero: a blankness, worth nothing. Demonstrations of magic with pen and paper in the shade of the fortified wall. Attractions of computation, of processes that produce the same result every time, of a calculable universe. Usmon informs us that the Tashkent earthquake occurred on April 26, 1966, and the Chernobyl disaster on the same date exactly twenty years later. A silence falls among us, as if this information is somehow significant, the coincidence itself a form of meaning. I consider sharing the fact that when I started researching the Great Trek I was forty-two, the same age as Claas Epp Jr. when he became a prophet, but decide it will just sound weird. Thirst can make you superstitious: thirst for meaning, for perfect understanding, for knowing when to stop.

How I would love to come home from this trip with a formula for cross-cultural interaction, one that would make sense out of the mosaic of my life, one that could act as a guide, for myself and anybody who needed it, explaining how to move in and out of the stories of others.

Walking with my group into the medieval inner town, where the streets are free of cars and rutted by ancient cartwheels, I retrace my long study of this problem, which seems to have lasted my entire life—all the theories, the concepts, the specialized terms. During my childhood, people were trying to chart a path between *nativism* and *assimilation*. In their effort to *decolonize* they emphasized the *agency* of the *colonized*, who had *roots* and traveled—usually forced, in some way—on *routes*. By the time I reached college, this discussion had yielded the notion of *hybridity*. Very quickly came *creolization, indigenization,* and *global flows*. I studied the methods of crossing: *mestizaje, mimicry,* and their delinquent cousin *cultural appropriation*. But none of these theories gave me what I needed, a way to live, and I think this is because they were made for looking backward, at things that had happened, rather than at the experience of the present: this present, for example, in the cavernous street, among booths selling DVDs and astrakhan hats. What to make of the flat roofs glinting with satellite dishes beneath the enormous Kalta Minor minaret with its rings of sea-green tiles? In the courtyard of the madrasa stands a wooden throne, painted gold; a robe hangs over it, and swords and sheepskin hats dangle from its arms. Three men approach this lonely imperial seat, take the hats, and stroll off to take pictures. A tour guide is shouting in German. At a well that, Usmon informs us, is 2,300 years old, I'm seized by a spirit of play, and flick Nozli with the ice-cold, primeval waters. She flicks me back, and soon we're chasing each other around the fountain. This is some kind of cross-cultural interaction, but what does it mean? Sure, I could just relax and enjoy a game of tag, but if social relations are important, they must be important down to the ground. They must have meaning in the moment, while they're happening. The theories I studied in school are useful for analyzing history, they're frankly excellent for skewering dumb comments on social media, but they're clumsy tools for figuring out what's going on right now, in this courtyard where our shadows flit back and forth over the stones.

The word *algorithm* comes from al-Khwarizmi. That's what I desire from Khiva: a set of instructions, a blueprint. If Muslims and Christians lived here amicably in the past, in peaceful exchange, then people could do the same today. If they lived without forcing their views on one another, without the rage for conversion, without the need to make others think and worship like themselves, then we could. And then I could. Live. This is backward divination, an experiment in sympathetic magic.

Eisegesis

I realize this is a quixotic notion. It might even be dangerous, like Claas Epp Jr.'s ill-fated hocus-pocus with the Book of Daniel. At the door of the small room in the Ichan-Kala Museum that houses an exhibit on Khudaybergen Divanov, the first Uzbek photographer, Frank gives me the word *eisegesis*: reading in. From what I understand, this means a bad way of doing theology. Instead of drawing out what's in the text, as in exegesis, a person involved in eisegesis enters the book. "You read your way into it," Frank explains. "You insert yourself. You put yourself there." This is what Epp did in his readings of Daniel and Revelation: he inserted himself, his world, Russia, Napoleon, Jung-Stilling's *Heimweh*. Everything important to him was there. And although I'm sure Frank doesn't mean to suggest this—he doesn't know—I have done the same thing with the story of the Great Trek. I have gone so far as to physically put myself here, in front of this door, with my hand on the warm, old wood, scared that something will go wrong at the last moment, the door will be locked, the exhibit closed on the one day I'm able to visit, I'm so anxious I can't help pushing the door a little, it gives, Frank chuckles at me, "Go ahead," he says, he'll wait here for the rest of the group to catch up, his hands in his pockets, his big camera on its strap resting on his stomach. He doesn't know about my study of Khudaybergen Divanov, but he reads my hunger, the passion of a fellow researcher. And I open the door on a room that reminds me at once of my Divanov study: a dense twilight flecked with pulsing points of light.

Photography and the angels

Every day for a month I woke up early and watched films from Central Asia. It was still dark outside and my bedroom was like a theater. My laptop screen lit up with historical dramas, documentaries, and popular movies churned out so fast they're known as *khon-takhta,* which means chopping-board. My thinking then was genealogical: I traced a direct line from the Mennonite photographer Wilhelm Penner of Ak Metchet to his pupil Khudaybergen Divanov to today's Uzbek film industry. More: as Divanov was the first indigenous photographer and filmmaker in the region, I saw him standing at the root of Central Asian cinema. Somehow, I thought, his presence, the fact that he lived, is flickering through this screen. Wilhelm Penner must be flickering too.

At the time, I was living in California, absorbed in my research on the Great Trek, which had already consumed a few years of my life. I plunged into a study of Khudaybergen Divanov, reading everything I could find about him in English, tracking down blogs, ordering obscure documentaries through the university library. With no knowledge of Uzbek or Russian, I couldn't undertake proper research; my notes wound up dotted with question marks, crisscrossed by contradictions. The most basic information seemed contested. After months of wrestling with conflicting documents, I concluded that he was born in 1879 and died in 1940.

My sources agree that he was born in the Khanate of Khiva and died in the Uzbek Soviet Socialist Republic. As a boy, he had his picture taken by Wilhelm Penner, a man known locally as *Panor-buva,* Grandfather Lantern, presumably because of the flash of his instrument. The young Khudaybergen was fascinated by the camera, and Penner taught him how to use it, then gave him a camera of his own. I copied in my notes that this gift was a German ZOT camera, a mystery that kept me occupied for some time. If you look up *German ZOT camera*, you mostly find Khudaybergen Divanov. For a researcher, this kind of loop is a bad sign. Still, I pursued it relentlessly, digging up finds like Le Zot (a camera repair shop in Vermont) and Bier Zot (a European gastropub located in the heart of Sister Bay, WI).

Tursunali Kuziev, author of the exhibition catalog *125 Years of Uzbek Photography*, is astonished by the unexpected beginnings of this photography, the improbable meeting of a boy and a wandering German. Divanov's life, he writes, is "a chain of surprising events full of deep meaning." This deep meaning seems to be a kind of fate. "Everything was predetermined," says Kuziev, referring to the arrival of the Germans of Ak Metchet, as if the entire journey, the millennial expectations, the effort, the suffering, the loss, had been orchestrated in order to produce Uzbek photography. And after all, why not? By 1903, Divanov was taking pictures of Khivan minarets piercing the blue cloudless sky, he was creating what would become the only photographic record of pre-Soviet Central Asia by an indigenous artist, he was establishing an oeuvre that would expand, after his 1907 visit to Russia, to include short films taken with the Pathé camera he brought back with him, an oeuvre that would eventually have to compensate, Kuziev suggests, for the deaths, presumably from illness, of both of Divanov's children, a pair of deaths that left the photographer only his wife and his darkroom, that left him like this, this man I gaze at in a photograph, solemn, dignified, almost startlingly handsome in his striped coat and broad sheepskin hat, with a delicacy of feature that somehow suggests he is not tall, a man with direct and tired eyes, whose black mustache flows into his sleek white beard, who exudes the calm self-respect proper to a retired minister of finance of the Republic, and who will one day, all too soon, go out to pick up his monthly pension and be arrested, imprisoned, and shot by Stalin's police.

A moving passage from Kuziev whose poignancy is only increased by its idiosyncratic translation: "It was a happy time for the photo. Its creative component wonderfully combined with the mass character. It could not grade up to the present, but anyhow was enough to reach our days through the stormy 20th century, considering the fact that only 10–20 percent of human products can avoid the decay and destruction."

Among the human products that have survived decay and destruction are several Latin spellings of the name Khudaybergen Divanov. Khudaibergen Divanov; Khudaibergen Devanov; Hudaibergen Divanov; Xudoybergan Devonov. During Divanov's lifetime, the Arabic script of the khanate was replaced by the Latin alphabet of the Uzbek Soviet Socialist Republic. He was a person who lived in orthographic transition. He didn't make it through all of them: he died as Cyrillic was introduced.

Kuziev tells a wonderful story of the transition to the world of photographic images. As Divanov began taking photographs, his father received a visit from a judge, who warned that photography was against Islamic law. It was a sin to represent the human figure. No angel, said the judge, will enter a room where there are portraits of human beings. "Well," answered Divanov's father, "my son keeps his photographs in one room; the angels may have the run of the other nine."

Photography appears here as an angel repellent. It edges the spirits out. Perhaps what the judge described as angels is what Walter Benjamin famously called the aura, a quality of uniqueness and authenticity that atrophies, for better or worse, in the age of photography. Certainly this judge was not the only one to recognize that as photography enters, something is lost. Balzac believed that our bodies are made up of thin spectral layers, one of which is removed with every photograph. It's as if a person's very essence were being peeled away. Consider the first Congolese to encounter Mennonites, who took the camera-wielding missionaries for sorcerers hunting people's shadows, or my grandfather, who, when my uncle last visited him in Somalia, refused to have his picture taken.

I pored over Divanov's photographs. A troupe of musicians, stoical and wary, poised with their instruments, one raising a flute to his lips. The elderly man seated on a wall, the thick, bare limbs of the trees around him webbing the sky, almost hiding the dome and minaret in the background. The crowds captured in sunlight, the blurred goats. Through these photographs, Divanov emerged as a risk-taker, a bit of a gambler, a person who didn't restrict himself to the studio but was willing to appear with his spooky equipment in the middle of a busy market. His images capture some of the excitement of early photography, its fragility, when pictures were so often marred by overexposure, by lines fan-shaped or forked like bolts of lightning, or those annoying air bubbles that materialized as black spots like malevolent moons. They were naïve days, a time of chaos, buckling negatives, indigo hours of development, and chemical fogs, when photography was both undisciplined and extremely demanding, requiring an equal measure of recklessness and patience.

Gazing at these pictures filled me with the wistfulness, the sense of futility and enchantment, that accompanies research in translation. I recognized something of what I was feeling in Roland Barthes's book on photography, *Camera Lucida*, in which the philosopher explains that photography tells us *something has been*. Although a photograph has a subject—musicians, an old man, a market scene—it's not simply a record but a relic, like a fingerprint on glass. It can't be reduced to its subject. To describe the strange bewitchment of photographs, Barthes identifies two elements, studium and punctum. The studium is what every photograph has, a cluster of aspects that give it cultural meaning: topic, purpose, style. The punctum is something much more personal and unpredictable, something which, Barthes writes, "rises from the scene, shoots out of it like an arrow, and pierces me." The studium, for example, might be a picture of children on a New York street; the punctum is one child's bad teeth. The punctum is what escapes intention, what just happened to be there, and the fact that it's *just there*, accidental yet inevitable, creates a shocking sense of presence.

Lacking the necessary research languages, I plunged into my Divanov study almost without access to the studium, the cultural apparatus that would have helped me understand his work in context. I was left with punctum: the piercing accident. Everything I encountered, from the phrase *German ZOT camera* to my favorite picture, the portrait of the hunters, struck me with poignant force, not in spite of the fact that I couldn't make any definitive claims about these things but precisely because of my inadequacy. Here are the hunters, one on a black horse, a pair of white hawks on his arm. The other lounges on the ground beside a dog. Patches of light and darkness form a pattern: dark hat, pale beard, pale coat, dark horse. The embroidered caparison adds a hint of luxury. This picture gives me a feeling of wandering far on a long day, but all I know for sure about these beings, these people and animals, is that they were. And this fact shakes me: the incontrovertible fact of a body, now lost, that imposed itself for an instant in front of the light.

———

Men in great black woolen hats are digging a canal with the swift, jerky movements of old film. Brightness. Slow shot of rooftops, towers, crenellation. This is footage from Divanov's Pathé camera, captured in 1908. It's part of a documentary made in 1970. The images are set to the sound of drums, the hum of a lute. There's a resounding Russian voiceover, with English subtitles that inform me, "You see the first shots of Uzbek cinema." Here is a stuttering waterwheel, a camel. Canal diggers scurry up and down the banks. The subtitles announce, "People fight for water in the distant Khorezm, in the country of forty thousand bushes." Whiteness reaches me, filtered through space and time. A sunlit wall disappears against the sky. I read a reference to the German Wilhelm Penner: "Vilgelm Paner." There are scenes I can't understand, some sort of gathering, a man blindfolded, stretched on the ground. Another man repeatedly steps on his abdomen, and a long rope, or something like twisted paper or ribbon, comes out of the blindfolded man's mouth. Through scenes like this, the subtitles claim, "Divanov expressed his world vision and his attitude to the hopeless destiny of people." Of course, I'm watching a propaganda film. It's meant to show the backwardness of the Uzbeks before their Soviet enlightenment. So I can't tell, I don't know if Divanov was trying to show me their hopeless destiny. I can see he was interested in movement. He was interested in wheels and spindles and plows and the long coil of ribbon unfurling from the mouth of the blindfolded man. He was also interested in the sky. The camera pans around, gazes up at a tree, a roof, seeing everything for the first time.

My ideas about photography changed during this period, for I saw that a photograph can work in more than one way. I had always distrusted the medium for its insistent claims to reality, the way it invites an acquisitive, violent gaze, and its usefulness to a worldview that crops and categorizes and frames, that reduces a human face to a racial type. But now I saw that there is also something else: a shadow. The imprint of an irreducible presence. If one side of a photograph gloats, "The eye can know everything," the other side murmurs, "The eye knows almost nothing."

Almost nothing. Only a flicker, a trace that can't be grasped, that can't be built up into an official record or a proper historical study. A mark that's not useful as evidence but simply evident. Untranslatable. "What I can name cannot really prick me," writes Barthes.

Divanov's widow appears briefly in the documentary and refers obliquely to his death. She mentions, the subtitles say, "the fatal 1937." An elderly woman, eighty-four years old, beside a dry tree. Her name, again according to the subtitles, is Ikakjan Ikakjanova. This image is captured in 1970; next year I'll be born. It will be many years before I go through Divanov's photographs looking for her, for someone who might be her, Ikakjan Ikakjanova. Is she the woman in the portrait who wears a high, round headdress crossed in front by the bold X of a white scarf, a woman with two black lines painted at the corner of her eye, whose cheek, though in black and white, gives an impression of burnished color? Is she the woman in the picture of Divanov and his camera, a woman who stands with her back to the viewer, her hands on her hips, apparently talking to Divanov who lightly touches his tripod, the two of them sunk knee-deep in flowers? The person who took this picture must be one of Divanov's students, one of the many young people he taught at his studio, for like Wilhelm Penner he was a teacher as well as an artist, mentoring a whole generation of photographers. The photographer must be a student, for it can't be Wilhelm Penner: judging by the whiteness of Divanov's beard, Penner, if still living, is no longer at Ak Metchet. So someone else takes the photograph of this intimate moment before or after the other photograph, the one Divanov will take, has taken.

It surrounds us, the ancient art. Khudaybergen Divanov steps outside. Spring has arrived, and Ikakjan has been cleaning the veranda. The outdoor carpet hangs on the garden wall, framed by the twin pear trees. It's an old carpet, leached of color by the sun. Yet, in its center, a large, irregular patch glows vibrant red and green. It's where the tea table usually stands, surrounded by cushions. The effect of the sun on the carpet has produced an image. How sensitive, he thinks, how deeply responsive objects are to the presence of light.

———

But I don't know and can't know if he ever thought this. *Something has been*, it's looking at me, the photograph regards me, but it doesn't see me. He's looking at me but he doesn't know I'm here. The gaze coming out of a photograph, says Barthes, is an aim without a target. That gaze is utterly distant, unreadable, like a foreign language, and yet it insists on presence, on what was once palpably, unavoidably there. And so perhaps the real significance of the conflict between photography and the angels, the idea that emanates so insistently from every photograph, burning like a ray from even the most indifferent, offhand shot, is that we ourselves are the angels and we are gone.

Grandfather Lantern

There's a photograph of Wilhelm Penner and Khudaybergen Divanov together: they're in the courtyard of a nondescript building, Divanov standing and Grandfather Lantern seated, wearing a brimmed cap that gives him a dapper air. They're gazing at a book, perhaps an album. Student and teacher. Wilhelm Penner was the schoolteacher of Ak Metchet, the brother of the fiery J. K. Penner who preached against Claas Epp Jr. at Serabulak. J. K. Penner left the group and emigrated to Nebraska, but Wilhelm Penner stayed in Ak Metchet, teaching, fishing, taking photographs, patiently awaiting a Rapture infinitely deferred. There were small satisfactions, in the meantime, such as the Uzbek boy, this child so curious about the camera, who took to it so quickly, becoming a devotee of light. While in Ak Metchet the walls slowly faded, the church was scrubbed with whitewash again, the children chanted in the schoolroom, and Wilhelm Penner, so loyal to his leader, was castigated by Claas Epp Jr., publicly shamed. "Thus saith the Lord," Epp declared. "Brother Penner uses two or three times as much fuel as any other family." A dreadful accusation of greed, or wastefulness, or both. This, although Penner had always been so close to the leader. Perhaps it was not possible to be close to Epp without receiving some wound.

From what I can tell, Penner endured his humiliation in silence. It seems he was a quiet man. Franz Bartsch, recording his own decision to leave the Bride Community, remembers Penner's wordless gaze. Other brothers remonstrated with Bartsch, sometimes harshly, but, he writes, "Wilhelm Penner and I looked at each other for a long time, reading the depths of emotion in our eyes. What moved us both so deeply could not be expressed in words."

Penner does speak, however, at the end of Bartsch's memoir, for it was

Penner who edited the final chapters, those that comment on the fate of the community in Khiva after the departure of Franz Bartsch. Penner's lengthiest addition, a detailed paragraph in parentheses, has to do with his income when he was teaching at Ak Metchet: how his wife's parents sent her a sewing machine from Aulie-Ata, how she supported the family by making coats, how Penner sold the garments in Khiva once a week. "I insert this explanatory passage," he writes, "only to show how wonderfully the Lord supports even his errant children." Yet it can also be read as a defense against Epp's denunciation, proffered years later, evidence of a lasting pain.

Penner writes, too, of the moment that severed him from Claas Epp. It happened when Epp had fallen ill. He asked Penner to bring communion to him in bed, but not give it to him: Epp would no longer accept the Lord's Supper from any human hand. For Penner, this was a breaking point. He spoke out against Claas Epp for the first time. Soon afterward, while Penner was giving a sermon, Epp burst into the church and accused him of denying God the Father. Penner records the events of that day, but he tells of its aftermath only through his silence, allowing Bartsch to write for him. "This pronouncement nearly drove Penner to despair and to the brink of insanity. As a result he suffered years of spiritual and mental anguish."

Wilhelm Penner and his family moved to Aulie-Ata. Apparently, he could no longer live at Ak Metchet, no longer calm himself, as he often had, with a line of his favorite hymn: *Es will die Augen schliessen und folgen blind.* To close one's eyes, to follow in blind faith. Such a strange vow for a photographer. Holding his camera at the level of his heart. Producing, from the box, his lucent images. Photographs of Penner show a face remarkable for its large, clear eyes.

The light thief

During the time of my Khudaybergen Divanov study, in California, in the predawn darkness before my workday began, hunched in bed with my laptop, I immersed myself in Central Asian films, seeking to trace a tradition that began with Wilhelm Penner and his camera. I watched everything I could find, from all over the region. I examined the angles, the shots, the gestures, the expressions, the woman making tea at an outdoor fire in the long, silent opening scene of Khodzhakuli Narliev's 1972 *Daughter-in-Law*. A film in which the protagonist barely speaks. She carries a bowl across the geometric pattern of light from a lattice. She flicks the floor with water. And how tender she is with the newborn lambs, cuddling their blackness against Turkmenistan's snowy peaks. The lambs are torn away, tossed from hand to hand by the men who have come to collect them, the woman is lonely, childless, her husband away at war, she tries to read her future in her tea leaves, a twig floating in reddish water, the lambs cry out, their voices echo. She drops a bowl of salt crystals that glitter like chips of ice. This is her language. At the end a voice begins to sing:

> *Will ill luck never abandon me?*
> *Will my heart never stop aching?*
> *In spring the steppe will bloom*
> *There'll be azure skies above*
> *If the bitter hour comes*
> *Let me have my share of trouble.*

The bitter hour, the lambs. *Daughter-in-Law*, with its wordless struggles, mirrors the parable of lonely labor, *Flight of the Bee*,

Jamshed Usmonov's 1998 collaboration with the Korean director Min Byung-hun. Scenes of burrowing, of bodies lowered into the earth. In *Daughter-in-Law*, the well must be cleaned: the woman lets her elderly father-in-law down the hole on ropes, slowly, anxiously, with immense effort. *Flight of the Bee* also portrays underground tunnel work, an exhausting labor of ropes and pulleys, a Tajik schoolteacher determined to make a statement by digging a public toilet in front of the house of a corrupt local leader. This toilet is the teacher's heroism. He quits his job for it. He's obsessed. And it becomes more and more difficult to watch him go down the hole, his skinny, resolute body sweating and straining, given over to a reckless, backbreaking project, until the end.

When *Flight of the Bee* was screened, the Iranian director Mohsen Makhmalbaf noticed scratches in one of the scenes. "Did you scratch the film on purpose?" he asked the directors. No, they admitted, it had been damaged during development, and they didn't have the money for a reshoot. "Don't tell anyone that," Makhmalbaf said. "Make up something about 'the aesthetics of poverty,' and those scratches will only help underscore the film's verisimilitude." Seize the terms under which you work. "Make up" an aesthetics of poverty when you actually don't have enough money to shoot the scene again. It's a glimpse of the working conditions of these filmmakers. Watching *Flight of the Bee*, I remembered reading about the Palace of Culture in Tashkent, which was handed over to the Komsomol Youth Association on independence in 1991. The members of the youth group suddenly found themselves in possession of a five-thousand-seat auditorium lit by chandeliers. They decided to revive the tradition of Uzbek cinema, but before they could manage it, the place was illegally sold out from under them. During their brief ownership, the group screened several films and cleaned out the toilets. The palace had been built without foundations; over time, the cellar, which housed these toilets, had become a slough, the staircase leading straight down into mud. *Flight of the Bee* reminded me of the youth group mucking out these toilets under a Palace of Culture that would soon be stolen, and of Murat Auezov, who said on becoming chief editor of Kazakhfilm in 1990, "The situation of Kazakh cinema is so difficult and hopeless that we have no other choice but to be brilliant."

On a dark, windy morning, I lay in bed watching Rashid Nugmanov's 1988 *The Needle*, sometimes described as the manifesto of the Kazakh New Wave. A film lit by the ragged, translucent beauty of Viktor Tsoi as Moro, the young drifter trying to save his girlfriend Dina from drug addiction. A black dog appears, then vanishes. A television rumbles, streaked with static. Dina wears a white Harlequin mask. "I want to go to the beach," she says. They go to the beach. There's a rusting ship on the sand. It's all sand. The Aral Sea is a desert. It's the desert of Bahadur Muzafarov's *Aralkum*, filmed in 1987, which documents the destruction of the sea, progressing in scenes of obliterating whiteness, salty winds, and ships beached on the sand, far from the receding shore. Children play on these stranded vessels. They've strung a rope from a pole to make a swing. But the ships are dangerous: sometimes they catch fire. The fuel in their tanks combusts in the heat, creating pillars of flame and dense black smoke to be empty signs in this manmade wilderness. Once, the Aral Sea provided fish so abundantly, and fed so many, the poet Ivan Drach called it a "magic tablecloth." Now the men who make their living from fishing have become itinerant. They are the nomad anglers, loading their boats on trucks to search for the Aral's remains. They park on the creamy, acid-green shores of the temporary lakes created by runoff from the cotton fields, momentary seas found on no map. "Now we have to move searching for fish," the fishermen say. Once the sea united people, now everybody leaves. Their heavy sheepskin hats ripple in the wind. Most of the fish have "hard roe," sterile from pesticides.

In *Aralkum*, these corroding ships and the massive derelict buildings marooned in the sands signify the loss of the environment. In *The Needle*, they are the environment. This is the world of the asphalt children, a term coined by Gulshat Omarova to describe the hero of her film *Schizo*. It's a world of fantastical factoryscapes, black insectile towers, mountains of coal. Men stand around, they squat to play cards, waiting for work. When a car drives up they cluster around it in their black leather jackets, carrying plastic bags. "What do you need? I've been standing here half the day." They'll do anything, scavenge wire from dead telephone poles, get themselves beaten to death in amateur boxing matches. Among them, a fifteen-year-old boy called Schizo, considered too slow for school. An asphalt child, a child of unfinished apartment blocks. Light shines through these desolate, alien structures as it shines through my screen, there's a broken-down house on stilts, a lone motorcycle in a blond field, a woman limping across the rocky ground in red high heels, vodka, cucumbers, money hidden inside a sewing machine.

When *Schizo* was released in Kazakhstan in 2004, the most famous Kazakh of international cinema was already appearing on TV, and would soon have his own movie, *Borat: Cultural Learnings of America for Make Benefit Glorious Nation of Kazakhstan*. The journalist Borat Sagdiyev isn't really a Kazakh but a character created and played by British comedian Sasha Baron Cohen. In a series of zany skits, Borat travels through the US, poking fun at American life by confronting it with a caricature of foreign backwardness. It's a hilariously discomfiting film, perhaps especially for disaffected Americans who enjoy seeing their collective weaknesses exposed. And as this pleasure washed over me in the theater, as

I burst out laughing, young Kazakh directors were making their grimy, unhappy films, movies so abrasive that at the 2008 Eurasia Film Festival, exasperated older filmmakers shouted, "Why is this all so ugly?" Films without pleasure and without national culture, made by asphalt children who have been set adrift, cut loose, who don't speak their ethnic languages, for whom the idea of Asia is emptied out. Rashid Nugmanov desired a film that was "perfectly meaningless—without meaning, without philosophy, without symbols—an empty shell."

I caught a gaze that wasn't looking my way. If I gaze back, am I a thief? Rashid Nugmanov stood in a temple garden in Kyoto. It was here that he conceived the idea of a film that rejected symbolism, philosophy, and even meaning itself. The stones of the garden seemed to him to be like that: speechless, void, and therefore ecstatically open to every kind of meaning. Their total stillness and detachment galvanized his heart. But of course the temple has history, the garden has history, the stones are cultural forms. So perhaps he was wrong, almost certainly he was wrong, this stranger in the black coat, but he lifted desire away from that garden, he breathed it in like vapor, he sank into it as I sank into the films of Central Asia, watching them in my dark bedroom, half asleep.

> The sun rises and sets behind the river.
> Someone is quietly singing ... ah, ah, ah.
> And in the algae, the green algae,
> The girl's body floats.

How often, in the films I watched, people began to sing. They sang out of nowhere, as if overwhelmed, in a dusty backyard, in a cell. Song knits these films together, forming a link between *Schizo* and a popular Uzbek hit like *Ali Baba and the Forty Thieves*, Latif Faiziyev's 1980 collaboration with the Indian director Umesh Mehra. The heroine in white, gazing beseechingly into the camera, unfolding one after the other her little plump palms. Her high, thin, meandering voice, floating over the ramparts of the city toward her rescuer, Ali Baba. Bollywood films are a major influence on Central Asian popular cinema, an influence scorned by young experimental directors like Adilkhan Yerzhanov of Kazakhstan, who declared that if people don't like reality, if they want entertainment, they should go and watch Indian films. But Aktan Arym Kubat knits up the attraction of Bollywood blockbusters, he sews it into his quiet 1998 film *Beshkempir: The Adopted Son*, a film that opens with a slow, deliberate shot of a quilt in lavish color: red, blue, green, pink. "My film is put together like patchwork," Arym Kubat explains. Most of the scenes are shot in black and white. Only at intervals a burst of color appears: a bird, a girl, a vivid screen showing an Indian movie. So Bollywood takes its place among scenes of fishing, winnowing, spinning. Arym Kubat describes *Beshkempir* as a funeral quilt. "Each piece of cloth contains information about a person who has passed away. According to custom, during the funeral such patches of material are distributed to all those who have come to remember the deceased. Then, a quilt is made from the collected scraps of fabric, which tells a story about each person who departs to the other world. My film is an attempt to create a collective memory of the Kyrgyz people." On reading this I wrote in my notebook, "Imagine a collective memory of the Mennonite people. The vastness of such a quilt." Except that instead of *quilt*, I wrote *guilt*, which indicates my distance from Aktan Arym Kubat, my admiration for his project and my gloom, because if I had trouble writing about Khudaybergen Divanov, it was just as hard to write about Claas Epp Jr., and I was hounded, I am still hounded by a feeling of having trespassed, of having committed, through writing, some dreadful, irreparable act, because I am writing not only across time but across bloodlines, across the border of race and also, what will be, to some people, of even greater significance, across the gap between my ancestors, who came from southern Germany and Switzerland, and those of the Bride Community, who came from northern Germany and Holland, and if you don't belong to one of these clans yourself, this probably seems like splitting hairs, but it doesn't look that way to the bearers of these bloodlines, who are, like the Kyrgyz, quilt-making people, but also accomplished quilt-tearers, prone to rupture, to cutting themselves off from one another, able to turn in an instant, it seems, from tight community to the flat rejection of shunning. In Pennsylvania's Big Valley, where my first ancestors to come to this country are buried, there are Amish groups, whose gene pool I share, who broke with each other long ago, and can now be distinguished by the colors of their buggies, the style of their suspenders, and whether or not they have screens on their doors. And it seems to me that no one who comes from a people who combine this maddening intolerance with an equally maddening attention to detail can ever achieve the lightness and openness of Aktan Arym Kubat, who sews a Bollywood movie so neatly into his quilt. I watched the effervescence of his films with a kind of ache. The scene of a game played on horseback in his 2010 *The Light Thief*, a very old game, what the Mennonite boys on the Great Trek called the devils-chase, the object of which is to seize a goat and carry it off on horseback. In the English credits for the film, the actors in this scene are listed under the delightful title "goat-grabbing players." I watched the goat-grabbing players entertain at a local festival, where people stood around in clumps, cheering, chatting. This scene was a gift to me, on a morning strafed by the hot Santa Ana winds, when I was forced to realize something I had suspected and then suppressed: the name Ikakjan Ikakjanova does not exist. It's simply not real. I had searched for it, in several forms, without finding a trace of it anywhere. On that blustery morning, I finally decided to give up the search. Surge of unhappiness, sudden desire for the films of Arym Kubat. Look: one of the spectators in *The Light Thief* has just been knocked off his bike in the crowd, and his friend whirls around on his horse, he picks up the fallen man. Now there are two of them on the horse, galloping off, settling themselves, wheeling, returning, reaching down together to snatch up the bicycle, hauling it up beside them and riding away again in rollicking triumph, just as if the bicycle were a goat.

> *Our hair is braided*
> *We don't know sadness*
> *It is time for us to sing love*
> *Like nightingales at dawn.*

That afternoon, I received an email from a friend, a professor of photography, informing me that there is no such thing as a German ZOT camera. Divanov used a Xit folding camera manufactured in London. Be true to history. Accept, at the same time, the spectral force. Admit that an image has pierced you across the stormy passage of years, changing your heartrate, and that this somatic effect may be of little use in an argument. When I had watched all the Central Asian films I could find, delved as deeply as my skills permitted into the history of photography in the region, I found no evidence of Wilhelm Penner or even Khudaybergen Divanov. Instead, I found a Kazakh director in Kyoto staring at stones. I found a light, a music. Images crossing me like sparks. Instead of gathering history, consolidating it, I felt myself dissolve. Radiated, strewn, I shimmered with pixelated feeling: a sense of being formed of myriad tiny points.

The lone curator

In Khiva, at the museum, I stand face-to-face with Khudaybergen Divanov's camera, the black cloth closed over it like an eyelid. I'm here, inside, at last. Nothing's gone wrong except that the lights aren't working today, so the blinds are slanted to let in the sun. I shift my position, sometimes crouching to see things more clearly, maneuvering in the glare. Here are his film canisters, his rifle case. A series of negatives under glass, the faces with their white eyes both phantasmal and strangely condensed, as if engraved. Everything calls for a tactile experience but can't be touched, oh his stylish little rounded sunglasses, his pocket watch, the beautiful Victrola like a black shell from the ocean tinged with green, cupped and fluted like an ear. Here are photographs I have never seen. Grinning men around a teapot. The musicians of the Khiva Theater, a man in the back row with his arm around a smiling woman in a scarf, pointing to her, half winking. An almost painful air of possibility. "Intelligentsia, 1930": fresh-faced women reclining in the foreground, young and summery in their slim white pumps. "Machine Operators, 1925": black hats, spectacles, again two women in the front row. And the woman in a vest, a circus performer, her curly hair, the way she stands half-turned between a pair of horses with bowed heads. As the room slowly fills up with the rest of my tour group, I walk in circles, ducking my head, experimenting with new angles of vision. In the flat glitter from the blinds, I feel like I'm reading by comet's light. I'm not close enough. It's not that I wish to possess the photograph of the circus performer, it's that I want to enter it, submerge myself in her glance, her slightly lost expression, her pallor, the practiced way she holds the horses, the space between her skirt and the animals' bodies, the scrap of coarse-looking grass, the layer of dust hanging over the earth, the air.

To document is to take on a project of cherishing. You decide, over and over, to honor a particular word, record, or memory. As your own work is constantly revised, you review the elements you've lifted from other texts again and again, as if rearranging objects in a museum. You are the lone curator of this work. You decide what to display, what to store in the endnotes, what to consign to the dark. Eventually, a permanent collection emerges: items you've chosen so many times that the sight of them brings up a flood of associations. These word-objects, polished with repeated cherishing, are your touchstones. Their presence alters your relationship to history, expanding your memory and infusing musty old books and blurry PDF files with a glow. For what was it that happened, really? I tried to enter a story and felt it disintegrate around me so that I had to hang it up on a few bare facts. Here are some bare facts: Khudaybergen Divanov went to the office to collect his pension. Three days later he was dead. How I hung it up. And now I'm feeling so close, so moved, but this feeling is based on nothing inevitable, I did it to myself. I gave myself this feeling of being disoriented in a strange room, of moving through spots of glaring light, of mourning a person I never knew, of missing a past that wasn't mine, of asking, Who is my neighbor?

The words *curate* and *cure*, I remember, are both related to *care*.

Everyone shines

Are you allowed to love a stranger? If so, what form should that love take? Is it permissible to identify with another? What if you're very ignorant, if you don't speak the other's language, if you're simply allowing the light to get into your eyes?

During my study of Central Asian film, I learned that cinema brought Langston Hughes to the Uzbek Soviet Socialist Republic. The poet was invited to act in a film called *Black and White*, written for a communist studio and set in the American South. Twenty-two Black Americans hired for the project set off from New York in June 1932. They reached Helsinki under the endless twilight of the white nights, then boarded a train for Moscow, where they stayed at the Grand Hotel, sleeping in gigantic beds from the czarist era and sampling caviar in the dark old dining room. They went to the opera, bathed nude in the Moscow River according to custom, and taught the locals the lindy hop in the bar at the Metropol, but they never made a movie. The script was ridiculous, according to Hughes, and to the dismay of the Russians, almost none of the Black comrades could sing. By September, plans for *Black and White* had collapsed. "In looking back at the saga of the twenty-two American Negroes who had spent their own money to go several thousand miles to make a picture with no contracts in front," wrote Hughes, "and, on the other hand, looking at a film concern that would bring to its studios such a group without exercising any sort of selectivity beforehand, I am amazed at the naiveté shown on both sides."

Most of the Americans went home once the project had failed, but Langston Hughes stayed and spent several months traveling around

Central Asia. This was his mirror, the place he longed to see: the Soviet Union's dusty, colored, cotton-growing South. His train passed Orenburg, where Asia begins, where he saw camels in the streets, then the sweeping steppe, then the silvery tip of the Aral Sea. His fellow passengers took out their balalaikas and danced in the aisle, and he reciprocated by playing them Louis Armstrong on his Victrola. "In the night air," he wrote, "there was the smell of the Orient—a kind of mixture of musk, melons and dust that seemed everywhere a part of the East. This smell, the tiny flares that in the early darkness augmented the streetlights, and here and there the sound of a muted lute, were my initial impressions of Tashkent." His welcome on the Tashkent platform, where Uzbeks, Turkmens, and Tartars in traditional dress approached him with fruit and flowers, differed dramatically from his arrival at the Ashkabad station a few days later, where he was dropped on a deserted platform without a town in sight. In the blazing sun, he carried his luggage into the silent station: first the heavy bags, then the smaller bag and lunchbox, and finally his typewriter, his Victrola, and the box of records, which seemed to weigh more than usual. A scorching wind filled the air with dust and sand. Wet with sweat and sticky with dirt, he gazed in helpless fury at the long empty track. The station master appeared and offered him a cigarette, saying *"Nichevo!"* which Hughes translates as "Anyhow, to hell with it!" Fortunately, he was rescued before too long by a car from town, which deposited him at a guesthouse near the public square, where a short time later he was jolted out of his nap by a bright-eyed, grinning youth in a spick-and-span Red Army uniform. This personage, who burst into the room after giving the door a single vigorous rap, shook Langston's hand while the poet was still in bed, addressing him with a long stream of speech, very musical and entirely incomprehensible. "There was at that time no one in Ashkabad who spoke English—not a human soul. My Red Army friend came from the high Pamirs up away near the Sinkiang border, and spoke only his own strange language. He was a captain of the border guard, and looked like a Chinese Negro, very brown, but with Oriental eyes. He was my friend for weeks, in fact my boon buddy, yet I never knew a word he said."

The captain's name was composed of two and a half or three syllables, and sounded like Yeah Tlang, Yaddle-oang, or Ya-Gekiang. Langston called him Yeah Man. Together they went to the circus, after which Yeah Man, a talented acrobat, repeated the performance of flips and flops all over Langston's room. They called on various girls in the town, bearing gifts of bread or brandy, crossing the park where the billboards of Lenin and Stalin stood veiled with dust. Yeah Man, Langston noticed, ate his fruit whole, including the seeds, cracking plum and apricot pits with his teeth. Outgoing, intensely active, a stout vodka drinker and woman chaser, Yeah Man stands in direct contrast to the other friend Langston made in Ashkabad: the writer Arthur Koestler, who knocked at his door one night when he was expecting Yeah Man, as if a conjurer's trick had substituted one man for the other. The young Koestler, then a communist, was researching a series of articles on Soviet achievements. He was restless and choleric, with a sharp face and sleek dark hair. Where Yeah Man distracted Langston from writing, Koestler, who never stopped working, shamed the poet into purchasing half a dozen oilcloth-covered notebooks. So Langston began to take notes. He took notes on the cotton mill, the botanical institute, and the school for railroad workers. He took notes on Arthur Koestler, whose German sense of sanitation made him miserable in the shabby guesthouse. "If the Revolution had only occurred in Germany," Koestler lamented, "at least it would have been a clean one." He was especially upset by the custom of sharing tea bowls: "slobbering in each other's bowls—a bloody disgusting filthy habit!" Langston, too, had been taken aback at first by the ritual of passing tea bowls around a circle, but he soon got over his squeamishness, and even resigned himself to the risk of catching tuberculosis from one of their visitors, a wizened Turkmen with a hacking cough. He resigned himself to letting something pass through him. He let go. He was moved by the Ashkabad film school, where Russians—*white* men!—taught acting, set building, and camera work. "I could not help but think how impregnable Hollywood had been to Negroes, and how all over America the union of motion-picture operators did not permit Negroes to operate projection machines, not even in theaters in Negro neighborhoods. Negro-owned establishments had to employ white projectionists. When I told this to Koestler, he said he could hardly believe it. But I was trying to make him understand why I observed the changes in Soviet Asia with *Negro* eyes."

———

His favorite film:

It is night. Snow. Across the Siberian border the soldier-provocateurs of Manchuria are firing into the Soviet defenses where Red Army men stand guard. The scene changes to the inside of the Soviet barracks. Officers and men are shown fraternizing together, laughing, shaving, playing cards. Suddenly the door opens and a man from the front is carried in dead. His body is placed in a bunk and the sheet drawn over him. A young Russian soldier, fists doubled, rises from the card game and begins to curse those slant-eyed bastards who have killed his comrade. Quietly, an officer goes toward the body, draws back the sheet so that the Russian boy may see the still, brown face there, and says simply, "Our comrade's eyes are slant eyes too."

A sentimental movie, obscuring inequalities with a saccharine haze. "A most beautiful film," wrote Langston, "with a powerful musical score." I am amazed at the naiveté shown on both sides. I read the poem dedicated to Langston by the Uzbek poet Karim Ahmedi:

> *Crossing many oceans, you've come*
> *Leaving your family behind.*
> *I saw you and felt wrapped in the curls of your hair.*

And how Langston responds. His poetry collection *The Weary Blues* is the first American book to appear in Uzbek translation. It includes six poems written in Uzbekistan, perhaps on the yellow paper of those oilcloth-covered notebooks. The English versions of these poems are lost. Retranslated from Uzbek by Muhabbat Bakaeva and Kevin Young, the poems throb with fellow feeling, they glimmer with dewy exaltation.

Look: here
Is a country
Where everyone shines

The cinema is a zone of sentiment. We go there to feel. Hamid Ismailov, in his novel *The Railway*, describes a movie theater in a small Uzbek town where people cry so hard their tears flood the aisles. Cinema is utopian because group feeling is utopian. It's utopian to believe you can share a feeling with someone else. At the same time, the gaze maintains its aggression. Someone must die on the screen, must be sacrificed to the communal river of tears. And so, you see, I don't know how to go on. I'm afraid to put a foot wrong. "I called him Yeah Man," wrote Langston, "and he called me Yang Zoon." It's sentimental to think you can be best friends without sharing a language. Langston was horrified by the script for *Black and White*. "With his heart in the right place, with the best will in the world, the Russian writer, who had never been to America, had committed errors so egregious they rendered the story impossible." In one scene, for example, a white man at a party asked a "lovely dark-skinned servant" to dance. In pre-Soviet Russia it might have been possible for a master, in the spirit of fun, to tread a measure with a maid, but in the Jim Crow South the proposed scene was ludicrous, grotesque. When Langston read the script, he laughed until he cried.

Saturated

Frank quirks an eyebrow at me. "Are you saturated?" he asks. Everybody else is filing out of the room, while I stare with fixed intensity at a portrait of a noble family, a little boy in the front smeared like wax because he couldn't hold still. "Yes," I sigh, and stash my notebook in my bag. Frank laughs good-naturedly at my stiffened claw-hand, cramped from taking notes. We catch up with the rest of the group on the way to the fortress of the khans, built in the twelfth century, the oldest structure in Khiva. Here Usmon, who was rather subdued in the Divanov room, bounces back into life, striding along the familiar ground of the Silk Road. The bricks of the palace, he informs us in a ringing voice, were made with straw and camel wool, to keep away the insects. Inside the walls, in the lofty, gorgeous, open-air Summer Mosque, the majolica tiles are white (lead), turquoise (copper sulfate), and indigo (original recipe lost). The butterflies of green stone sunk in the bricks outside the khan's bedroom are Zoroastrian, the origin of the symbols on modern public restrooms. I have trouble matching these bow-tie shapes with anything I've seen on a bathroom door, but Usmon is leading us on, to the khan's Complaining Room—"Every house should have one of those," Arnie murmurs—where the ruler received petitions from his subjects, including the Mennonites. The Complaining Room is a courtyard with a large stone dais where, in winter, the khan would pitch his yurt and listen to grievances in its snug warmth. Musicians would play from the upper floors. The Mennonites, Frank says, would have entered the court through the middle door, the one for foreigners.

For a moment I'm struck by the elegant arrangement of the khans of Khiva. They built three doors: one for commoners, one for foreigners, and one for local dignitaries. Everybody knew how to enter the story. This neat organization impresses me exactly as long as it takes to stroll over to the little former prison. "Mind you head!" an attendant calls out gently as we enter, her concern almost immediately taking on an ironic tinge, since as soon as we've ducked through the doorway, we come face-to-face with a painting of Tomyris, a local Scythian queen, holding a decapitated head. This head belonged to Cyrus the Great, Emperor of Persia and, according to Herodotus and Usmon, a treacherous jerk, who got the Scythians drunk and then slaughtered them (wine was unknown to these nomads, whose party drink was fermented mare's milk spiked with hash). In revenge, Tomyris chopped off Cyrus's head and dunked it in a wineskin full of human blood. The painting hangs among antique knouts and shackles. The room is incredibly hot. Usmon describes the punishments of the khans, which include lashes, dismemberment, and being sewn up in a bag of live cats. That's the end of my admiration for the khan's three doors, because there's always a fourth door, and it leads in here. I want to get back outside, but I'm brought up short by a little collection of black-and-white photographs of policemen, taken, of course, by Khudaybergen Divanov.

I wonder if he was arrested by some of these very cops before he entered the fourth door and died in some desolate place. Now their faces adorn the wall of this room where the attendant smiles indulgently from her chair, knitting, despite the cauldron-like heat, something large, complicated, and floral in design, like a lighter, more flexible form of the Summer Mosque, and occasionally cautioning "Mind you head!" in a flutelike voice. Two balls of yarn, blue and white, lie beside her on a ledge, along with her plugged-in cell phone, under a rack of swords. The scene is so surreal, I feel almost dazed, but the photographs also spark something in my memory: according to Frank, who mentioned it earlier today, Kholid is a distant relative of Khudaybergen Divanov.

"Kholid!" I say in excitement. "Do you know the name of Divanov's wife?"

Yes, he knows. He writes it in my notebook: *Bikajanbika Atajanova*. And this feels like the conclusion to my Divanov study: not the map of a tradition that began with Wilhelm Penner, but two words written by another's hand, identifying a woman long dead, in an old torture chamber, among the empty chains.

I'm not local

I never touched Divanov, never found him, yet I can feel that something has been. Out in the courtyard, the air is still hot but looser, finer. It must be very safe here, because someone has left a cell phone charger and ID badge on a table: evidence of another of those ghostly attendants of Uzbek museums, who, when not knitting, seem to be always off on mysterious errands.

We cross the courtyard and enter a garden with a double lamppost. Invisible birds are shrilling in the trees. Are these the famous nightingales? They sound frantic, like alarms, or more precisely (if you're familiar) like a hundred Egyptian doorbells. Here is the mausoleum of a local saint, Pahlavan Mahmoud (I admit to having looked this name up later, and to having written down at the time *Baklava Mahmoud*). He was a poet, says Usmon, a Sufi, and a wrestler. This is very exotic to the Mennonites in our party, since our tradition is long on spiritual wrestlers but short on guys who will actually pin you. Unlike the rest of the complex, the mausoleum has a number of visitors, mostly local families, their children running around. At the door, the women tourists in our group respectfully cover up with the headscarves we always carry as instructed by the tour company. We are the only ones so veiled. Nozli trips in comfortably bareheaded, like all the other women who live here, who feel at home in the shrine. This reminds me of days in Egypt when, knowing Egyptians are always at least an hour late for any scheduled appointment, my husband and I would take our time preparing for guests to arrive. Meanwhile, our guests, knowing Americans are at least an hour early for everything, would show up long before the agreed time. Snazzily dressed, bearing sweets and flowers, they'd find me scrubbing the floor in a t-shirt and my husband standing over a pot of raw potatoes. Sometimes getting along with people is like doing research in translation. I can hear the birds in the garden yammering like a presage of early guests, the noise weaving in and out of the sound of a red-haired young imam who kneels in the shrine, chanting in a strong head voice. Kholid says he's reciting a prayer for the repose of the dead. People come here to listen and take a blessing. Some of the women are probably here to pray for children: there's a well in the garden where they voice this particular appeal. After she prays, if a woman sees a sun inside the well, she'll have a boy, and if she sees the moon, she'll have a girl. Sometimes, Kholid adds, a boy is brought here for a blessing after his circumcision, dressed like a little khan.

Enveloped in sound, I remember my notes on the distant city of Shakhrisabz, especially the story of a shrine located there, the grave of a man known as Faqiri, a Sufi poet, like Pahlavan Mahmoud, but born into different times, his education disrupted by Soviet laws. First the madrasas were closed, and then his sheikh was banned from public teaching, requiring his students to study by correspondence. Due to this break in his training, Faqiri believed himself incapable of passing on a spiritual legacy dating back to the sixteenth century. He died in 1980, a blind recluse. But his grave immediately became a place of pilgrimage.

Faqiri thought he was finished. He didn't believe in distance learning. But other people reestablished the links. As we walk back to the hotel, I ask Kholid if he knows the work of Langston Hughes, the first American writer published in Uzbek translation. I'm hoping to hear that *The Weary Blues* is an Uzbek bestseller and part of the high school curriculum. But Kholid, a bookish person, has never heard of the poet. After the sweltering afternoon, a milky sheen is slipping over the sky, so that the sun seems both diluted and broader, blurred at the edges. In the deep streets of the old town, the shade has the color of dried rose petals. TV sets babble behind the medieval walls. Kholid asks if I've heard of the famous Uzbek poets Hamid Olimjon and his wife Zulfiya. I haven't, so it's Kholid's turn to feel deflated. "They are considered," he says in a melancholy tone, "a romantic and trustworthy couple." I promise to look them up. I stop at a cart where women are selling woolen mittens with intricate black-and-white designs. It's an odd thing to buy, or sell, in Uzbekistan in June, but I instantly fall in love with these mittens and buy a pair. Kholid says German women who came to Uzbekistan in the 1940s taught women to knit mittens, but Khivan women already knew how: they'd learned from the Mennonites.

The sky grows denser, curdled, and there's no accounting for all the ways we enter each other's stories, no algorithm. As if reminded by the mittens, Kholid tells me the Mennonites brought several new vegetables to Khiva, so people here cooked with them while they were still unknown to the rest of Central Asia. Tomatoes, cucumbers, cabbages, eggplants. A popular dish called *nan qavurdaq* was developed with the new produce, a stew of cabbage, tomatoes, and sweet peppers. Poor people dip their bread in it. It's one of Kholid's childhood favorites. Brightness quivers in the brown water of the pond outside the hotel. My skin tingles; I think an electrical storm is coming. I feel crossed by currents of energy, as on those mornings when I watched Central Asian films: open, atomized, and stray, not as if I'm lost but as if I'm turning into a cloud of dots. I can feel the hours of my Divanov study, my dark bedroom, the light of the laptop on my face, the images flooding me like water, the syllables of Uzbek (a clatter) and Russian (dispensed in thick bursts, as if forced through a tube) going into my ears, my brain, my blood. How to keep track of such echoes darting through every single person? And how much can you really learn from a genealogical study, when the genes belong to people traversed by so many wild, fleeting influences? Even Menno Simons, Kholid has read, was interested in the East.

Before he leaves for the evening, Kholid tells a joke that feels like a warning against a certain nervous hyperawareness of borders (or maybe I take it that way because I have that kind of nerves). In the joke, a guy is walking through a strange town. A second guy, native to the town, comes up to him and asks, "Hey! Is that the moon or the sun in the sky?" This part confuses me, honestly: why didn't Guy Number Two know if it was the moon or the sun? Was he drunk? Convalescent? Befuddled by a long nap? But the point of the joke isn't Guy Number Two, it's Guy Number One, the traveler, who raises his hands, as Kholid demonstrates, with an exaggerated show of caution, and answers with a claim so absurd, it pokes fun at Guy Number Two and slyly emphasizes the oneness of the world: "I'm not local."

Love story

Thunder over the city. My wet hair tied on top of my head, I dig through my suitcase while Diane takes her turn in the shower. Compressed between one of my flip-flops and Elizabeth's diary is an essay on the Mennonites by the Uzbek scholar Dilaram Inoyatova. This is what I'm looking for: the shadow of a love story, a passion that lives on in a pair of sentences. "People who had lived in the colony for a long time remember how one young Khoresani who had worked in the German colony fell in love with a Mennonite. The young people married, but they were shunned by the community."

I see a young woman unlatching a door, so quietly, holding her breath. She opens it just wide enough to slip through. It's after midnight, a moonless night, sheer black, the darkness so complete she can't make out the wall of the church. Analyze culture, history, studium to your heart's content; there will still be punctum, the unexpected, dazzling accident. What Kuziev called "a chain of surprising events full of deep meaning." I wonder how it was for this young woman of Ak Metchet, this shade, this footnote. I wonder about the "young Khoresani," if he was the worker described to Ella Maillart, the one who spoke "our Platt-Deutsch," who couldn't accept the idea of fifteen plates. I wonder what life was like for the new bride. I imagine she had a Muslim wedding somewhere in the town. I wonder how she left the house, if there were arguments, tears, a glacial silence, perhaps a gift of money shoved hastily into her hand. I wonder if she left in secret. She closes the door behind her with infinite prudence, infinite solicitude. He's outside the wall, waiting with a horse. He helps her up. The deep night. His cold belt against her wrist.

EIGHT

Ak Metchet

the world didn't end

This is our valley

The Mennonites of Ak Metchet board a boat on the Amu Darya. They wave their white handkerchiefs. They are being deported into the desert. Goodbye, goodbye. They weep. They sing, "God be with us till we meet again." The moon rises above the river.

Rain on the road, rare for the time of year. The asphalt gleams, the canals run high, and a hard patter falls like beads on the roof of the bus. We turn off onto a rough, muddy road, crossing stream after stream, or perhaps it's all the same stream, I wipe the steamy windowpane with my sleeve, there's a vista of wet green banks, the steel-gray ponds of the fishery reflecting the clouds, and little pale flashes as the rain falls on the canals. How different it all is from the image that brought me here:

Ella Maillart's photograph of Ak Metchet in its arid stillness! In this watery landscape, everything moves. Rivulets course down the sheepskins hanging on courtyard walls. Women wave from a window: red and gold sleeves.

The bus pulls over. We disembark, a jostling and eager line of pilgrims, opening our umbrellas under a row of dripping trees, taking deep breaths of the springy, resinous air—*their* air, I can't help thinking, though I know it's not possible to taste the air of the past. Still, I breathe. The sky between the branches looks spongy, distended, ready to leak out water and light at the touch of a finger. Our hosts come to greet us: the retired headmaster and his brother, and Mr. Karimov, the leader of a project to open a Mennonite museum in Khiva. Frank shakes hands with them, exuberant, shouting introductions, so happy to be here at last, drops bouncing from the brim of his canvas hat, and me, I've got my head tilted, umbrella gripped in the crook of my neck, notebook balanced on one arm, I'm writing. *Shelter of the porch*, I write as we enter that shelter. *Yellow brick floor. A ladder of trimmed branches against the wall. Roof of branches, logs, sacks. Rope on a windowsill. Trowel. Window frame of iron pipes.* There's nothing here I could have predicted, nothing that speaks to me of the past. Yet everything seems to tell me they were here. It's absence that fills me, absence I've come here to feel, like a long ache. Of pilgrimage, Usmon says, "It's better to go once than to hear about it a million times."

In Shakhrisabz, I have read, the *chakar* is used as a spatial measure: the distance a shout can travel across the mountains.

I wish I could get close enough to shout. Standing in this porch, I imagine what happened here, what it must have been like: waking up the day after the failure of prophecy. Imagine the second time, the second promise and disappointment, two years after the first. That's the one that demands my attention: the day all hope was lost. In my mind, it's a mirror of the day the Mennonites were deported. In the deportation, they were torn from the world of Ak Metchet. In the breakdown of prophecy, their world, the cosmos they knew, was torn from them.

Picture the time. The beginning of spring. Buds on the poplar trees. But they were not meant to witness this earthly growth. They were meant to be with God. How to come back from such a fall? I imagine the hushed village. People staying indoors as much as they can, unwilling to meet each other. A child, alone, trotting along a wall, carrying a pail, off to the desert to collect dried dung for fuel.

Go to the well. The bucket. The bright white walls. Water the garden. Weed the cold earth. Dirt in the nails. Keep moving. Hands.

It is no sin to be angry with God. *Wherefore hast thou brought me forth out of the womb?* cries Job. *Oh that I had given up the ghost, and no eye had seen me!*

Anger. Grief. And is there also a certain lightness? The walls of Ak Metchet are steeped in silver, clarified by mourning. In the raw March air a smell of relief. The lamps have gone out, the Bridegroom has failed to arrive, and the Bride sits silent, numb. It's over.

Over. And the sky comes in. And all the clouds.

Behold, he cometh with clouds.

Read the Bible, always. As the day draws to a close. The mosque call lingering in the brown sky. Against the curtains, a last peach-colored ray. And then the benediction of night.

In the stillness, a sound of footsteps in the square. Lean to the window. It's the night fisherman, with his silken beard. They call him Grandfather Lantern. He is going down to the river, a lamp on a pole over his shoulder. The orange light turns the whole scene blue.

It must be a matter of going on like this, one day after another.

Tentatively tracing the contours of the new world. The Bridegroom will not come. Instead, the irises will bloom. In May the heat will rise, and the mulberries will ripen. June will bring the wheat, July the grapes and corn, the airless nights, and the torment of the mosquitoes and the sand flies. And they will still be here, among the stunted olive trees, the drooping figs. Buying meat from the butcher's shop, by the sooty wall studded with nails. On these nails, pieces of a ram's carcass are arranged for display. The butcher stands in his greasy robe and sharpens his knife. And perhaps they will begin to feel that this is becoming their world, this knife, these nails, the shouts of the boys driving crows and starlings from the millet fields, the alarmed birds rising, the silver poplars, the plowmen singing ghazals, and the shepherds grazing their sheep in the cemetery. The merchant with his rugs spread under a tree, his stacks of cotton and chintz, his rows of buttons, tin mirrors, and cones of soap. The girls looking over his wares, buying pine tar to chew, their saffron-colored palms, their earrings so heavy they wear them in their hair. Perhaps, on a summer evening when the merchants of Khiva are closing up their stalls, when the women, cloaked in blue and gray, are hurrying home, when the wind drops and the earth releases a quiet, humid breath, while a pink luminescence streaks the waist-high seas of alfalfa—perhaps then they will think, *This is our valley. We have no other.* And this strange land, where they never intended to stay for very long, will draw them gently in and hold them close, like a woman who, to hatch a silkworm egg, carries it under her breast.

The historians

A sodden tour of the village. The edges of our umbrellas knock together as we walk. Voices fly back and forth around us: the voices of our hosts, and of Kholid's father, the scholar of Mennonite history, who has joined us for the day. Also, of course, the voices of Kholid and Usmon translating, interpreting, explaining. We step carefully in the deep mud, in the rain that retreats and then returns. This is Ak Metchet. This was the Mennonite graveyard: a broken wall and a lonely stretch of grass, mud, and straw. Here is a pear tree descended from Mennonite trees. This was their well. And this blackened, craggy stump at the edge of a drowned field: it's all that remains of an elm planted by the Mennonites long ago. We slip in the muck; a child dressed in turquoise and pink watches us from a doorway. "Ladies and gentlemen," Usmon calls out, testing the planks of a bridge with his foot, "I wouldn't suggest you to rely on this bridge." Laughing, we cross over. In a stable we see a spotted cow, black and white, partly descended from Mennonite Holsteins.

"Holsteins are mean," says Evelyn. She remembers growing up on a farm, and a certain malevolent Holstein named Blue Cheer. Even hobbled, Blue Cheer could kick the pail over. "How did we fasten the tail?" Evelyn wonders, stumbling over a gap in her memory. Lois answers promptly, "You had to catch it in the hobble." This knowledgeable talk of cattle reminds me of my Mennonite aunts and uncles, raised on a dairy farm, but it's now that I learn Evelyn isn't Mennonite: her background is German Catholic, and she's a member of the American Historical Society of Germans from Russia. It's the Russian and German connections that have brought her on this tour. Although I didn't recognize her surname, I thought she must be Mennonite, because of her youth on a farm, because I've heard her talk about gardening and canning, because she's here. I couldn't tell the difference.

Our hosts all talk to us at once: the retired headmaster, his brother, and Mr. Karimov of the Mennonite museum project. They wear crisp hats— two embroidered, one smart flat cap—and beautifully creased shirts and trousers. They take us to the school, to a classroom furnished with modern desks and chairs and then, at the back of the room, the Mennonite desks. These centenarian benches are massive, heavy, gnarled, as if chopped from petrified logs, as if dredged up from the bottom of the sea. I have to wonder what it means to sit here, in the back, if the children like it or if it's a kind of punishment. The desks are lumpy yet shiny, abraded by paper, burnished by fingers, almost black. The room can't assimilate them; they're alien with age. Above them hang eight colored drawings of Uzbek intellectuals, five of whom lost their lives in the Great Terror. It's summer, there's no school, but slowly the room begins to fill up, teenage girls sneak in whispering, smaller children gather at the door, perhaps the ones who will later receive the candy we've brought for the headmaster, the notebooks, the pens and pencils, the balloons. The room grows crowded and noisy, everyone angling to take photographs. A cardboard model is carried in like a great cake. It's a model of the old Mennonite village, created by some of the children as a history project: trees cut out with scissors, houses constructed with paste. Here are the trim white buildings, here is the cemetery we saw, the one that's overgrown now. In the crush I can only glimpse the model in sections. Overlaid with shoulders, arms, and cell phones, it's a collage. One paper tree won't stand, and a hand keeps coming down to straighten it, tenderly.

It happens under the portrait of Alisher Navoi, the great defender of Turkic, the father of literary Uzbek. The one who proved that Turkic, like Persian, was suitable for poetry, that it wasn't just a military language.

Out in the schoolyard, the children give us sprigs of basil. A piece of the garden in the hand, later crushed in a pocket, diffusing scent. They cluster around us, gesturing, they want to have their pictures taken, then look at the photographs, the cell phones' tiny mirrors. A child in red, clutching a red umbrella. Some razor-winged bird flies into an apple tree, releasing a spray of drops. The Mennonites always had their own school, separate from the Soviet schools, staffed only by themselves, like a madrasa. They had their scrubbed white church, their Ak Metchet. I ask if it's true that the village was named for their church. As usual, there's more than one answer. In one version, yes, people named this place Ak Metchet because of the church. In another version, it already had that name: it was *waqf* land, donated for the purposes of charity, an endowment named for the Ak Metchet mosque in Khiva.

Behind the school, in the shelter of the eaves, the retired headmaster's brother has arranged a display of things the Mennonites left behind. Irons like chunks of volcanic stone. Once, these heavy instruments, filled with hot coals, pressed the coats and pleated dresses of Ak Metchet. A metal pitcher, a window frame, a pot. A skeletal sewing machine, attenuated, with a long, sharp beak. I lean over these objects with my fellow pilgrims, with Frank and Kholid, with Kholid's father, our hosts, and the teachers from the school. All of us admiring, as if before a tray of jewels, the metal pail, the battered wooden box, and the rusty cage of an old lantern, inside which a candle or vessel of oil was once placed to light the way across the bridge to the dark stable. Strange how the Mennonite trek, a journey in anticipation of the world's end, has produced this pilgrimage to mundane things, this group of people enthralled by flaking paint and dented tin. We are historians, documentarists: we love this world.

Love story (second draft)

Frank asks our hosts about the rumored love affair. He has found a different version of the story, according to which it wasn't, as Dilaram Inoyatova heard, an Uzbek man who married a Mennonite woman, but a Mennonite man who married an Uzbek woman.

At this, the retired headmaster steps forward, in front of his brother. Each of these brothers received a Mennonite inheritance from their father: one got the objects, the other got the stories. The retired headmaster, custodian of the stories, says that both versions of the rumor circulate, though it's believed there was only one affair. The more popular version claims that a Mennonite girl ran off with an Uzbek man. But Frank says he asked some Mennonites in Germany about it, some of the descendants of the Ak Metchet group, and one woman insisted there *was* a Mennonite man involved—it was her father! A widower with three children, he abandoned them to elope with a Khivan woman and was excommunicated. I can feel the story shifting, finding its way at a slightly different angle, adjusting itself like a joint in a socket. The woman I imagined slipping out of a house evaporates. In her place stands a man in a dark hat. The story inverts, reinvents itself in this courtyard scattered with apricot pits, against a bright background of grass, the deeper green of the pear trees. Here where the rough old Mennonite objects are laid out with great care, as on an altar. Yes, the retired headmaster says, there was an Uzbek woman. She outlived her Mennonite husband by many years. Twenty years ago, she could still be seen in the village. He himself saw her standing on her feet.

Prayer

A history constantly revised. I have read that at Ak Metchet, in springtime, they pray for the health of the crops at the old Mennonite cemetery, and return at harvest time to offer prayers of thanksgiving. This, because the Mennonites were such fine farmers. But now, no, I'm told something else, that these are not prayers for the crops but simply prayers for the dead, for the souls of the dead, because they were good neighbors. The Mennonites are still being held, cared for, in this place. I think of Shakhrisabz, where, at the grave of Timur's beloved son Jehangir, twenty sheep were cooked daily and distributed to the poor: the father's ritualized remembrance of his son.

The retired headmaster tells us how the Mennonites were taken away. It was June 18, 1935. (Today, I mark in my notebook, is June 14, so it was summer then, too, though most likely hot and sunny, without this rain that, we've been told, falls in this season no more than twice in a century.) Eighteen trucks drove into the village. Each deportee was permitted to pack one sack of belongings. The rest of their things were loaded onto the trucks, separate from the people, except for a few items hurriedly given away, like the ones inherited by the retired headmaster's family. It was around lunchtime, very sudden. The Khivans who worked for the Mennonites or lived nearby were in an uproar, running after the trucks, shouting and weeping for their neighbors. And that was the end: a community snatched up, removed in the blink of an eye, in a chilling parody of the Rapture.

But the end was not the end, because here we are. The rain thins until it seems to be no longer falling but hanging in the air. Walking through the vineyard of the khan's summer palace, among the green vines, in the gold shimmer of the last drops, is like being wrapped in some rare brocade. The doors of this palace were constructed by Mennonites. "They're as good as the day they were made," says Frank, touching a jamb, and his palpable happiness, his pride in these sturdy, handsome doors, seems to me to carry a feeling just as durable, a reverence toward work that links him to the vanished craftsmen.

Inside, in a carpeted nineteenth-century hall, we attend a music performance: a series of songs by a group wearing brilliant satin outfits, the women tinkling with coins, the men and the two little boys in sheepskin caps. The whole troupe bears a strong family resemblance. The men play the accordion, horn, and drum; the boys click castanets. A woman in red takes center stage, executing a stately whirl, the coins on her bodice and her gold tooth flashing. The highlight of the performance is a dance by the two slim, active little boys, who shake their fingers at each other and puff out their cheeks. They're doing this, Kholid explains, because they're gophers; the dance is meant to represent a gopher hunt. The adult musicians shout encouragingly at the boys, whose wooly white hats stand out against the richly decorated walls, and I wonder how old this dance is, if it was ever performed for Muhammad Rahim Khan II, the owner of the palace and protector of the Mennonites, plump and dignified in his portrait by Khudaybergen Divanov, under his tall black hat, a sword across his knees.

Above us, a crystal chandelier. The strings of beads reflect the electric candles, creating a blaze, an effulgence of starry light, so that I have to squint through my lashes in order to make out the painted ceiling, the clump of gaudy curlicues around the base of the chandelier, a tacky painting, I would say if I had no connection to it, the colors pasty and flat, the border a spindly peacock-feather design, and at the center a rural landscape painted by Mennonite artists: yellow-green Russian fields, the blue Volga, and a windmill.

The drum throbs. There is another life in Paradise, Kholid has told us. There is a life that starts when the heart stops beating. We must pray for the souls of the dead because they need it, because these prayers are their sustenance. Prayer for them is like food for us.

The returnee

I want to know if Otto Toews made the *plov*. The visitor from Tajikistan, the one who returned in the 1970s—did he fulfill his father's directive to cook plov for their former neighbors? Outside the bus, as we get ready to board and return to Khiva, Kholid asks his father, the specialist in the history of the Ak Metchet Mennonites, who tells us, yes, Otto Toews did make the plov. He purchased ten kilos of rice, as well as the necessary meat and carrots. He hired men to cook it, and fifty people were served. Kholid's father speaks in a quiet tone, very much like his son, so that when Kholid delivers the translation it sounds as if the same voice is magically rippling into English without breaking its flow. The rain has stopped, leaving behind a soft, purplish sky; mist clings among the poplar and mulberry trees. The *Aksakal*, the village elder, gave Otto Toews a formal introduction, Kholid's father tells us, and people rose to embrace the returnee. There is a way of greeting a holy person: you touch the person's shoulder, near the heart, then bring your hand to your own forehead. This gesture recognizes that the person is surrounded by a sanctuary. Otto Toews was greeted this way, because of collective memory. He was staying in a Soviet hotel, a miserable place, but he was polite and humble. He felt happy there.

The leaky caravanserai

And yet it's not enough, is it? Hospitality. It's not enough, because the guest is never at home. There's always this discomfort. You're not sure which towel to use. A guest, no matter how kindly treated, feels a certain alienation, a pressure toward gratitude and conformity. On the bus, Frank asks me to talk to the group about my dad, so I tell one of Dad's favorite stories: the one about the traveler and the leaky caravanserai. This story was told by a medieval Arab philosopher, I believe, though I can't remember who it was. This philosopher was asked which religion was best: Christianity or Islam? And in response, he told a story about a traveler. I'm retelling this story into a microphone on a swaying bus, as it makes its way through the outskirts of Khiva. The traveler stopped at a caravanserai, but the roof in his room started leaking, so he switched to another room. However, the roof in that room also leaked! Both Islam and Christianity are leaky rooms, according to the philosopher. The point is, you might as well stay in the room you started out with. It occurs to me that this is sort of a mean story to tell to a group of Mennonites, a way of saying my dad felt weary or disgusted about religion, that he regretted having joined the Mennonite Church, yes, I can feel that telling this story is a bit passive-aggressive, a mode of interaction Swiss Mennonites are geniuses at by the way, and I also wonder what our Uzbek hosts are thinking, especially Kholid, who asked me about my dad's religion over lunch. It's not enough to let people into your story, you also have to let them out. You have to allow your own children to go and be guests somewhere else. That's what people can't bear. In Egypt I was told it might be dangerous to tell people my dad was Somali, because then they'd know he was, or had been, Muslim. I heard different things about what might happen then. It might just cause a change

in the atmosphere, a jolt, like when I told my Arabic teacher, the way
her face fell, the tightness in her voice as she said, "We don't have that
here." Or some might say I should be punished for marrying a Christian
man, I should get a hundred lashes. For a while this really scared me.
When I visited Khartoum I told people my dad was Ethiopian. Then I
got tired of this, and I'm still tired. I think of Paul retelling the story
of his conversion, the story that made him: *And last of all he was seen of
me also, as of one born out of due time.* That weird phrase, "one born out of
due time," which my Bible glosses as "an abortive." I once read a com-
mentary that said Paul's talking about being a convert: that he's "born
out of due time" because he wasn't born naturally into Christianity but
hauled there in some kind of divine caesarian section. I don't really get
this, but I get that a convert is a misborn person. I get what it means to
be considered tainted, shameful—in Arabic, *haram*—and on the other
hand to be regarded as a trophy. To be reviled by one group, sometimes
almost against their will, as they instinctively recoil, and to be held up
by the other group as a symbol of missionary success.

Hospitality isn't enough. What's needed, I think more and more, is
the transformation of home into an alien place. In Khiva, Mr. Karimov
unlocks the door of the Mennonite museum: a special gift to us, as
the museum has not officially opened. Here, in a bare gallery that was
once a trading house, we view a heavily annotated photograph album,
packed with descriptions and dates, from which the museum team has
reconstructed Mennonite clothing of the last century. A woman from
the team, standing in the light from a doorway, shows us a dark dress
with a small lace collar and cuffs, meticulously copied by someone—
perhaps the woman herself—who must have spent hours poring over
these photographs. Mr. Karimov holds up a child's outfit to show us
the little white apron. How gently they are carrying our ghosts. How
persistently, despite opposition from the state, which has denied them a

permit to open the museum, they are preserving this strange episode in Khiva's history. Here, it seems possible to recognize home as the site of transit, not ownership, a zone shot through with innumerable rays. The moral of the story of the leaky caravanserai is that we're all travelers and it's raining everywhere.

At night, in the hotel, I begin to write. Not to record, not to take notes on the day just past, but simply to write, in a stream, for hours. My knees drawn up, Diane asleep in the next bed, the neon light of the hotel sign coming in at the window, I enter memory.

Stories of brown girlhood

At fourteen, the child is sent to a Mennonite school in Pennsylvania. She is glad to go, for she is a delicate child who reads too much, and reading too much has made her socially backward in a way that creates problems for her at the rough New Jersey high school. She is transported over a green expanse with her suitcase, her pillow, her laundry hamper, her boxed set of J. R. R. Tolkien books. At her new school, she notices immediately and with a thrill that while there are lockers, there are no locks. So this is a land without crime.

She walks clasping her books. She wears a red shirt with a yellow jumper made by her mother, an outfit her best friend calls ketchup and mustard. The child has made several best friends. In the dormitory the phone peals down the hall and everyone rushes to answer it. There is a yellow light. There is a lounge where you can sit and the boys will give you backrubs. There is a cafeteria where the child washes dishes. The women who work at the cafeteria wear little white net coverings on their heads, or sometimes a piece of lace fastened with a pin. The round covering is known among the dormitory girls as the Egg McMuffin, the piece of lace is called a doily. Dimly the child understands that she exists somewhere between the cafeteria women and the Ethiopian students who receive hot spices from home in plastic bags.

In the dorm you can wear whatever you want, but at school you have to wear skirts. You can't wear earrings, though some girls get away with it by claiming they've just had their ears pierced: they have to keep their studs in, they whine, or the holes will grow shut. For boys, the hair must be short enough that it doesn't hide the collar. Shoulders must be covered, and in music class, on a hot spring day, the child, who has taken off her blazer, is told to put it back on, to conceal the bony brown shoulders and the colorful flowered shell she made in a sewing class. The teacher is annoyed, and the child feels frightened but also powerful, like a bad girl. She rolls her eyes, putting on the dull blue blazer, a garment she also made in sewing class, very badly, a near-impossible architectural project. She bends to her work: she is writing, as an assignment, a hymn in four parts. Another near-impossible architectural project. As a text she has chosen Matthew 11:28: *Come unto me, all ye that labor and are heavy laden, and I will give you rest.*

An era of experiments in clothing, of clothes worn like fabulous beasts. The dormitory girls exchange clothing so often, it seems they dwell in a single marvelous closet, a Narnian wardrobe filled with mountains, seas, phantasmagorical islands. Clothes become detached from their owners and are known by their names, like heads of state. The Purple Sweater. The Brown Skirt. To teach herself to dress, the child restricts herself, for one year, to the colors black, red, and white. The experiment ends when her uncle gives her a gift of one hundred dollars, a fantastic sum. The child walks down the highway to the mall. Carefully she searches for things on sale. She buys ten items, mostly peach-colored and pale green: recently popular, now defunct colors. She returns to the dorm proudly, a frugal queen. There, another girl—an intelligent girl, one with advanced knowledge of the world, the very girl, in fact, who told the child to start shaving her legs—this girl says that, given a hundred dollars, she would have bought only two things. A nice sweater, this wise girl says, and a bottle of perfume. The child sits open-mouthed in

the lounge where the girls are going through her purchases, astounded
at the thought of spending fifty dollars—a whole fifty dollars!—on one
object of any kind. Several of the other girls sit dumbstruck, too, almost
catatonic, as if somebody has knocked their heads together; they hadn't
even come to terms with the haul the child dragged in from the mall
before this new idea exploded among them. These girls, in their sweat-
shirts and denim skirts, strain to imagine the kind of uncle who gives
a person a hundred dollars, the dark and profligate uncle possessed by
the child and also, apparently, by the wise girl, who is Puerto Rican, and
possibly from New York.

Fields, churches, malls. It's a landscape of highways and hills. You travel
by car. On the weekends, the dormitory is closed. Some of the students
go home, but the child lives too far away for that, so she stays with a local host family who take her to church. Sometimes she goes to her best
friend's house. The walls creak. In winter the roads are an endless mist.
You look out, you see a gray field cut in two by the window frame. Only
many years later will it occur to the child—now a woman—that there is
anything drab or oppressive about this landscape.

At dawn the clouds are lit from below with fiery pink light. Gold pours
through the trees, which appear black, like burned-out torches.

In the dormitory, there are entertainments. There is a Wednesday
Night Bible Study in the lounge. The child attends once or twice, for
something to do, but she feels inadequate there, daunted by all the language she doesn't know. The boys and girls at Bible Study are experts in

this language, they can work praises seamlessly into any sentence, they have shining eyes and glossy hair and t-shirts from their summer Bible camps, and the child feels subtly wrong among them. She goes down the hall, sliding in her socks. She goes to Movie Night in the basement: *Monty Python's Holy Grail.* At first this too seems like a foreign language, but soon it catches hold of everyone, all the kids screaming with laughter, rolling on the carpet. This will become the child's favorite film. Afterward someone says she felt bad about laughing so hard at a movie that mocked Christianity, but somebody else says no, it's okay: the movie wasn't making fun of Christians, it was making fun of Catholics.

The child has a red leather Bible, a gift from her mother. She reads it at the window when her roommate isn't there. She's trying to catch up. She underlines phrases that strike her. She writes in the margin: *Hallelujah!* There's a white light on the page, from the sky streaked with telephone wires.

She tries to consider the lilies of the field. She also experiments with makeup. She consults her best friend on the dormitory phone. One day she sits at the phone with wet hair, she's just gotten out of the shower, and another girl walks by and waves hello. Afterward this girl tells the child, "You're the only person I know whose hair looks better wet than dry." It's a pronouncement of huge significance, as if from an oracle, it descends to the place where the child has begun to suspect her hair might be a problem and it lodges there like a weight. The child searches for ways to make her hair look wet all the time, or at least smooth. Mousses, gels, hot instruments plugged in by the mirror. If a little bit of smoke comes out it's good. Without being aware of it, she is launched on a lengthy voyage regarding her hair. If her hair were shorter, she thinks, it would be easier to straighten, so she finds a picture of a nice short haircut in a magazine, and because she doesn't have enough money to go to a salon, she cuts it herself on the weekend, at the bathroom mirror in her host family's house. She uses a hand mirror, angling it to see when she cuts the back. Afterward she carefully cleans up the fallen hair with wet toilet paper. The little garbage can under the sink brims with clumped paper and hair. She looks in the mirror. She's shorn, her head looks rectangular, ghastly. There's a bald spot at the back of her head, the size of a postage stamp, where she clipped too close. A thin hank descends from the nape of her neck. She knows she will have to find a way to save herself when she goes back to school, and on Monday she arrives laughing, bold-faced, very loud. She wants to make this haircut a madcap story, an adventure and not a tragedy, an example of her special daring and carefree spirit, and through her gift for storytelling, combined with a frantic gaiety she maintains by the force of her will, she succeeds.

The window. The hissing radiator. Falling into heavy after-school naps to the sound of other girls' voices through the wall.

Every morning the students file into chapel. It's warm and bright, even in winter. They sing from a red-backed hymnal that opens like a dark rose. The child stands with her best friends, who have grown up with this hymnal and know how to sing: one of them sings alto, another tenor. A third, a soprano, will one day become a professional opera singer. The singing is a marvel to the child. She can only manage soprano, even though some of the notes are too high for her, she can only ever sing the melody. In a year or two, it's true, she will be able to sing the alto line of some hymns, either because they are simple, a whole page of E and D, or because she has picked out the notes on the piano during the summer vacation and taught herself, as with her favorite hymn "O Thou in Whose Presence." But she will never have the facility of her friends, who can harmonize even without the notes. They sing alto and tenor to pop songs and advertising jingles. To the child, it's a kind of sorcery. The chapel isn't like school. It's a *cleft of the rock*, a place of *torrents*, of *delight*.

The child dwells in magic time. On the one hand she is going to school, on the other hand she inhabits a world of giants, dragons, and witches. The witches are people with familiar spirits who must be stoned with stones. The child reads about them and about the giant with six fingers on each hand. She can see everything, the valley of salt, the wood where honey falls out of the trees, the hero who slays a thousand enemies with the jaw of an ass, another who kills six hundred men with an ox goad. While the heroes are fighting, the ladies stand at the window lattice and sigh, "Why tarry the wheels of his chariots?" There are dreadful diseases, consumption and fever, something called extreme burning, something called blasting. You can even be stricken with mildew. Little children are torn by bears, and a villain chops a lady up in twelve pieces and mails the parts all over the country. But what are mandrakes? What is a lign aloe? What does it mean when cattle are ringstraked? What does it mean to be girded with a linen ephod? The child loves most the words she doesn't know. How can you come unto someone delicately, or dwell in a several house? After reading these words the child runs up and down the stairs of the dormitory, *a smoking furnace*, she doesn't know what to do. She puts on bizarre makeup, strips off her clothes, and slips silently into other girls' rooms, so they look up and scream. But often it's study time, and she isn't allowed to leave her room. She lies on her bed and writes. A keen electricity runs up and down her body. Especially in the pit of her stomach there is a little storm, and as she writes she rocks from side to side to calm it.

Pages of writing. She writes for school. *Dorm living is both fun and rewarding. Very good friends can be made in a short amount of time. These friendships last forever, especially those of roommates. Learning to live with others is probably the most important part of living in a dorm.* She transforms a school notebook into a journal. She writes in class while the teacher lectures. *You know something? I am still a kid. I am only fifteen years old and I am still very much a child. What hurts is when people treat me like one.* She writes: *I make jokes and laugh at people and give ego trips for free and make a fool out of myself. I do tricks, like a lapdog.* By the end of the year, her handwriting will have altered to a startling degree, becoming much smaller and more controlled. She writes: *The sky was the color of plums that night.* She writes: *Am I a genius?* She makes lists of words that go together. *Trees—gnarled, stunted. Sea—wide gray void. Eyes—blue, slanting. Hair—pale.* She collects the words, arranging them in lines, as if in response to some huge, never-ending assignment. *In the twelfth year of the reign of Dolmanen Kandor VI, also known as the Mad Monarch, whose hair grew down to his feet until it began to fall out, a tree was planted in the center of Mormere, the capital city.*

There are not many outings from the dormitory and not many places to go. One of the assistants takes some girls to see the movie *Platoon.* They go in a van, there's a theater with a red carpet, buckets of popcorn, and then they're trapped in the thundering onslaught of the film. The child knew it was a war movie and had no interest in it, she just came along because it meant going outside at night, and now the men are crying in the mud so hurt and close among the bursts of light and relentless hammering sound. Afterward the girls are stunned. The parking lot seems vast, the streetlamps like planets. The child can count the silences all the way to the road. Even the dormitory assistant, who took the girls to this film as a learning experience, is subdued. The expected discussion never starts. Instead there's the whoosh and then the thud of the sliding door of the van. The child sits close to the window, watching the watery streaks of highway lights. At last another girl speaks: The saddest thing, she says, is that the men who fought in Vietnam all went to Hell when they died. They went straight to Hell to suffer forever, for fighting is a sin. The child answers savagely, "They didn't go to Hell." She says there can't be a Hell, for a loving God would never torment someone who had already been so tormented in life. Again a stillness descends. The child feels the others disagreeing with her in silence. Here are the steps of the dormitory, the yellow light. The child is finished crying and she is finished with Hell, which doesn't exist and will never exist, no matter what anyone says.

The child's host parents are kind people with no children of their own, as in a fairy tale. The child, like a wish fulfillment, is both gratifying and troublesome. On her first weekend, she makes herself at home in the upper story of the house, where she has her own bedroom and bathroom. The following weekend, when the child's host mother picks her up at the dormitory, there is a cold fury in the car. For a time the child tries to make conversation into this fury, but the air around her keeps freezing and she gives up. She asks if she can go to her best friend's house on Saturday. And the host mother answers, "Maybe, if you learn to clean up your room." It emerges that the host mother took some visitors on a tour of the house last week and was embarrassed by the mess upstairs. The host mother's house is decorated in two colors: country blue and dusky rose. There are many small wooden ornaments garnished with dried grass. The child, whose house in New Jersey is decorated in all colors and no color, is unfamiliar with the practice of giving tours of the place where you live. Her bed was unmade, the host mother informs her, gripping the steering wheel, there were dirty clothes on the floor, there were Tampax on the dresser! The word *Tampax* ricochets all over the car. Years ago, the host mother and father were missionaries in Somalia. Now, having opened her country-blue and dusky-rose home to the child, the host mother is being forced to pronounce *Tampax* in broad daylight. The child feels Somalia, dusty and far away, and herself, dirty and very near, with Tampax connecting them like a bridge. This is silly, because, as another former missionary informs the child at church, Somalis don't even know what Tampax means. This former missionary once took tampons with her in her luggage, and the Somali customs officers opened them all up! They were looking for contraband, perhaps rolled-up dollars. They pulled all the missionary's tampons apart, making them useless! This story is told in the church bathroom, which echoes with the laughter of nice ladies who are pulling up their nylons.

December fields, brown and frozen before the snow. White flicker of birds on a distant fence. The wind drops at the end of the day, going down with the sun. Now it's so quiet you can hear the cows lowing. The walnut trees are bare. The last of the wild asparagus hangs its feathers.

The child and her best friend go bumping over the ridges of the winter fields, whooping and laughing on something called a four-wheeler, a little car you're allowed to drive before you have your license. Wind burns their faces, the dog runs beside them. The roaring four-wheeler breaks up the mist in the hollows. The child wears old green coveralls that belong to the best friend's mother, she wears a pair of borrowed boots, she's a city girl with nothing good for wearing out here in the open, on the farm. At her best friend's house, they eat deer burgers, fetching the meat from the deep-freeze in the garage. The deer are shot by the best friend's dad. The best friend knows how to shoot, too, because she's the oldest of three girls with no brothers, the strongest, the most practical, she hunts and helps her dad with the hogs. Folded laundry on the piano bench for the girls to take upstairs, and, on Sundays, a miracle: ice cream and pretzels for supper. The best friend does a handstand. She turns cartwheels in the cold. When she was little she wanted to be a ballerina, but wasn't allowed, because dancing is wrong.

How to dance: jump, wiggle, step from side to side. The child and her best friend practice upstairs in the best friend's room. At some point they add arm and hand movements to their repertoire, for the child has observed this technique in one of their friends who transferred from public school. The former public school friend dresses all in black, with combat boots from the army surplus store. She has been to a live concert. It wasn't even a concert of the Christian rock the best friend listens to, the only rock music allowed in her house. No, it was a concert of a real band in Lancaster City, where the public school friend got a bruise on her arm from moshing. She rolls up her sleeve to show the bruise. There's a darker, red notch in the middle of it, because the person who hit her was wearing a ring. This is completely fantastic, but eventually, when the child gets a boyfriend who drives, when she finally goes to one of these concerts in Lancaster City, it will turn out to be horrible, and she won't even spend a whole song in the mosh pit in front of the stage where pale boys in tank tops are beating everyone up. It will be like her first party, where the host, a big restless boy whose parents are gone for the weekend, a friend of the child's—though she's not in his inner circle, the ones who take codeine tablets—will choke her in the foyer for a joke. She'll be on her knees, surprised because she's really choking, while he laughs. But that's in the future, his hands on her neck, the dark wood of the banister, the studio portraits of his family slanting up the wall. Now she's teaching herself to dance, her wrists in the air like smoke. Her best friend jumps up and down. "Control," they sing. "Control."

In Lancaster City the streets are lined with lights in paper bags. A glowing trail, because it's nearly Christmas. It's lovely there, but the child almost never goes. She goes to the mall. She sits in fluorescent light and drinks from a plastic cup.

One way for the dormitory students to go places at night is to join Gospel Team, so the child joins Gospel Team. Gospel Team is a group of girls led by the dormitory assistant, who wears a doily on top of her long brown hair. The assistant plays the piano and the girls sing and act in plays. They ride in the van, far out in the dry leaf-smelling night. They ride up and down the hills, on unlighted roads where isolated houses gleam in the distance, shielded by screens of trees. In this way they arrive at churches that smell of old winter coats and bleach. Sometimes when they go in there's nobody in the lobby, or maybe there's just a child running around, or the sound of a photocopier working somewhere in the hushed, suspended air of the night church. But the lights are on, and at last somebody comes. The Gospel Team sits in the front row, or, if they're lucky, in a small room behind the pulpit, for some of the churches have a room full of cabinets and dusty ornaments where the girls can cluster as if in a real backstage. The dormitory assistant begins to bang on the piano and the Gospel Team advances, all in black. They sing contemporary praise songs, which the child secretly hates, to a small audience of old people and children. They perform a play called *Frustration* which is about a teenager who is sad and confused until she discovers Jesus. It's a very modern play in which the girls stand motionless in a row and bark out all the lines one after another. The first lines are:

> *Frustration!*
> *Frustration!*
> *Frustration!*
> *Stop!*

The girls have spent many hours practicing this play, which is hard to memorize because there isn't any dialogue and no one moves. Sometimes when they practice they shout:

> *Menstruation!*
> *Menstruation!*
> *Menstruation!*
> *Stop!*

But everyone agrees the play is really good in the end, it's their signature piece, the star of their show. And nobody knows how, one night, they get the lines confused, so out of order they can't find their place at all. The teenager they represent, who is going through such a difficult time in her life, begins to yelp out totally disconnected phrases, she's gone aphasic, and worse, she's shaking, the Gospel Team is shaking, paralyzed with laughter, tears running down her face. The child, part of this hydra-headed, twitching, stuttering monster, finds to her horror that she can't stop laughing. Everything sets her off: her teammates jerking and sniffling beside her, the desperate silences, the wrong words emitted in a sudden shriek. Her strength fails, and she sinks, mortified, to the floor. Two other girls crouch with her, undone. The child sees the dorm assistant's white, lightly pimpled, enraged face, she sees the stony expression of an elderly lady in a cape dress as she watches the Gospel Team break down onstage. And the child is powerless, breached. She'll have a similar experience next year, performing the beautiful Bach hymn "Jesus, Priceless Treasure" at her church: she (soprano) and her two friends from youth group (alto and tenor) will waver their way to the end through tears of mirth. Something happens with other people that makes you a liquid being. One heroic girl concludes the *Frustration* play. The Gospel Team crawls offstage. They cling together, gasping and wiping away mascara-black tears, best friends forever. They have all wet themselves.

To sum it up you could say: a liquid era. A borderless era, an era of the breach. Or you could say: an era of bursting and finding, of realization, of the flow that begins to recognize the trench. Weekends at camp with the church youth group, the snow, the rush of inner tubes down a hill, the chilly faces, freezing fingers in wet gloves, and then at night the roar of praise songs, hot hands waving in the air, the fires, the tears. There's a constant whirl, a sensation of vertigo, of speed. The child feels excited and carsick. There's oatmeal at breakfast, you wear pajamas around boys, you cuddle up with boys in sleeping bags in the lounge, there's some kind of movie on, like the one where the boy kills himself because of that Dungeons and Dragons game, there's a dark smell of popcorn and wood. The child glances over at her best friend who is also curled up with a boy, she can make out her best friend's face in the glancing light of the screen that shows teenagers crying, their eyes meet, exchange a sparkling glance, the eyebrows wriggling furiously, later the best friend says she could feel something *jagging into her hip.* The child did, too, she could feel it: the boy's thing! And after that all they have to do, the child and her best friend, especially around boys, is wriggle their eyebrows and say "*Jag, jag!*" in order to collapse in giggles, just the two of them, sometimes laughing so hard they have to run out of the room. Waves of contagious feeling, as when in the evening there are praise songs and guitars. The child doesn't like the songs, but she cries because people are crying. Kids exhausted from snowball fights and cuddling and staying up all night: they cry as they praise the Lord, they get saved in droves.

There is something strange about it all, especially the weird adults who lead the singing at camp, who want to hang out with kids all the time. One song leader from the youth camp is also a dorm assistant on the boys' side: white t-shirt, white jeans, a wooden cross on a leather strap. He plays the guitar at Bible Study and often explains that Jesus is a cool dude. What must it be like inside his room? Sad rooms of dormitory assistants, worn Bibles, high school soccer or field hockey jerseys on the wall, instant coffee and dirty mugs. These enthusiastic grownups, who never seem to go on dates, must pray a lot, the child imagines, to keep from getting depressed. Their lonely desire to work with children gives them a damp aura: they seem always sweaty, like the visiting preacher who does an altar call at chapel. An altar call is when the preacher summons the sinners up to the front to get saved.

The visiting preacher stamps and hollers in his blue suit. Six hundred pairs of eyes stare at him. What if nobody goes? It's too awful, the child stands up, she floats to the front of the chapel in a red dress. Later she thinks this was marvelous, the red dress, as if she were a kind of Hester Prynne. Up close the preacher gives off waves of heat, like a stove. She bows her head and he touches her brow with a hand like a piece of ham. The blood of Jesus flows from this hand, or perhaps from the ceiling. The child is drenched, the visiting preacher tells her in his resounding, trembling voice, cleansed of her sins, and she's sad, she even cries a little, she cries from being so bad, because once she said her little brother was fat and once she slid a mean note underneath another girl's door. But she's happy, too, content to have done something nice for the visiting preacher, who will go back to his hotel room, or, more likely, a friend's couch, with the knowledge that he has saved a child today. Her eyes half-closed, she can see his polished shoes, his briefcase against the podium.

After she's saved in front of the whole school, the child is invited to be in a presentation at chapel. It is about abortion. Some students have made a poster showing a tiny pink baby surrounded by words in big black letters: WOULD YOU KILL ME? The child's role is to read a short story from the baby's perspective. The stage of the chapel is huge, the audience dizzying, it goes on forever. She looks down at the paper she's been given, reads into the microphone. At first her voice shakes, then it grows stronger, then softer, pure. The softness comes as she enters into the voice of the baby, describing its growing body inside the mother, its heat, its comfort, its round world. She finds that her voice responds to her thoughts, like those plants that respond to touch. She can deepen it, lengthen it, modulate it in countless ways. Afterward everyone agrees the child's reading was very moving, she really made them sorry for the unborn baby. The child is elated. She has a beautiful voice! As for abortion, that's something distant, completely alien to the child and the people she knows. For the child and her friends would never, ever, even two years from now when they have boyfriends, when they're under blankets with these boyfriends in nothing but underwear, they would never, ever do that, the child only knows of one person who maybe has done it, a girl in the dormitory who, shockingly, wears an Egg McMuffin on her hair, a girl with blond hair and bad skin who goes around, sometimes, with a boy from the basketball team, an impossibly handsome boy who never calls her his girlfriend, who tells her not to show up to games but waits for her afterward in his car, who takes her to barns. They drink whiskey, it's said, and the girl comes back covered with straw. At the podium, reading her doomed baby story, the child doesn't think about this girl, who sits in a back pew picking at her nails.

It's true the kids in the dormitory are rumored to be very bad. Some parents use the Mennonite school as a kind of reform school. They threaten their kids: "Do it again and I'll send you to the Mennonites!" There's a chastened girl who arrives in tears, her eyes slits in a wash of eyeliner. There are some rough boys too. The child has a pair of worn-out jeans, one knee a hole, and she wears them for a joke as the hole gets bigger and bigger, until one day on the stairs one of the rough boys grabs the edges of the hole and rips the jeans down to her ankle and up her thigh. The girls know a lot about these boys, more than you would think. They know that a certain gentle, red-haired boy made cider in his closet, and got so drunk he fell and broke his nose. They know, but will never tell, who tried to drop a jar of peanut butter on the security guard. The night security guard is also the chemistry teacher, a distant man in glasses, the butt of many jokes, his house smacked with eggs every Halloween, and one night as he patrols the grounds a jar of peanut butter falls from the second story and smashes right beside him. It's a serious offense, he could have been injured, even killed. The girls say nothing, bound by an ancient code. They whisper about the perpetrators at night by the bathroom sinks, in the cold flat light that stays on all night, the scene of conspiracy. They breathe the names of the criminals only in this sacred place, as they whisper the name of the boy who won the penis-size contest, as well as the name of the boy who almost won but lost in the end because his penis, though long, is also very thin. They creep from the bathroom into the room of some girls with a view of the courtyard where the night guard walks. Only years later will the child think about this guard. How can he teach all day and work here at night? What is his life—what was his life? Now she ducks, snickering, as he appears across the yard. He walks with his flashlight, sweeping it to and fro, raising an uneven glimmer from the broken glass on the pavement, where the peanut butter, mingled with rain, will slowly dissolve over the next few weeks, until you can't see it anymore.

Places to go: church. Camp. Other churches. The mall. Dunkin' Donuts. You can reach Dunkin' Donuts by walking down the highway. There's barely room to walk. Your feet slip. Wind of the passing cars. When trucks go by, pump your fist in the air and maybe they'll honk the horn. Girls shrieking and dancing with glee by the road because a truck driver, who comes from somewhere and is going somewhere, has honked at them. These girls are in their pajamas. They've sneaked out for donuts after midnight. They're going to get caught. For punishment, they'll scrub the floors. The punishment won't bother them at all: they'll make it a joke, singing mournful gospel melodies as they work, pretending to be slaves. They occupy an enchanted circle that makes them impervious to harm. Every event is transmuted into laughter. When the night guard catches them creeping back into the dorm, his flashlight will kindle them like bulbs. Now, at the twenty-four-hour Dunkin' Donuts, they float amid clouds of sparkling, crinkled paper, their foreheads flecked with halos of icing sugar.

Buoyed by her success on the chapel stage, the child tries out for the school play and receives the role of Calpurnia in *To Kill a Mockingbird*. She wears a long skirt and a kerchief and carries a broom. A boy like her—his mom Mennonite, his dad Somali—plays the doomed Tom Robinson. In the courtroom scene, the Ethiopian students from the dormitory line the back row, wrapped in drab clothes, the girls with their hair in bandannas. They're so shy, the child can't imagine they tried out for this play; the teacher directing it must have fetched them out of the dorm. Anyway, they don't have speaking parts. The lights are hot. The child wishes she had Atticus's line: "If I had my druthers, I'd take a shotgun!" The gruff novelty of *druthers*. Of her own lines, her favorite is the wide-eyed "Sweet Jesus, help him!" because it makes the audience laugh.

Didn't she know? Well, no, she didn't know, or only vaguely. She doesn't know. She knows the girls envy her for having a tan year-round. She never has their springtime problem of pasty skin, the white flesh, hidden away all winter, suddenly exposed in shorts. She knows that her hair is no good but she doesn't know why. It's just bad luck. Then one day in class she asks another girl for some White-Out. "Why," the other girl grins, "to paint your face?" The child laughs along. After school, the other girl comes to her room in the dorm to apologize. She really doesn't believe there's anything wrong with being African American, this girl explains, it was just a joke. It's like being slapped. The child is slapped by race and, even more, by her own stupidity: she didn't catch the slur. She just thought it was a joke about being erased.

And so she becomes a brown girl. She develops a passion for Frida Kahlo. She acquires an artist boyfriend and calls him Diego. In her senior year she sprains her ankle and wears a plastic boot for six weeks, and she thinks of Frida as she limps up and down the stairs. It's the time of the sadness experiments. The child lies in bed for hours, listening to music and crying in a kind of voluptuous trance. She writes down her dreams, and the dreams grow worse and worse. There is a ten-day series of nightmares. *I was riding a bicycle and my foot was caught in the spokes.* In these dreams the gutters run with blood. The child sees her eyes on the floor. She is put in a freezer. A witch with a white face arrives, a hand sticking out of her neck. Everything translates into a steady buzzing sensation, like a hum, that comes to surround the child, and into which she dissolves. The child remains essentially feral, an organ of experience. After her first heartbreak, when she sobs on the floor with her head half under the bed, she feels the nap of the carpet and even the shadow of the bed so intensely her blood thrums, as it does when she looks at paintings.

As if everything were a prelude to ecstasy. In the mornings before school starts, she sits on a bench in the lobby, her injured leg stretched out. A prim authoritarian in red lipstick, she makes her friends sit down and listen as she reads James Joyce aloud.

She drifts. She writes: *What is life without writing?* She's a writer, and so she writes. It's her only intelligence, the one thing she knows for sure. In all other matters, she's blank. She won't even remember what's happened to her at school until, thirty years from now, she starts to read her journals.

When you leave the Mennonite high school, you go to a Mennonite college. There are two main ones. The jocks and business majors go to the one in Virginia. The artists go to the one in Indiana, so the child and her friends will go to lovely, windswept Indiana for four years. Everything is arranged, but then the child finds, to her shock, that her dad won't allow her to go to the Mennonite college. He refuses absolutely. He insists she apply to Harvard. She fights, she cries. Her mother wanders to and fro in the background with a drawn face. The world becomes unreal, as in one of the child's nightmares. She goes upstairs slowly, lifting her feet extra high, not trusting the shape of the steps. How can her dad have allowed her to attend the Mennonite high school and then suddenly refuse her the Mennonite college? Why this sudden resistance to his own alma mater? For he once trudged across that Indiana campus in the snow. Something is burning in his eyes, an obscure bitterness related, the child feels, to the fact that he never goes to church. She can see he's been caught off guard, he didn't know what would happen, he didn't know that the Mennonite school would produce this girl in his house, this Mennonite child, but as for her, she doesn't care, she's developed a code of feeling that binds her irrevocably to her friends and to the texture of that world. A code of feeling deeper than faith or tribe. She lies on her childhood bed with the blue dust ruffle and cries herself to sleep. In the morning she finds an envelope her dad slipped under her door, containing a letter of apology and fifty dollars.

At church, a foot-washing ceremony. The ladies take off their shoes but not their nylon stockings. You kneel by a basin and take your partner's foot. You hold the foot over the basin and splash a little water onto it. The water beads on the nylon and then turns dark. Afterward you walk around with one foot cold and tingly from the wet nylon. You have to shake hands with people and say, "The peace of Christ." These old, wan, faded faces in snow-light. It's awkward, yes, so awkward it's hard to explain how much she loved it all.

And how the sight of a hill with a grove of bare trees, ashen as if sketched in charcoal, retains the power to move her even now.

Today there's a swath of darkness across the sky. Above it, a layer of cold silver. As the child goes down the dormitory steps, a startled crow springs from a wire, rising with a snap of wings that makes the whole day vibrate like a bell.

NINE

Tashkent

a land gleams at us from afar

In a carpet, Usmon says, everything depends on the knots.

We fly back to Tashkent on a small, packed plane, swiftly passing the desert that took us a day to cross going the other direction, that took the Mennonite travelers three weeks. Most of my companions are asleep. A sudden illness has struck our group, affecting all the North Americans except Frank and myself: Frank, we think, because he's been to Uzbekistan before, and me, we don't know, maybe it's all those years in Egypt and South Sudan, or maybe I just have, Micah says, "a leather gut." Arnie jokes lugubriously that the tour is designed to reproduce the Great Trek right down to the typhoid. Somebody nicknames the illness "the Khiva Fever." And I tell myself not to be foolish when I feel slightly left out, as if the trip didn't want to touch me as deeply as the others.

Desire for evidence. Particles of cotton oil in my blood from the *plov* of Tashkent. As if you could record a journey through the language of a changing cuisine, make a map from what was swallowed at each point. The red carrots, and then, as we moved farther south, the yellow carrots. I think again of the Kyrgyz symbol, the raven's claw: "to leave a trace." And I make bird-like tracks in my notebook, scratching with my pen, inscribing, as if etching into the surface of a tin spoon with a pin. I write what pierces me.

Sky of Tashkent, nacreous and shifting like a caged dove. Those of us who feel well enough go to the Chorsu Bazaar, the city's main food market, where we walk beneath the steely modern dome among sides of beef, stacks of trotters, and slabs of fat folded like blankets. Only a few booths carry tourist souvenirs; more offer clothes, shoes, electronics, and household items. The major object on display is food. There are pyramids of cucumbers, spices heaped like sand dunes, troughs of almonds, dried apricots, and figs.

Everything is in motion but to represent it requires such stillness. The eyes of a miniature, says Kholid, are painted with the hair of a three-day-old cat. Oniony smoke billows from the kabab stand. He says Ibn Sina, the first pharmacist, prescribed plov as a cure for exhaustion. Bukhara, he says, has a stamping dance; Tashkent has a bird dance. He says a piece of silk paper can last for two thousand years. When a baby boy is born, he says, you should plant poplar trees, so that when he grows up you'll be able to build him a house.

He tells me of a magical people who live among the mountains. They fast all day, every day, and eat only at night. They live on mulberries, apricots, and sprouted wheat. They eat no meat, because they can't cook it; in the high peaks, there's not enough oxygen for fire. They drink from the mountain streams. Many are blond. They're so healthy and hardy, the women bear children until they're sixty years old. In one of their rituals, they kill a black cock and sprinkle everyone with the blood. Their lives are long. At ninety, they get a third set of teeth.

In the covered walkways, you can smell the fruit. Nozli is happy with her purchase of fuzzy pink high-heeled bedroom slippers.

Al-Kindi: "It is manifest that everything in this world, whether it be substance or accident, produces rays in its own manner like a star."

At the tea stall, we sip from cups with a blue and white design. Usmon tells us the secrets of the transformation of milk. He tells us of *kaymak*, a kind of butter made by skimming the surface of boiling milk with a ceramic bowl in the shape of a triple flower. He tells us of *qatiq*, a near relative of clabber, and *suzma*, which is prepared with herbs and pepper. "If you apply suzma to your horny feet for an hour," he says, "you will not recognize your feet and heels, so smooth and velvety they will be." You will not recognize your own body. You will be someone else. I think of the long poem "The Community of Christ," written in 1934 to celebrate Ak Metchet's fiftieth anniversary, and how the historian Walter Ratliff compares it to Khivan epic poetry. Like the compositions of Uzbek poets, "The Community of Christ" mingles history with prayers and religious lessons, and it was recited aloud by the village youth, like a poem in the local tradition. As if the literary genre had entered their pores like scent.

We fill each other's cups with darkening, astringent green tea. Nozli feeds a scrap of bread to a small stray dog. That book by Menno Simons, *Why I Do Not Cease Teaching and Writing*—I've never read it. But I think there is only one reason: to cross the border of skin.

Eat this book. In its final transformation, milk is made into balls called *kurt*. It's salty, says Usmon, loved by children, and eaten with beer. I wonder if the word *kurt* is related to the English *curd*, or if the similarity of the sounds is just a coincidence, or, again, if it's not simply chance but experience that developed this nice firm word, with its yielding center, that feels like a curd in the mouth. I doubt this last possibility—I think language is more arbitrary than that—but I don't doubt the effects of experience on the body, the effects of time, of movement, of particular days lived one after the other, of certain weather, of teaching and writing, or of the dazed, contingent feeling of the present. Boarding the bus again, I remember the essay by Dilaram Inoyatova, and her claim that the Mennonites of Ak Metchet absorbed some of the local customs. She writes of their traditional Khivan hospitality, the way the village elder would go out to welcome passing travelers. The men would set out coffee, tea, milk, and bread for their guests. From living so long in Khiva, they had been transformed.

And now it's our last night. The walls of the hotel are decked with paintings. This is the same hotel we stayed in at the beginning of our trip, but only tonight do I see that these paintings are copies, in colored oils, of Khudaybergen Divanov photographs. They cluster about us. The man at the well. The last khan.

At dinner there's a dance troupe in kaleidoscopic light. There's a live singer. It's too loud for conversation. Frank passes me his phone, which holds a PDF of a Soviet document he has recently had translated. This document lists all the people deported from Ak Metchet. Each head of household has received a block of text. I start reading, then read faster, too fast, so that everything goes blurry, the scrolling screen, my thumb, the figured tablecloth. The impression is one of devastating accuracy. Heart thudding. Each name of man, woman, and child, each age and re-lationship. Number of cows and chickens. Number of objects in posses-sion. In the room where I sit, there is a woman who dances like a snake. There is a woman who dances like a peacock. There are some tourists clapping. There are some tourists recording on their phones. There is a man who attempts to croon like Elvis: *Fools rush in.* There is a famous Uzbek song about a teahouse.

A wind inside everything. A feeling of storm. Lights cracking, lanterns blown over, fire.

What remains after the end of the world? Fragments. Stray DNA. A smear of cells. In the 1970s, when Fred Belk wrote his history of the Great Trek, he estimated that approximately one hundred thousand people living in Siberia and Central Asia had "German Mennonite eth-nic background."

After the end of a world, the fall of a city, the ruin of a distinct way of life, there is ethnic background. After faith dwindles, there is music. There is, in winter, the ritual of the lighted tree. And how it persists, how strongly, with what marvelous elasticity, not desired or planned but felt in every pore. I remember, on one of my visits home during my Egypt years, standing by a bonfire one July night, on a farm in Pennsylvania, talking about church with an old college friend. We were staying there with our families, helping another old friend, the owner of the farm, to tear down an ancient barn and destroy some invasive plants. Every night a crackling fire of debris. My friend was telling me that he still went to church, though he didn't believe in God. He went for tradition, community, mutual aid, and the chance to do activist work with like-minded people, because he believed in those things. He said the church was full of people like him. I thought this was awful. Going to church when you don't believe—doesn't this make a mockery of faith?

My friend laughed. "I think you have a romantic idea of church." He was right. Today, he and I are part of the same congregation. It's a wonderful grab bag of singers and readers and prodigals and seekers, a miscellany of *either/or* and *both/and*. And today, if you asked me to name the strength of the Mennonite Church, I would say it's precisely what looks like weakness and contradiction, the patchwork of people brought together in such different ways, by birth and faith and thirst, to build a house of effort and care. I would say our strength is that we can't get everyone on the same page. I would say my church almost looks like my idea of utopia. And I'd have to add that on a typical Sunday, with around three hundred in attendance, you can count the people of color on your two hands.

Ethnicity is a knot that's hard to sever. When I look at Mennonite communities, it seems clear that those who are joined by blood retain a means of attachment even if they no longer have faith. But those who are joined by faith can be detached by its disappearance. I understand that someone like my father, deeply influenced by the Mennonite story, had no place in it once he was no longer a practicing Mennonite, unlike other nonpracticing Mennonites who carry the banner of blood. But experience, just like blood, endures. How I wish this could be recognized, acknowledged, and celebrated, stories granted a status equal to that of DNA, perhaps even greater! It's the days spent together that make us part of each other. There is a genetics of storytelling, for stories too are encoded, inherited, lodged in the flesh.

No one knows the exact location of the place of refuge, but after dinner, out in the lobby where it's quieter, Kholid tells me that Jesus, peace be upon him, will one day return to Damascus. He will arrive at a mosque called the White Mosque—that is, in the Uzbek language, Ak Metchet. Every Friday, at a white minaret—"which I hope still exists," Kholid adds—the imam puts down a white prayer rug, in case this is the day when Jesus son of Mary, peace be upon him, comes there to pray with the community.

We say goodbye to Kholid, Usmon, and Nozli. Embraces. Email addresses recorded in cellphones, written on a notebook page. We wave goodbye from the doorway of the hotel, and some of us linger there, watching the three of them move into the night. They talk and laugh together. Soon we can't hear them, then we can't see them. My last glimpse is the wink of Nozli's white t-shirt as she bends to get into a taxi, and the watery gleam of the plastic bag that holds her new fuzzy slippers throwing back the headlights of the passing cars.

If home is a story, then home is both resilient and malleable. Total strangers can read themselves in. Home can become an alien place. Perhaps this fragility, this slippery quality of stories, leads to the fear that they will be changed out of all recognition. It's understandable that, in the grip of this anxiety, people cling to their stories, repeat them with strident insistence, or, in a process that's probably more common, simply forget, allow themselves to forget, suppress, omit the strangeness, unsee the uncanny glint at the heart of home. But the mutability of stories is also a source of hope. Walter S. Friesen, in his essay "Pilgrimage as Healing," writes about a woman whose life was haunted by the sentence "I am an illegitimate child." One day, when she was twenty-two years old, this woman realized that she was no longer a child, and as for the word *illegitimate*, that had to do with being born, it wasn't something with power over her life anymore. "I am an illegitimate child" became simply *I Am*. "Such *I Am* events," Friesen explains, "include and embrace everything in the pure light of belovedness."

Hafiz: "I too begin to so sweetly cast light like a lamp through the streets of this world."

In that essay, Friesen writes about his own journey to Ak Metchet. He defines *Heimweh*, or home-ache, as "longing for at-homeness." He also calls it a "driving homesickness."

In my hotel room, I break my rule about never paying for international data so that I can watch a video on my phone, one I discovered before this trip: the popular music group Yalla, singing their hit song "Shakhrisabz." It's a video of a live performance, the crowd singing along, the dancers on stage twirling fiery batons. The members of the band wear boxy coats encrusted with rhinestones. The lead singer comes out in a lustrous magenta robe. Casting it off, he reveals a pair of oversized silver epaulettes. He claps and snaps his fingers. *Shakhrisabz. Shakhrisabz.*

It's the only word in the song I can understand. The music feels warm and tinged with longing, as if sung by someone who loves the city, who knows it intimately enough to praise it in detail, who perhaps has not been there in some time. I look up the lyrics online, generating one of those quirky translations, the internet's global, distorted, misbehaving language.

> *Like many cities in the world*
> *But the best unvarnished*
> *It lies in the spurs of the mountains high*
> *Green City Shakhrisabz*

Some sites say the song was released in the eighties, others say the nineties. Either way, I was alive.

A few hours of sleep. At dawn, I watch the clouds around Tashkent touched with yellow and red. They're lit from beneath, because I'm on a planet.

I don't have a telescope; I'm inside one. The practice of research length-
ens the line of sight. Yet the vision of a person on a planet is defined
by what can't be seen, by all the world that's in the dark. I realize now
that I've carried Shakhrisabz, where I'm not going, as a kind of amu-
let, a reminder of the incomplete nature of my journey. Shakhrisabz
maintains the driving homesickness. It keeps its distance like an un-
assimilable punctum, point, or star. It reminds me of what refuses to
be disciplined, absorbed, and brought in line with a given story: all
those as-yet-invisible gleams. For I would keep my affinity for stray,
discarded things. I would perceive in every studium the punctum. A
magpie method, if you like, averse to the main idea, ready to champion
the insignificant detail. It's not a mode of thinking that builds author-
ity; to search outside the known constellations, gazing into the dark, is
to make yourself vulnerable to error. You might mistake a church for a
mosque, or a foreign country for home. Don't forget: in *The Wizard of Oz*,
the Emerald City wasn't green at all! It just looked that way through the
colored spectacles. And Shakhrisabz, my symbol, is at the same time a
real place, sunny and pleasant today, with a high of eighty-eight degrees
and a low of sixty-two.

> *Rich in carpets, cotton, bread*
> *Blooming edge, green hail*

And what a joy it is to know you don't know. It is *joy* to dwell in the place
of hunger, to recognize that the acrobat of thought, climbing the rope
of imagination, will never reach the top of this minaret! And so when
I say that Shakhrisabz recalls the gaps in my knowledge, I don't just
mean that I'm trying to respect difference, although that's part of it, and
I don't just mean that humility is a good thing, and we should take care

with the stories of others. I mean that I want to feel alive. If the studium belongs to purpose, argument, and expertise, the punctum belongs to passion. It bursts the numbness of the known. I want to believe that this is always possible: the charge, the leap, the quake of story moving through the skin.

A child at the theater crying, "Oh curtain, curtain, please don't come down!"

Perhaps for the Mennonites of Ak Metchet, the Green City evoked some unreachable promised land, perhaps it meant disappointment, but to me it means simply that there is always more, that the story is never over. And this, too, is paradise.

> *Shakhrisabz, Shakhrisabz*
> *Filled with joy and light*

And how I love their wrongness. Their beautiful error. The collapse of their intent. It's failure that saves these wanderers from the old lines, the known gestures, the missionary effect. Every new story happens by accident.

Yellow circle of lamplight on the hotel pillowcase. Fold the clothes, collect the last items. Toothbrush, sandals, books. As a farewell, I read the night journey of Elizabeth Unruh, a story from her crossing to America.

Now I will relate a stirring incident. One still, clear moonlit night on the ocean. We were all on deck, those that were well, enjoying the nice music, that we could hear there. All of a sudden the ships' officers came hurrying; the music stopped— told us all to go to our cabins... For in a short while, there would be a very dense fog, which we could cut with a knife; and that shortly we would be meeting an American passenger ship.

Down to the lobby, dragging my wheeled suitcase over the tiles. In the courtyard, morning holds its breath. The birds chatter.

On deck no passengers were allowed, only a few men were overlooked, and they never knew of any of these orders. They told later, that the fog was so black, there was nothing to be seen, they stayed just where they were. The lights on deck looked like little sparks. Down below we could only always hear the fog horns, over and over, our ship barely moved. All of a sudden we felt as though our ship was being shoved sideways, we heard a kind of scraping, the whole ship quivered—what feelings went through us one cannot describe, whether all of a sudden they would say: the ship is sinking.

The bus, the Golden Dragon, for the last time. It swings through a city still half asleep. Juniper trees bristle in the parks.

Then the door opened and they said we could come on deck. Were we thankful. We went on deck as fast as we could, then we could hear the ship's organ playing, "We Thank Thee, O God." When we got on deck, the ships were side by side, calling salutations to each other. They were playing the same songs on both ships, both decks were packed with people. The fog had lifted—the moon was shining on the water. Both ships were undamaged, ours was scraped some.

A beautiful goal: to emerge from any encounter undamaged, but scraped some.

My companions gaze out the windows, some still a little wan from illness. Soon, in our own way, we will be crossing Elizabeth's sea. "There's so much to learn," sighs Evelyn, "so much to look up when we get back!" I nod without really taking in the significance of her words, without knowing how right she is, in my case at least, unaware of the years of research that will follow this trip, ignorant, as I must be, of the future.

June 2016. By the end of the year, there will be new governments in both the United States and Uzbekistan. In Uzbekistan, certain strictures will be relaxed, and Mr. Karimov and his team will at last acquire the permit they need to open the Mennonite museum in Khiva. And in the US, in my Virginia town, in this bleak period, I will go on with my research project amid new pressures and cares, I will ride my bike across town to the campus of Eastern Mennonite University and climb the stairs to the little historical library. My photocopy of a few chapters from Franz Bartsch's *Our Trek to Central Asia* is insufficient; I need to read the whole book, again and again. Outside, a line of mountains. Shadowed stacks. Something like twilight seeps from the case displaying a collection of blue Dutch plates. There's a rack of books for sale, cheap, no more than a dollar: old yearbooks from Mennonite schools from the 1970s. I will spend a long time crouched on the floor, paging through these books, looking for photographs of my father.

I will continue studying German. I will publish my interview with Mohamud Siad Togane in a Mennonite journal. I will seek out the poets Kholid mentioned, Hamid Olimjon and Zulfiya, gleaning phrases from academic articles, sensing a poetry steeped in landscape: sleepy cotton fields at dusk, mountains wandering like shepherds, white seas of snow. I will learn—with pleasure, but not too much surprise—that Frank and I are distant cousins. With a thrill, I'll discover the website of a thrift store selling a coat designed by Irina Sharipova, and beg my husband to buy it for me for Christmas. "Are you serious?" he'll ask, when I request him to spend eighty dollars on a second-hand "flowered military trench." "Dead!" I'll reply. "It's all I want!" I'll get the coat. I will also, in the throes of my Irene Worth obsession, spend sixty-five dollars on her perfume. I will feel that I absolutely must possess this rare elixir that contains, I imagine, the essence of her sublime elegance. The perfume arrives. I breathe it in. It smells—familiar. It smells—I have to admit—elderly. Well, of course it does! She was born in 1916! The divine distillation of Irene Worth smells like a clean Oldsmobile, a faux leather purse, tinted pantyhose, and Juicy Fruit gum. It smells like church.

I will reread "Melanctha." I'll be amazed at how much of this story is occupied by a marathon breakup: an agonizing, circular conversation between Melanctha and her doctor boyfriend, who seem to be splitting up from the day they meet. I didn't remember this at all. Clearly, as a teenager with a high tolerance for repetitive talks, happy to spend whole evenings sifting through the minutiae of a relationship, I found this a normal way of carrying on. I will cringe through the racial characteristics Stein describes in such authoritative tones, wince my way into the text, to find the story deep in shuttered rooms. And I will see, not what I share with Melanctha, but what I share with Stein: the desire for language.

And very often, I will recall a bus ride in Uzbekistan, when Kholid confessed to me that he was struggling with his dissertation. I told him the method I used to finish my own: write one page a day. Surely any educated person can manage one page a day!

"But didn't you get exhausted sometimes?" he asked. "Didn't you get desperate?"

"Yes," I said, a bit helplessly, "but you have to trust it."

Trust the process, the transformation you can't see yet. This material that will never be enough: it is enough.

The point of healing pilgrimage, Walter S. Friesen writes, is "not to *close* the book but to keep it openable."

And how I have loved literature and language for this: the openness. The capacity for being opened again. Shar-i-Sabs becomes Shakhrisabz, acquiring a completely new valence, a fresh tonality, as when you touch down in a different country. When Otto Toews came to Ak Metchet, they called him *Ottovoy*. This is a title given to a dervish. They called him Ottovoy because he was considered a spiritual leader, and also because of the sound of his German names. To make a sound is to make something happen in the body. It's like a miracle. In my notebook, I've underlined the word *Panor-buva*, a word I first read with the translation "Grandfather Lantern," the nickname of Wilhelm Penner, the Mennonite photographer. But in Ak Metchet I learned that it doesn't really mean Grandfather Lantern. It means Grandfather Penner. There's a word, *fanar*, that means a kind of lantern. Somewhere along the line a researcher or translator misunderstood and took the name *Penner* for *fanar*, a light.

The story has become luminous. At the airport we stand in lines, we board the plane, we shuffle down the aisle and stow our bags overhead. I am seated beside Frank. He asks me if, when the time comes, I'll help edit the English translation of Kholid's father's book on the Khivan Mennonites. Of course I will, of course. No one knows the exact location of the place of refuge because the place of refuge *is* the place of exile. And it is also the place of hunger. Shar-i-Sabs is Shakhrisabz. Langston Hughes is Yang Zoon, his best friend is Yeah Man. The White Mosque is a church. Mangled stories, errors of history, consensual hallucinations, they light my way. I go on maneuvering in the glare. It comes from every direction; I can't see straight. How do we enter the stories of others? We are already there. We are inhabited by archives, steeped in collective memory, permeated with images and impressions, porous to myth.

I gather them up, Franz Bartsch and Herman Jantzen, Jacob Jantzen and Jacob Klaassen, Elizabeth Unruh and Johann Drake and Claas Epp Jr., Khudaybergen Divanov and Wilhelm Penner and Langston Hughes and Ella Maillart and Irene Worth, my knots, my conductors, my shadow tribe. These are only a few of the lives that intersect with mine. They remind me of how many more have touched me, sometimes acknowledged, sometimes missed, how each of us belongs to the unimaginable lives of others, to what we can't see and what we'll never know. How long I lived with my link to Uzbekistan without realizing it! So the ships endlessly pass, invisible in the fog. Sometimes they scrape us, sometimes not. People stand on their decks like phantoms, muffled shapes that might release, if the moonlight pierces the cloud for an instant, a face like a mirror, dazzlingly familiar. Call out to them. Like the Bride Community in their ardor, give up the formal pronoun.

What kind of cry? Something unintelligible, distorted. Maybe only a grunt of surprise, as if in reaction to some unlikely tale, a gasp or a bark of laughter at the unexpected conjunction. A pressure in the throat. A human sound.

And was this trip my *I Am* event? Did I find the language of wholeness? I push up the white plastic window-shade for a last look at the place of refuge. The pane is thick and scratched, the runway flushed with lilac light. I would call this trip my *They Were* event. For what was it that made the glow, the excitement that brought me here? I thought it was the promise of integration, of seeing myself as one, of finally claiming emphatically *I Am*, but instead I saw them, those others, how variously and chaotically *They Were*.

It wasn't me. It was them. The glow wasn't that I was reflected whole. It was that they were reflected prismatically, as mosaic. It wasn't a sense of my own wholeness that drew me to this story, but a sense of the fragmented nature of others: of everyone.

Now the plane gathers speed. The windows shudder, and we are lifting into blue. As always, my hands tighten slightly on the arms of my seat. The plane peels away from the city of Tashkent, reaching toward Istanbul through a bright density like a lake, like the turquoise dome of a Samarkand mosque, like the ceiling of the summer palace in Khiva where Mennonite artists painted, out of the depths of their thirst, their longing, their inexhaustible home-ache, a landscape from their history, or perhaps their imaginations, rendered in blunt strokes of unmixed color that still glaze the air of that empty hall: a scene of a river, a windmill, a sky, above all a land as green as life, exhaling the air of the lost, the last, the past, the future home.

Acknowledgments

This book has benefited from the attention and support of many people and institutions. My conversations with Kate Zambreno energized this project and helped clarify my ideas—thank you, Kate! Thank you, Bhanu Kapil, for inspiring the title and material of "Stories of brown girlhood." Thanks also to those who read and commented on early drafts: Aaron Bady, Amina Cain, Jennifer Lockard Connerley, Michael Ann Courtney, Ashon Crawley, Jacob Sider Jost, Laura Sider Jost, Julia Spicher Kasdorf, K'eguro Macharia, Annetta Miller, Harold F. Miller, Jeremy Nafziger, David Connerley Nahm, David Naimon, Mary Rickert, Benjamin Rosenbaum, Lydia Samatar, Shirley Showalter, and Mohamud Siad Togane.

Thank you to California State University Channel Islands for two grants that afforded me time to write, to University Studies at James Madison University for a summer research grant, and to the English Department in the College of Arts and Letters at James Madison University for covering image permissions and cartography. To Ann Hostetler and Julia Spicher Kasdorf: thank you for your encouragement and for publishing an excerpt in the "Documentary Writing" issue of the *CMW Journal*.

Thank you, Andy Vosper, for your careful fact-checking, Mary Rostad for your beautiful map, and Khushnudbek Abdurasulov for giving the manuscript the benefit of your expertise. I'd also like to thank Maksudbek Abdurasulov of the Ichan-Kala State Museum, Pascale Pahud of the Musée de l'Élysée, and Molly Cusick of International Literary Properties for their help with the photographs; John Thiesen of the Mennonite Library and Archives for his invaluable assistance; Walter Ratliff and Ben Goossen for generously answering research questions; Holly Yanacek for checking my German; and Mary Sprunger for her advice on seventeenth-century Dutch spelling.

To my agent, Sally Harding, to Ron Eckel at CookeMcDermid, and to my editor, Mensah Demary: thank you for your unfailing belief in this project through all its metamorphoses.

To the wonderful people who traveled with me to Khiva: thank you for being my companions on the road, and for your comments on the manuscript, which brought this book to completion.

To Keith Miller, who has read this book assiduously and often, my gratitude and love.

Further Reading

The following is a partial list of secondary sources for those who would like to know more about the various subjects of this book.

Allworth, Edward A., *The Modern Uzbeks: From the Fourteenth Century to the Present: A Cultural History* (Stanford, CA: Hoover Institution Press, 1990).

Barthes, Roland, *Camera Lucida*, trans. Richard Howard (New York, NY: Farrar, Straus, and Giroux, 1981).

Bartsch, Franz, *Our Trek to Central Asia*, trans. Elizabeth Peters and Gerhard Ens (Winnepeg, MB, Canada: CMBC Publications, 1993).

Beachy, Kirsten Eve, ed., *Tongue Screws and Testimonies: Poems, Stories, and Essays Inspired by the Martyrs Mirror* (Harrisonburg, VA: Herald Press, 2010).

Beaton, Cecil, *The Unexpurgated Beaton: The Cecil Beaton Diaries as He Wrote Them, 1970–1980* (New York, NY: Knopf, 2003).

Beck, Ervin, *Mennofolk: Mennonite and Amish Folk Traditions* (Harrisonburg, VA: Herald Press, 2004).

Belk, Fred, *The Great Trek of the Russian Mennonites to Central Asia, 1880–1884* (Harrisonburg, VA: Herald Press, 1976).

Brandt, Di, "On *A Cappella*: Hybrids and Half-Severed Roots," *Mennonite Life*, 59, no. 2 (2004).

Brandt, Di, *questions i asked my mother* (Winnipeg, MB, Canada: Turnstone Press, 1987).

Drieu, Cloé, *Cinema, Nation, and Empire in Uzbekistan, 1919–1937*, trans. Adrian Morfee (Bloomington, IN: Indiana University Press, 2018).

Eby, Omar, *The Boy and the Old Man: Three Years in Somalia* (Bloomington, IN: Xlibris, 2009).

Eby, Omar, ed., *Fifty Years, Fifty Stories: The Mennonite Mission in Somalia, 1953–2003* (Telford, PA: Dreamseeker Books, 2003).

Enns, Elaine L., "Trauma and Memory: Challenges to Settler Solidarity," *Consensus*, 37, no. 1 (2016).

Epp, Claas Jr., *The Unsealed Prophecy of the Prophet Daniel and the Meaning of the Revelation of Jesus Christ*, trans. Dallas Wiebe and Kevin Dyck (North Newton, KS: Mennonite Library and Archives, 1997).

Friesen, Walter S., "Pilgrimage as Healing," *Mennonite Life*, 62, no. 2 (2007).

Friesen, Patrick, *The Shunning* (Winnipeg, Canada: Turnstone Press, 1980).

Gill, Peter, "Irene Worth," *The Times of London* (March 12, 2002).

Goossen, Benjamin W., *Chosen Nation: Mennonites and Germany in a Global Era* (Princeton, NJ: Princeton University Press, 2017).

Gundy, Jeff, *Spoken Among the Trees* (Akron, OH: The University of Akron Press, 2007).

Haile, Ahmed Ali and David W. Shenk, *Teatime in Mogadishu: My Journey as a Peace Ambassador in the World of Islam* (Harrisonburg, VA: Herald Press, 2011).

Hostetler, Ann, ed., *A Cappella: Mennonite Voices in Poetry* (Iowa City, IA: University of Iowa Press, 2003).

Hughes, Langston, *I Wonder as I Wander*, 1956 (New York, NY: Hill and Wang, 1993).

——, *Poems, Photos and Notebooks from Turkestan* (New York, NY: Center for the Humanities, City University of New York, 2015).

Inoyatova, Dilaram, "The Khivan Mennonites," *Mennonite Life*, 62, no. 2 (2007).

Jantzen, Herman, *Journey of Faith in a Hostile World: Memoirs of Herman Jantzen*, trans. Joseph A. Kleinasser (Bloomington, IN: iUniverse, 2008).

Jantzen, Jacob, *Memories of Our Journey to Asia*, trans. Margaret Horn (self-published, 1958).

Janzen, Jean, *Snake in the Parsonage* (Intercourse, PA: Good Books, 1995).

Janzen, Rhoda, *Mennonite in a Little Black Dress: A Memoir of Going Home* (New York, NY: Henry Holt and Co., 2009).

Jung-Stilling, Johann Heinrich, *Das Heimweh: Erster Band*, 1794 (Charleston, SC: Nabu Press, 2011).

——, *The Autobiography of Heinrich Stilling*, trans. Samuel Jackson (New York, NY: Harper and Brothers, 1844).

Kasdorf, Julia Spicher, *The Body and the Book: Writing from a Mennonite Life* (Baltimore, MD: Johns Hopkins University Press, 2001).

Khalid, Adeeb, *Making Uzbekistan: Nation, Empire, and Revolution in the Early USSR* (Ithaca, NY: Cornell University Press, 2019).

Klaassen, Jacob, *Asienreise: Grandfather's Description of the Trip to Central Asia 1880*, trans. Henry Klaassen (self-published, 1964), ketiltrout.net/asienreise/.

Kluge, Alexander, *Cinema Stories*, trans. Martin Brady and Helen Hughes (New York, NY: New Directions, 2007).

Kuziev, Tursunali, *125 Years of Uzbek Photography* (Tashkent, Uzbekistan: Academy of Arts of Uzbekistan, 2005).

Kyle, Richard G., *Apocalyptic Fever: End-Time Prophecies in Modern America* (Eugene, OR: Cascade Books, 2012).

Loewen, Harry, ed., *Why I Am a Mennonite: Essays on Mennonite Identity* (Harrisonburg, VA: Herald Press, 1988).

Maillart, Ella, *Turkestan Solo: A Journey through Central Asia*, 1934 (The Long Riders' Guild Press, 2001), http://www.horsetravelbooks .com/.

Miller, Gerald L., and Shari Miller Wagner, *A Hundred Camels: A Mission Doctor's Sojourn and Murder Trial in Somalia* (Telford, PA: Dreamseeker Books, 2009).

Nathan, Jesse, "The Unfinished Great Trek," *Mennonite Life*, 62, no. 2 (2007).

Ratliff, Walter R., *Pilgrims on the Silk Road: A Muslim-Christian Encounter in Khiva* (Eugene, OR: Wipf & Stock Publishers, 2010).

Reimer, Al, *Mennonite Literary Voices: Past and Present* (Mishawaka, IN: Bethel College, 1993).

Reimer, Priscilla, *Mennonite Artist: Insider as Outsider* (Manitoba, Canada: Manitoba Mennonite Historical Society, 1990).

Rouland, Michael, Gulnara Abikeyeva, and Birgit Beumers, eds., *Cinema in Central Asia: Rewriting Cultural Histories* (London, UK: I. B. Tauris, Bloomsbury Publishing, 2011).

Ruth, John L., *Mennonite Identity and Literary Art* (Harrisonburg, VA: Herald Press, 1978).

Sahadeo, Jeff, *Russian Colonial Society in Tashkent, 1865–1923* (Bloomington, IN: Indiana University Press, 2010).

Saydumarova, Mahmuda, ed. and trans., *A Collection of Uzbek Short Stories* (Bloomington, IN: AuthorHouse, 2012).

Schultz, Elizabeth Unruh, *What a Heritage: Autobiography of Mrs. Elizabeth Schultz née Unruh*, trans. Annie Schultz Keys (self-published, 1985).

Shenk, David W., *A Study of Mennonite Presence and Church Development in Somalia from 1950 through 1970* (PhD dissertation, New York University, 1972).

Thoreson, Frank-Ole, *A Reconciled Community of Suffering Disciples: Aspects of a Contextual Somali Ecclesiology* (New York, NY: Peter Lang, 2014).

Thubron, Colin, *The Lost Heart of Asia* (New York, NY: HarperCollins, 1994).

Tiessen, Hildi Froese, and Peter Hinchcliffe, eds., *Acts of Concealment: Mennonite/s Writing in Canada* (Waterloo, ON, Canada: University of Waterloo Press, 1991).

Togane, Mohamud Siad, *The Bottle and the Bushman: Poems of the Prodigal Son* (Sainte-Anne-de-Bellevue, QC, Canada: Muses' Company, 1986).

Weaver-Zercher, David L., *Martyrs Mirror: A Social History* (Baltimore, MD: Johns Hopkins University Press, 2016).

Wiebe, Dallas, *Our Asian Journey* (Mishawaka, IN: Bethel University, MLR Editions, 1997).

Yaroshevski, Dov, "Central Asian Context for the Khivan Mennonites' Story," *Central Asia on Display: Proceedings of the VII. Conference* (European Society for Central Asian Studies, 2004).

Zacharias, Robert, ed., *After Identity: Mennonite Writing in North America* (University Park, PA: Pennsylvania State University Press, 2015).

Illustration Credits

Figure 0: Mennonite Journey to Central Asia, 1880–1884. Map by Mary Rostad. Commissioned by the author.

Figure 1: The church at Ak Metchet. Ella Maillart, 1932. Musée de l'Élysée. Used with permission.

Figure 2: Mennonite woman. Friedrich Keiter, *Rußlanddeutsche Bauern und ihre Stammesgenossen in Deutschland*, 1934, Tafel VII. Public domain.

Figure 3: Dirk Willems rescuing his pursuer. Jan Luyken, 1685. Mennonite Library and Archives. Used with permission.

Figure 4: Torture of teacher Ursula. Jan Luyken, 1685. Mennonite Library and Archives. Used with permission.

Figure 5: Burning of Anneken Hendriks. Jan Luyken, 1685. Mennonite Library and Archives. Used with permission.

Figure 6: Torture of Hans Bret. Jan Luyken, 1685. Mennonite Library and Archives. Used with permission.

Figure 7: Khudaybergen Divanov. The Ichan-Kala State Museum-Reserve. Used with permission.

Figure 8: Photograph by Khudaybergen Divanov. The Ichan-Kala State Museum-Reserve. Used with permission.

Figure 9: Khudaybergen Divanov at work. The Ichan-Kala State Museum-Reserve. Used with permission.

Figure 10: Wilhelm Penner. Photographer unknown, 1904. Mennonite Library and Archives. Used with permission.

Figure 11: Langston Hughes in Central Asia. Photographer unknown, c. 1932. Beinecke Rare Book and Manuscript Library. Permission granted via the Langston Hughes Estate and Harold Ober Associates.

SOFIA SAMATAR is the author of the novels *A Stranger in Olondria* and *The Winged Histories*, the short story collection *Tender*, and *Monster Portraits*, a collaboration with her brother, the artist Del Samatar.